SPENSER'S CRITICS
Changing Currents in Literary Taste

SPENSER'S CRITICS

Changing Currents in Literary Taste

William R. Mueller

SYRACUSE UNIVERSITY PRESS — 1959

Library of Congress Catalog Card Number: 58-12183

© 1959, SYRACUSE UNIVERSITY PRESS

MANUFACTURED IN THE UNITED STATES OF AMERICA BY
BOOK CRAFTSMEN ASSOCIATES, INC., NEW YORK

To Douglas Bush

"A gentleman or noble person in vertuous and gentle discipline"

PREFACE

The original planning of this volume included the hope that it might appear in the year marking the four-hundredth anniversary of Edmund Spenser's birth, 1952. Comprised of critical essays on Spenser dating from John Hughes' "Remarks on the *Fairy Queen*" (1715) to W.B.C. Watkins' "The Kingdom of Our Language" (1949), the volume was to serve as a companion piece to *That Soueraine Light: Essays in Honor of Edmund Spenser, 1552-1952*, a collection of essays especially written for the quadricentennial year, co-edited by Professor Don Cameron Allen and myself, and published by the Johns Hopkins Press in 1952. Various circumstances have delayed the appearance of this present volume; I have, nevertheless, not taken account in my introductory "A Brief History of Spenser Criticism" of any scholarship appearing after 1951.

To the following publishing houses and journals I express my indebtedness for permissions: Houghton Mifflin Company for the Lowell essay; *Modern Philology* and the Johns Hopkins Press for the Greenlaw essay; Edward Arnold and Company for the Renwick essay; *The Johns Hopkins Alumni Magazine* for the Osgood essay; the Cambridge University Press for the Davis essay; the Clarendon Press, Oxford for the Lewis essay; *The Hudson Review* and the Princeton University Press for the Watkins essay. To Professors Renwick, Osgood, Davis, Lewis, and Watkins I am deeply appreciative for their willingness to let me reprint their essays.

Two generous grants from the Committee on Research of the Santa Barbara College of the University of California were helpful in the assembling and preparation of material. The Johns Hopkins University Library and its superb Spenser collection were invaluable, and I wish in particular to mention the numerous kindnesses of Mr. J. Louis Kuethe, Assistant Librarian. Mrs. Violet Shue, Reference Librarian of the Santa Barbara College Library, made my work easier in many ways, and I warmly recall her graciousness. Professor Merritt Y. Hughes of the University of Wisconsin and Professor Marvin Mudrick of the Santa Barbara College both gave me the benefit of their critical acumen by commenting on an early draft of my introduction. The microfilm office of the Johns Hopkins University and the Photoduplication Service of the Library of Congress have been of assistance. Finally, I wish to thank my wife, whose sharp eye and patient temperament contributed much to the accuracy of my manuscript.

William R. Mueller

The Woman's College of
The University of North Carolina

CONTENTS

INTRODUCTION

A Brief History of Spenser Criticism

Spenser criticism began in 1579 with E. K.'s prefatory apology to the *Shepheardes Calender* and was at its best in the half century between 1715 and 1762, and again during the past half century. Before 1715 we have little more than a series of incidental remarks on Spenser—exemplified by such familiar judgments as those expressed by Sidney, Jonson, Milton, and others. The only extended treatment of Spenser prior to the eighteenth century was Sir Kenelm Digby's most ingenious explication of the twenty-second stanza of the ninth canto of Book II, and even this essay, of course, made no attempt to judge the whole of Spenser's work. John Hughes, in the critical essays of his 1715 edition, was the first writer to consider the sum of Spenser's work, and not merely fragments of it. A half century of interesting and revealing criticism was climaxed by Thomas Warton's monumental work of 1754, revised and published in two volumes in 1762.

Romantic criticism of Spenser was hardly so satisfactory, principally because the early nineteenth-century writers refused to take seriously Spenser's expressed premises and statements of intention. Spenser would have been somewhat disconcerted by Hazlitt's advice (1818) to disregard the allegory, and sick at heart to note Lowell's later suggestion (1875) that the *Faerie Queene* could best be appreciated as a series of lovely pictures. The romantic critics were too busy re-creating earlier authors in their own image to pay much attention to what the earlier writers had explicitly set out to do. Certainly the best statement of the romantic position is Lowell's essay, a brilliant exposition whether or not one agrees with it. Lowell was promptly challenged by Edward Dowden (1884), who looked upon the *Faerie Queene* as an epic directed more toward our moral sense than our physical senses.

Our own century has seen a renaissance of Spenser criticism spear-

1

headed by the Johns Hopkins Variorum edition and the criticism of B. E. C. Davis, Edwin Greenlaw, Ray Heffner, Charles Grosvenor Osgood, Frederick Morgan Padelford, W. L. Renwick, and others. The last decade (1942-1951) has seen the learned contribution of Josephine Waters Bennett on the evolution of Spenser's epic, the monograph on Spenser's religious beliefs by Virgil K. Whitaker, the excellent critical study by W. B. C. Watkins, and the edition of one of the most perceptive Spenserians since Warton: W. L. Renwick.

The large majority of Spenser criticism is directed, as one might expect, toward the *Faerie Queene,* and virtually all of this criticism has to do with one or more of four topics: Spenser's poetic technique—his language and verse form; the structure—or lack of it—of the epic; the allegory and the question of whether it is excrescent or organic to the poet's work; and finally, the total effect of the epic, whether it be principally that of a picture gallery or that of a book of conduct with serious moral intention. This brief essay on the history of Spenser criticism will discuss these topics in turn and will trace representative opinions through the nearly four centuries of their expression. A far more detailed discussion of Spenser scholarship and criticism through Todd's Variorum edition of 1805 is found in Jewel Wurtsbaugh's *Two Centuries of Spenserian Scholarship (1609-1805).*

Ben Jonson's fondness for off-the-cuff remarks has been a benefit to Spenser criticism. Such a compact and unequivocal statement as *"Spencer,* in affecting the Ancients, writ no Language," was bound to attract much attention; indeed, Jonson has been answered by critics extending all the way from Digby and Fuller in the seventeenth century to certain scholars in our own. Moreover, Jonson's remark was quite in keeping with the first century of Spenser criticism, set in motion by E. K. and obsessed with the question of the propriety of the author's diction.

E. K.'s preface to the *Shepheardes Calender* bears some relationship to Wordsworth's later and more famous *Preface:* it is a declaration of literary theory and seeks to forestall hostile criticism, just as Wordsworth's seeks to divert it. E. K. proudly calls the reader's attention to Spenser's "pithinesse in vttering" and "dewe obseruing of Decorum euerye where" and then goes on to the more controversial matter of diction. It is true that the diction will seem strange, "the words them

selues being so aunticent," but such a choice has been purposeful. In the
first place, the attributing of rustic words to shepherds is a part of the
"dewe obseruing of Decorum." But far more importantly, Spenser is
playing the role of the patriotic Englishman in laboring "to restore, as
to theyr rightfull heritage such good and naturall English words, as haue
ben long time out of vse and almost cleane disherited." E. K. decries
the fact that some Englishmen, viewing their native tongue as barren,
have "patched vp the holes with peces and rags of other languages" so
that English has now become "a gallimaufray or hodgepodge of al other
speches." E. K.'s preface, then, is perhaps no more an apology for Spenser's use of ancient words than it is an attack on the ink-horners who
adulterated the "pure" English with unpatriotic borrowings from the
French, Italian, and Latin.

Sir Philip Sidney, writing a few years later, praised the *Shepheardes
Calender* as one of the few notable contributions to his country's literature, but he did feel that Spenser's language was a blemish. Sidney and
Jonson were soon answered. Sir Kenelm Digby insisted that those who
caviled against Spenser's use of obsolete words blamed that which should
be praised; Spenser used such words not in affectation, but in a desire
for precise expression. Digby's position became as extreme as Jonson's
when he expressed the hope that what Spenser had written "will be a
meanes that the English tongue will now receiue no more alterations and
changes, but will remaine and continue settled in that forme it now
hath." Thomas Fuller neatly put Jonson in his place when he wrote that,
in Spenser's works, "the many *Chaucerisms* used (for I will not say
affected by him) are thought by the ignorant to be blemishes, known
by the learned to be beauties, to his book."

Finally, to bring the argument down to our time of more scientific
scholarship, we can turn to the relatively recent pronouncements of
Emma Field Pope[1] and Bruce Robert McElderry, Jr.[2] Miss Pope argues
that Spenser's vocabulary is largely that of his contemporaries and that
his archaisms add color to his diction without obscuring it. McElderry,
making extensive use of the Oxford English Dictionary, contends that
Spenser's deliberate archaism is found in no more than 320 words; that
his use of dialect is slight in the *Shepheardes Calender* and almost neg-
ligible in the later poetry; and that his innovations are purposeful,
seldom stemming from carelessness or ignorance.

If the Elizabethan and Jacobean critics of Spenser's poetic technique were interested mainly in his diction, those of the Restoration and eighteenth century turned their attention to his verse form. Rymer blamed the Italians for bequeathing to Spenser "the unlucky choice of the *stanza,* which in no wise is proper for our Language." Dryden bestowed a questionable compliment when he praised Spenser for doing so well with such an inappropriate stanza—an even more questionable one when he stated that "only Mr. Waller among the English" surpassed Spenser in the art of verse making. Hughes found the stanza tiresome, but harmonious. Upton felt that Spenser had needlessly fettered himself by his choice of verse. The most complete comments on the stanza were made by Warton, who suggested among other things that the necessity of repeating one rhyme four times and another three times in a stanza led Spenser into many absurdities: it led to "trifling and tedious circumlocutions"; it led, particularly toward the close of a stanza, to redundancy; it led to the introduction of puerile or impertinent ideas. But the stanza had its advantages, especially for descriptive passages. Warton's final word in the matter is representative of eighteenth-century opinion: "It is indeed surprising upon the whole, that Spenser should execute a poem of uncommon length, with so much spirit and ease, laden as he was with so many shackles, and embarrassed with so complicated a BONDAGE of RIMING."

The greatest chorus of praise for Spenser's poetic technique came from the romantic critics. It was in a spirit of high praise that Hazlitt found the effect of Spenser's musical verse similar to that of the waves of the sea, "lulling the senses into a deep oblivion of the jarring noises of the world, from which we have no wish to be ever recalled." Coleridge called attention to the "indescribable sweetness and fluent projection of his verse," and Hunt found the stanza to be accompanied with "endless grace and dreaming pleasure." But we must turn for the last word to Lowell, who was to nineteenth-century Spenser criticism what Warton had been to the criticism of the preceding century. "No man," wrote Lowell, "contributed so much to the transformation of style and language as Spenser." The poet had a superb sense of harmony, was soothing yet not monotonous, was a composer whose magnificent control over his verse gave great spirit and energy to his writings. And Lowell went on to chide Warton for his paltry criticisms of the Spenserian stanza.

Brief notice should be paid to three twentieth-century judgments on Spenser's technique. Mr. Renwick, finding in Spenser considerable prosodic variety, points out that the style of each poem is determined by the principle of decorum. Further, Spenser's unity of effect is wrought by his skillful blending of meaning, style, and verse. Mr. Davis suggests that Spenser's language is "the supreme achievement of Elizabethan poetic invention" and that he has influenced English poetic diction more than any other single author, with the possible exceptions of Shakespeare and Milton. Finally, Mr. Watkins writes that "[Spenser] and Shakespeare represent two great traditions, narrative and dramatic, two primary ways of using language, direct and oblique. . . . The technical triumph of the Elizabethan age and the richness of its poetic language cannot be illustrated by Shakespeare alone, or by Shakespeare in combination with any other poet than Spenser."

A study of the remarks made upon the structure of the *Faerie Queene* provides a reasonably accurate barometer to the history of English literary criticism. In these remarks we find a microcosmic reflection of the main trends in criticism from the Age of Reason to the present time.

The first comments on the epic's structure, those made by the neoclassical writers of the late seventeenth century, were, as we might expect, not wholly complimentary. Thomas Rymer, though he could praise Spenser as the most gifted heroic poet since Virgil, complained that the Elizabethan neglected the excellent models of Homer and Virgil and rambled on blindly after the fashion of Ariosto. The epic lacks uniformity and direction, eminent classical virtues, and "we must blame the *Italians* for debauching great Spenser's judgment." Sir William Temple complained about Spenser's poor design, and Sir Richard Blackmore, lamenting that Ariosto and Spenser overlooked classical rules, commented that their "way of writing mightily offends in this Age; and 'tis a wonder how it came to please in any." Dryden summed up the neoclassical argument against Spenser's structure by criticizing the absence of uniformity in the design and of unity in the action, and by arguing that the heroes of the six books were of equal eminence with no proper epic subordination among them. In partial defense of Spenser, Dryden, relying perhaps more on the Letter to Raleigh than on the epic itself, asserted that Prince Arthur "shines throughout the whole poem; and succors the rest, when they are in distress."

Spenser's first editor, John Hughes, was an important transitional figure in his remarks on the epic's structure, for he both carried on the neoclassical point of view and yet planted the seeds of the later preromantic position of apology and defense. Hughes was enough of a classicist to be disappointed by the lack of unity and lack of interdependence among the various books and the various knights. And he went a step beyond Dryden in observing that Prince Arthur plays far too minor a part in the epic to be considered in any way a central hero. Such criticism was very much in the tradition of the preceding half century. But Hughes went beyond this and looked forward to the preromantic criticism of some fifty years later. He pointed out that the epic must indeed appear monstrous if examined according to the practice of Greek and Roman epic, that Spenser was attempting a different kind of epic, and that "to compare it therefore with the Models of Antiquity, would be like drawing a Parallel between the *Roman* and the *Gothick* Architecture." Such a judgment was followed in part by Warton and became the basis of Hurd's essay. Hughes continued with the statement that different writers had different talents and that Spenser's kind of epic gave much greater scope to his peculiar kind of talent than a classical model would have given.

The next Spenser critic of importance, John Upton, was excessive in his praise as he attempted to rescue Spenser from neoclassical criticism. He focused his attack on Dryden and Hughes and their view that the *Faerie Queene* was lacking in unity. Asserting that Homer's critics had abused him in the same way, he set out to vindicate both Homer and Spenser. Upton found in Spenser's epic a structural unity with the requisite beginning, middle, and end: "The beginning is, the British Prince saw in a vision the Fairy Queen, and fell in love with her: the middle, his search after her, with the adventures that he underwent: the end, his finding whom he sought." The case for Spenser is hardly so simple and clear.

Warton's remarks followed fairly closely those of Hughes: Spenser chose a plan which would give widest scope to his unlimited imagination; he chose Arthur as his unifying hero but failed to give him the important position necessary to achieve such a unity; unity of action is found in each separate book rather than in the epic as a whole; and finally, it is foolish to judge Spenser by rules to which he did not attend

—he did not live in a classical age, and "his poetry is the careless exuberance of a warm imagination and a strong sensibility."

If Dryden summed up the neoclassical sentiment, and if Hughes provided a transition from neoclassic to preromantic criticism, then Richard Hurd, in "Letter VIII" of his *Letters on Chivalry and Romance,* is most representative of the latter viewpoint. Hurd stated his thesis early in the Letter: "Under this idea then of a *Gothic,* not classical poem, the *Faery Queen* is to be read and criticized. And on these principles, it would not be difficult to unfold its merit in another way than has been hitherto attempted." If one will judge the epic by Gothic rules he will find a kind of order not apparent to classical taste. The *Faerie Queene* derives both its method and its characters, not from Homer or Virgil, but "from the established modes and ideas of Chivalry." Thus it was as necessary for Spenser's epic to revolve around the adventures of twelve knights as it was for Homer's to confine itself to the adventures of one hero. Spenser's unity consists in the fact that all the adventures are related to a common source, the orders of Gloriana at the twelve-day Feast; and all are related to a common conclusion, the return of the successful knights to the Feast one year later. Hurd made clear that this is not a classical unity, one which requires a single action. Rather, it is a "unity resulting from the respect which a number of related actions have to one common purpose. In other words, it is a unity of *design,* and not of action." Had Spenser been content to depend exclusively on this Gothic unity he would have been more successful than he was. But he could not completely overlook the classical influence, with the result that the *Faerie Queene* is an unfortunate hybrid. In the first place he deemed it necessary to give the appearance of unified action to his epic by interlocking within one book various subsidiary actions of other books; instead of bringing about the desired sense of unity among the books, this simply interrupted the principal story of each book. Secondly, the creation of Prince Arthur to superimpose a unity on the entire fable was an unhappy afterthought which did violence to the Gothic design; Arthur was perhaps necessary to the carrying out of Spenser's moral or allegorical plan, but he fitted only awkwardly into the poet's narrative. Hurd made a convenient summary of his argument:

The conclusion is, that, as an *allegorical* poem, the method of the *Faery Queen* is governed by the justness of the *moral:* as a *narrative* poem, it is conducted on the ideas and usages of *Chivalry*. In either view, if taken by itself, the plan is defensible. But from the union of the two designs there arises a perplexity and confusion, which is the proper, and only considerable, defect of this extraordinary poem.

The romantic critics let the case rest. True to form, they showed more interest in the small unit, the phrase, the stanza, or the episode than in the over-all structure. Thus the neoclassics criticized the structure, the preromantics defended it, and the romantic critics were simply not interested. The problem of Spenser's structure, which had been so central an issue during the century extending from Rymer to Hurd, was a matter of little concern from 1762 to 1934. This is not to say that the matter was entirely forgotten; there has been no lack of argument, for example, regarding the debt of Spenser's plan to Aristotle. But it was not until Janet Spens' *Spenser's Faerie Queene* (1934); J. H. Walter's *"The Faerie Queene;* Alterations and Structure" (1914);[3] and Mrs. Bennett's *The Evolution of "The Faerie Queene"* (1942), that a concerted attempt was made to carry on from where Hurd had left off. We find that these contemporary critics are as representative of their time as Dryden, Hughes, and Hurd were of their own. Present emphasis is on scientific sleuthing; the tools in the case of Spenser scholarship are a thorough knowledge of classical, medieval, and Renaissance literary documents and critical premises; a close reading of Spenser's text; and a fertile— sometimes, perhaps, an unlicensed—imagination. The best example of what can be done with such a method is not in the field of Spenser: it is John Livingston Lowes' *The Road to Xanadu*.

Miss Spens, Mr. Walter, and Mrs. Bennett are not interested either in exposing the weakness of the structure or in defending it. They have made an intensive study of the text, seeking to explain how it came to be as it is; they are concerned, as Mrs. Bennett's title suggests, with the evolution of the epic. The results are fascinating, if perhaps occasionally overingenious; the following summaries will be too brief to do full justice to the careful and detailed arguments of these scholars.

Miss Spens, arguing that the plan of the poem was altered after nearly half of it had been written, sets out to prove that there was a change of plan and to suggest the nature of the original structure. Spenser originally planned an epic of eight books containing eight cantos each. The conception of the twelve Aristotelian virtues and the twelve-day Feast at Gloriana's Court were late additions, the latter perhaps suggested by Raleigh to curry favor with the Queen. Prince Arthur was a part of the original plan, and the first seven books were to be devoted to his overcoming the Seven Deadly Sins; for example, Book II was built around the sin of avarice, Book III of lechery, Book IV of wrath. The eighth book was to record Prince Arthur's successful realization of his vision, his reward for his conquest of the Seven Deadly Sins. It is perhaps needless to say that Miss Spens gives substantiating arguments for which there is no room here.

The most interesting part of Mr. Walter's essay has not to do so much with the probable nature of Spenser's original plan (though he does consider this), as it does with Spenser's frequently expressed interest in the seasons and the influence which this preoccupation may have had on the structure of the epic. Mr. Walter cites the months of the *Shepheardes Calender,* the passing of time in the *Amoretti,* the parade of the seasons in the Mutabilitie Cantos, and the medieval and Renaissance commonplace of representing the seasons of the year as symbolic of the life of man. Suggesting that the books of the *Faerie Queene* may have borne some relationship to the months of the year, he lists those qualities which were popularly assumed to predominate in the various months: "January, the month of the circumcision or initiation; February, the month of Lent and abstinence; March, the month of boisterousness and love; April, likewise the month of love; May, the month of mildness (mercy); June, the month of grace (courtesy); July, the month of change or the turn of the year." [4]

Mrs. Bennett, in her elaborate study of the epic's structure and the stages through which it passed, argues that Spenser did not write according to a preconceived plan which was eventually expressed in the Letter to Raleigh; instead the Letter was "a piece of apologetics" for what had already been done. The epic was written along experimental lines and piecemeal, not in an order beginning with Book I and ending with the Mutabilitie Cantos. Arguing that the criticism in Harvey's letter of 1580 could hardly be directed against Book I as we now have it, Mrs. Bennett suggests that most of Spenser's early writing is to be found in Books III and IV, books largely under Ariosto's influence. Spenser then turned his more serious attention to an exposition of the moral virtues and composed the legends of Red Crosse and Guyon, with Virgil supplanting Ariosto as his principal guide. Then at some time before 1589 Spenser was won back to Ariosto, and there were added the story of Britomart and an elaboration of Florimell's adventures. The role of Arthur and the emphasis on the twelve Aristotelian virtues were also late developments. Though in agreement with Miss Spens that the so-called twelve virtues were no part of the original scheme, Mrs. Bennett suggests that the earlier emphasis was not on the Seven Deadly Sins, but on the four cardinal virtues.

The above summaries of what are perhaps the most interesting contemporary speculations about Spenser may send the curious to the works which they summarize. Presentation of the critics' conclusions without the substantiating arguments obviously gives neither a full nor a just picture.

The history of the criticism of Spenser's allegory falls into no such convenient pattern as that of his structure. For example, we can find no more diverse points of view about the nature and importance of the allegory than those expressed by two romantic critics whom we might expect to have rather similar viewpoints. In 1818 Hazlitt, writing of the merits of the *Faerie Queene,* assured the literary world that readers should not be afraid of the allegory, pointing out that "if they do not meddle with the allegory, the allegory will not meddle with them." Coleridge, in a lecture delivered in the same year, took issue with such a statement and asserted that "no one can appreciate Spenser without some reflection on the nature of allegorical writing." Thus in one year we have diametrically opposite statements on the most important issue of all: whether the allegory is an excrescence which might just as well be disregarded or whether it is so organic to Spenser's method that one must understand it to understand Spenser.

There are also subsidiary problems relating to Spenser's allegory, some critics asserting that the demands of his allegory do violence to his narrative, forcing it into unnatural and self-contradictory situations; others that all allegory is inherently dull and is incapable of presenting vital and interesting characters. Still another allegorical problem grew out of Dryden's statement that "the original of every knight was then living in the court of Queen Elizabeth"; this marked the beginning of an identification hunt which reached its highest intensity in this century, only to be attacked by the late Professor Greenlaw in his essay "Elizabethan Fact and Modern Fancy." [5]

The first extended study of Spenser's allegory did not come until 1747, in which year was published Joseph Spence's unsympathetic chapter on the "Defects of Spenser's Allegory." Spence, a classical scholar, devoted one chapter of his *Polymetis* to a minute dissection of Spenser's allegorical method and presented the faults thereof under three general headings. The faults arise from the poet's mixing heathen fables with Christian truths, from his misrepresenting the allegories of classical writers, and from his being inept in the invention of his own allegories. Virtually the entire essay is an elaboration of the third charge, which, to say the least, is presented with most careful documentation. In the first place, Spence found some of the allegorical figures too complicated, such as those of Scandal, Discord, and Pride. Secondly, he was revolted by what he considered "filthy ideas," asserting that the description of Error "half turns one's stomach." Thirdly, he felt that the allegories were occasionally extravagant rather than great, ridiculous rather than admirable. The most heinous example of this fault was the dragon which succumbed to the Red Crosse Knight; the extravagant and ridiculous examples cited are that the dragon's tail was too long—three furlongs; its spurting blood too powerful—powerful enough to drive a water-mill; and its roar too loud—like that of a hundred hungry lions. These examples will suffice to give an accurate picture of Spence's method. He was subjecting Spenser to the kind of criticism which men of his own century—Hughes, Warton, Hurd—thought unfair, namely to a criticism governed by classical rules. Toward the close of his essay he made explicit the basis of his critical judgments: "Had Spenser formed his allegories on the plan of the ancient poets and artists as much as he did from Ariosto and the Italian allegorists, he might have followed nature much more closely and would not have wandered so often into such strange and inconsistent imaginations."

Most of the major problems concerning Spenser's allegorical writing are touched upon by Warton. His criticism that Spenser "frequently introduces an allegory, under which no meaning is couched" is related to Henry Reynolds' earlier charge (1633) that the narrative is too closely tied to the allegory. It is the argument in reverse, however, for Reynolds thought that the loss was on the side of the story, whereas Warton argued that the allegory was sometimes forgotten in the development of the fiction. He cited the episode of Alma and her Castle as a good example of Spenser's failure to maintain a consistent allegory due to the demands of the fictional, as distinguished from the allegorical, situation. In 1933 Mr. Davis agreed with, and elaborated upon, the judgment made by Reynolds exactly three centuries before. Mr. Davis pointed out that the narrative suffers from the rigid allegorical demands; for example, the reader is forced by the allegory to condemn the fraternal affection of the Brothers Sans, though such affection should be praised on the narrative level; and the reader is forced to approve Artegall's harshness, which on a purely narrative level is hardly commendable. The criticisms of Reynolds, Warton, and Davis have in common the complaint that the allegory and the narrative interfere with each other.

Warton introduced a devastating criticism of Spenser's allegory in his expressed agreement with the Abbé du Bos that allegorical action is by its very nature lacking in interest. Macaulay, in essential agreement, believed that Bunyan alone had given the allegorical form a strong human interest; Spenser is tedious, and it is the unusual reader who can struggle to the end of even the first book of the *Faerie Queene*. Lowell also praised Bunyan and yet found Spenser's allegory boring. We must turn to an anonymous essay appearing in the *Edinburgh Review* in January, 1885, for the highest praise of Spenser's method: "It is true that he dealt much in allegory; but though allegory is commonly a cold thing—always, indeed, if it be mere allegory—yet whenever Spenser's genius is true to itself, his allegory catches fire and raises to the height of song themes which would otherwise have descended to the level of ordinary prose."

Dryden's remark that Spenser's knights were drawn from Elizabethan courtier models was pursued by Upton, who suggested some identifications; and by Warton, who questioned whether the epic was not as much a historical or political poem as it was a moral poem: the allegory is based on "the history, and intrigues, of queen Elizabeth's courtiers," though the whole is presented with moral overtones and didactic intent. Sir Walter Scott lamented in 1806 that Spenser commentators had not paid more attention to the "many particular and minute allusions to persons and events in the court of Queen Elizabeth." Lowell asserted that all the leading figures of the day appeared in the epic under a thin disguise, and that all of them were once easily identifiable. Since Lowell's time, many scholars have sought to remedy the deficiency which Scott had mentioned. No one has gone to greater lengths in this respect than Lilian Winstanley; in the introduction to her edition of Book I, we find a historical identification for virtually every character in the book. Her ingenious essay is worth noting, as is Greenlaw's answer to it and to others of its kind. Greenlaw insisted that Miss Winstanley had taken an untenable position in regarding Book I "as a transcript of English history of the time of Henry VIII and Mary Tudor" (Greenlaw's quotation), and that Spenser's "continued allegory" must be interpreted mainly in philosophic terms, not in terms of historical allusion. Greenlaw summed up his position by stating that Spenser's allegory "is simple, makes its presence known, has a general rather than a minute application."

The most significant issue regarding Spenser's allegory goes back to the diverse opinions of Hazlitt and Coleridge. Lowell gave support to Hazlitt's view that the allegory might well be disregarded by suggesting that Spenser perhaps "adopted it only for the reason that it was in fashion, and put it on as he did his ruff, not because it was becoming, but because it was the only wear"; the "holy function" or allegorical substance of the entire epic was forgotten by a poet who lost himself in lavish adornment. Emile Legouis and Denis Saurat also discount the allegory. On the other hand there have been critics unwilling to discard so lightly Spenser's expressed purpose and plan. Davis, for example, writes that Spenser's "philosophic allegory . . . represents the fullest expression not merely of one poet's ethic but of the whole humanistic idea concerning poetry and its function. If poetry is to be regarded as means to an end, a delectable way of righteousness, the poet will best fulfill his priestly function by investing his creations with moral significance." And certainly C. S. Lewis' excellent chapter on Spenser in *The Allegory of Love* suggests that to read Spenser without an understanding of the allegory is hardly to do full justice to the epic or to the poet.

Perhaps the most sympathetic criticism of Spenser's allegory is that of Mr. Watkins, who intelligently meets the objections of many of his predecessors. He points out that "to an idealist of a Platonic cast allegory is an inevitable technique"; such an idealist is constantly suspended between the world of facts and the world of ideas. Thus Spenser's use of the allegory is perfectly natural and seldom perfunctory. With Hazlitt in mind, Watkins states that "the basic allegory of the *Faerie Queene* is the most important element in its structure, and this is one reason why allegory meddles with any reader of the poem." And with considerably more insight than that possessed by most of Spenser's detractors, he concludes that the poet's "greatest beauty is often achieved not despite but because of allegory."

Mention should also be made of Isabel E. Rathborne's *The Meaning of Spenser's Fairyland*. Miss Rathborne's careful study of Spenser's fairy mythology leads to an allegorical interpretation of Book II, Canto 10, which makes far more meaningful the chronicle of British kings and the roll of elfin emperors.

When Hazlitt stated in 1818 that the moving principle of Spenser's mind was the love of beauty and not of truth, he gave a new direction to Spenser criticism. The implications of this statement have been developed by Lowell, Courthope, Yeats, Jusserand, Legouis, Saurat, and others. There have been many variations on the general theme that, whatever Spenser may have set out to accomplish in the writing of his epic, his actual accomplishment was a harmonious and restful blending of color and scene, a sequence of beautiful pictures to be enjoyed in and for themselves. In a sense, the *Faerie Queene* has been looked upon as a supremely successful example of art for art's sake. It is evident that among those who take this viewpoint are some of Spenser's most ardent admirers, and it is equally evident that such praise carries with it the belief that Spenser failed in his expressed intention: "the generall end therefore of all the booke is to fashion a gentleman or noble person in vertuous and gentle discipline." If we can take seriously this and many other statements of intention, then Spenser obviously set out to write a courtesy book, a book which would follow in the general tradition of Plato, Aristotle, Cicero, Erasmus, Castiglione, Elyot, and others. For the past century and a half one of the main issues of Spenser criticism has been whether the *Faerie Queene* is primarily a courtesy book or, to use Lowell's term, primarily a "gallery of pictures."

Such a question never occurred to Spenser's early critics. Drayton expressed in 1627 what undoubtedly was the sentiment of his time when he wrote of the "Grave morrall *Spencer*." And Milton, accepting the distinction which Sidney had made between poetry and philosophy, found the "sage and serious" Spenser a better teacher than Scotus or Aquinas because the poet, in describing the virtue of temperance for example, gave not only abstract precepts but also concrete pictures of

Guyon overcoming the temptations of the Cave of Mammon and the Bower of Bliss. Sir Kenelm Digby thought the famous twenty-second stanza "to be dictated by such a learned Spirit, and so generally a knowing Soul, that were there nothing else extant of *Spencers* writing, yet these few words would make me esteeme him no whit inferiour to the most famous men that ever have been in any age." Drayton, Milton, and Digby would argue that Spenser conscientiously followed his own poetic ideal as expressed by Piers in "October," by the Letter to Raleigh, and by the Proem to Book I of the epic.

It is interesting to note that the successful marriage of Spenser's stated intention and ultimate achievement was not questioned until over two centuries after the publication of the *Faerie Queene*. Hazlitt, by implication, questioned the successful fusion of intent and achievement, and the matter was brought into its sharpest focus by the famous and divergent essays of Lowell and Dowden in 1875 and 1884. Lowell's general point of view has already been discussed, and one of the delights of his essay is that his position, stated so unequivocally, is the perfect summation of the entire romantic school. No one expresses more clearly than he the judgment that Spenser, however magnificent a poem he may have written, failed to fulfill his intention: "So entirely are beauty and delight in it the native element of Spenser, that whenever in the 'Faery Queen' you come suddenly on the moral, it gives you a shock of unpleasant surprise, a kind of grit, as when one's teeth close on a bit of gravel in a dish of strawberries and cream."

Dowden's essay is a direct answer to Lowell's and is a perfect companion piece. If a reader were confined to two essays in his study of Spenser criticism, he could do no better than to read Lowell and Dowden, for their essays not only epitomize the two main schools of Spenser criticism but also manage to discuss most of the significant problems which have confronted Spenser critics for the past three and a half centuries. Dowden begins by attacking Lowell and the romantic critics and goes on to insist that the *Faerie Queene* was written in the spirit of Sidney's *Apologie*. Spenser thought of his poem to a great extent as a study in ethics, and the aim of the poem was to stimulate virtuous action. This is not to say, of course, that Sidney and Spenser made no distinction between the moral philosopher and the poet; if their view on this matter needed any clarification by example, Milton made it in his distinction between the philosophers Scotus and Aquinas and the poet Spenser.

Dowden finds Spenser's particular genius in his poetic ability to unite "sense and soul, moral seriousness and the Renaissance appetite for beauty." "While Spenser sees the abundant beauty of the world, and the splendour of man and of the life of man," writes Dowden, "his vision of human life is grave and even stern. For life he regards as a warfare, a warfare needing all our foresight, strength, and skill."

This very signficant argument did not die with Lowell and Dowden, for each has his retinue of supporters. But they brought the argument into its clearest terms, and their followers do not advance or resolve the argument so much as they echo it. Courthope could speak of the *Faerie Queene* most highly when he viewed it as a picture gallery. Yeats averred that Spenser "was always to love the journey more than its end, the landscape more than the man, and reason more than life, and the tale less than its telling." Legouis, challenging the views of Milton and Dowden, followed Hazlitt in finding that Spenser was more enchanted by beauty than by truth and followed Lowell in suggesting that little of the epic would be lost if we viewed it simply as "an immense gallery of separate pictures." Saurat, in essence, followed Legouis.

The most eminent critics in the other camp are Renwick, Osgood, Davis, and Watkins. Renwick believes with Dowden that the key to Spenser is to be found in Sidney, and that Spenser viewed poetry as above all "an efficient cause of action in the world"; the purpose of the *Faerie Queene* was to inspire mankind to "right thinking and right doing." Osgood, criticizing the disparagement of moral values in art and literature, also follows in the tradition of Dowden. Davis, attacking Legouis, suggests that the *Faerie Queene* would be reduced to an epic of nonsense if the moral values are overlooked and that the attempt to dissociate the poetry from the teaching "is to raise an artificial barrier between content and form." And Watkins writes that poetry, to both Spenser and Shakespeare, "is the finest expression of human wisdom, the highest form of human experience." It is clear that both sides of this important question have had considerable representation and elaboration.

Criticism of Spenser, like all literary criticism, is as informative about the age in which it was written as it is about its subject. The critical essays which make up this selection throw light on the major periods in the history of English literary taste. Indeed, recognition that a history of Spenser criticism could also approximate a history of English literary criticism was a major factor in the selection. The eighteenth, nineteenth, and twentieth centuries are all amply represented, as are the four main issues which have confronted the critics: the poetic technique, the structure of the epic, the allegory, and the ultimate effect.

NOTES

1. "Renaissance Criticism and the Diction of *The Faerie Queene*," *Publications of the Modern Language Association*, XLI (1926), 575-619.

2. "Archaism and Innovation in Spenser's Poetic Diction," *Publications of the Modern Language Association*, XLVII (1932), 144-170.

3. *Modern Language Review*, XXXVI (1941), 37-58.

4. *Modern Language Review*, XXXVI (1941), 54.

5. *Studies in Spenser's Historical Allegory* (Baltimore: The Johns Hopkins Press, 1932), pp. 59-103.

ONE

JOHN HUGHES

Remarks on the "Fairy Queen" (1715)*

By what has been offer'd in the foregoing Discourse on *Allegorical Poetry,* we may be able, not only to discover many Beauties in the *Fairy Queen,* but likewise to excuse some of its Irregularities. The chief Merit of this Poem consists in that surprizing Vein of fabulous Invention, which runs thro it, and enriches it every where with Imagery and Descriptions more than we meet with in any other modern Poem. The Author seems to be possess'd of a kind of Poetical Magick; and the Figures he calls up to our View rise so thick upon us, that we are at once pleased and distracted by the exhaustless Variety of them; so that his Faults may in a manner be imputed to his Excellencies: His Abundance betrays him into Excess, and his Judgment is overborne by the Torrent of his Imagination.

That which seems the most liable to Exception in this Work, is the Model of it, and the Choice the Author has made of so romantick a Story. The several Books appear rather like so many several Poems, than one entire Fable: Each of them has its peculiar Knight, and is independent of the rest; and tho some of the Persons make their Appearance in different Books, yet this has very little Effect in connecting them. Prince *Arthur* is indeed the principal Person, and has therefore a share given him in every Legend; but his Part is not considerable enough in any one of them: He appears and vanishes again like a Spirit; and we lose sight of him too soon, to consider him as the Hero of the Poem.

---

*John Hughes edited the works of Spenser in 6 volumes in 1715. Reprinted from the chapter, "Remarks on the *Fairy Queen*," are pp. lviii-lxxvii and xciii-xcvi; from the chapter, "Remarks on the *Shepherd's Calendar,* &c.," pp. xcvii-cv.

18

These are the most obvious Defects in the Fable of the *Fairy Queen*. The want of Unity in the Story makes it difficult for the Reader to carry it in his Mind, and distracts too much his Attention to the several Parts of it; and indeed the whole Frame of it wou'd appear monstrous, if it were to be examin'd by the Rules of Epick Poetry, as they have been drawn from the Practice of *Homer* and *Virgil*. But as it is plain the Author never design'd it by those Rules, I think it ought rather to be consider'd as a Poem of a particular kind, describing in a Series of Allegorical Adventures or Episodes the most noted Virtues and Vices: to compare it therefore with the Models of Antiquity, wou'd be like drawing a Parallel between the *Roman* and the *Gothick* Architecture. In the first there is doubtless a more natural Grandeur and Simplicity: in the latter, we find great Mixtures of Beauty and Barbarism, yet assisted by the Invention of a Variety of inferior Ornaments; and tho the former is more majestick in the whole, the latter may be very surprizing and agreeable in its Parts.

It may seem strange indeed, since *Spenser* appears to have been well acquainted with the best Writers of Antiquity, that he has not imitated them in the Structure of his Story. Two Reasons may be given for this: The first is, That at the time when he wrote, the *Italian* Poets, whom he has chiefly imitated, and who were the first Revivers of this Art among the Moderns, were in the highest vogue, and were universally read and admir'd. But the chief Reason was probably, that he chose to frame his Fable after a Model which might give the greatest Scope to that Range of Fancy which was so remarkably his Talent. There is a Bent in Nature, which is apt to determine Men that particular way in which they are most capable of excelling; and tho it is certain he might have form'd a better Plan, it is to be question'd whether he cou'd have executed any other so well.

It is probably for the same reason, that among the *Italian* Poets, he rather follow'd *Ariosto*, whom he found more agreeable to his Genius, than *Tasso*, who had form'd a better Plan, and from whom he has only borrow'd some particular Ornaments; yet it is but Justice to say, that his Plan is much more regular than that of *Ariosto*. In the *Orlando Furioso*, we every where meet with an exuberant Invention, join'd with great Liveliness and Facility of Description, yet debas'd by frequent Mixtures of the comick Genius, as well as many shocking Indecorums. Besides, in the Huddle and Distraction of the Adventures, we are for the most part only amus'd with extravagant Stories, without being instructed in any Moral. On the other hand, *Spenser's* Fable, tho often wild, is, as I have observ'd, always emblematical: And this may very much excuse likewise that Air of Romance in which he has follow'd the *Italian* Author. The perpetual Stories of Knights, Giants, Castles, and Enchantments, and all that Train of Legendary Adventures, wou'd indeed appear very trifling, if *Spenser* had not found a way to turn them all into Allegory, or if a less masterly Hand had fill'd up his Draught. But it is surprizing to observe how much the Strength of the Painting is superior to the Design. It ought to be consider'd too, that at the time when our Author wrote, the Remains of the old *Gothick* Chivalry were not quite abolish'd: It was not many Years before, that the famous Earl of *Surry,* remarkable for his Wit and Poetry in the Reign of King *Henry* the Eighth, took a ro-mantick Journey to *Florence,* the Place of his Mistress's Birth, and pub-lish'd there a Challenge against all Nations in Defence of her Beauty. Justs and Turnaments were held in *England* in the Time of Queen *Elizabeth.* Sir *Philip Sidney* tilted at one of these Entertainments, which was made for the *French* Ambassador, when the Treaty of Marriage was on foot with the Duke of *Anjou:* and some of our Historians have given us a very particular and formal Account of Preparations, by marking out Lists, and appointing Judges, for a Tryal by Combat, in the same Reign, which was to have decided the Title to a considerable Estate; and in which the whole Ceremony was perfectly agreeable to the fabu-lous Descriptions in Books of Knight-Errantry. This might render his Story more familiar to his first Readers; tho Knights in Armour, and Ladies Errant are as antiquated Figures to us, as the Court of that time wou'd appear, if we cou'd see them now in their Ruffs and Fardingales.

There are two other Objections to the Plan of the *Fairy Queen,* which, I confess, I am more at a loss to answer. I need not, I think, be scrupulous in mentioning freely the Defects of a Poem, which, tho it was never suppos'd to be perfect, has always been allow'd to be admirable.

The first is, that the Scene is laid in *Fairy-Land,* and the chief Actors are *Fairies.* The Reader may see their imaginary Race and His-tory in the Second Book, at the end of the Tenth Canto: but if he is not prepar'd before-hand, he may expect to find them acting agreeably to the common Stories and Traditions about such fancy'd Beings. Thus *Shakespear,* who has introduc'd them in his *Midsummer-Night's Dream,* has made them speak and act in a manner perfectly adapted to their suppos'd Characters; but the *Fairies* in this Poem are not distinguish'd from other Persons. There is this Misfortune likewise attends the Choice of such Actors, that having been accustom'd to conceive of them in a diminutive way, we find it difficult to raise our Ideas, and to imagine a *Fairy* encountring with a Monster or a Giant. *Homer* has pursu'd a contrary Method, and represented his Heroes above the Size and Strength of ordinary Men; and it is certain that the Actions of the Iliad wou'd have appear'd but ill proportion'd to the Characters, if we were to have imagin'd them all perform'd by Pigmies.

But as the Actors our Author has chosen, are only fancy'd Beings, he might possibly think himself at liberty to give them what Stature, Customs and Manners he pleas'd. I will not say he was in the right in this: but it is plain that by the literal Sense of *Fairy-Land,* he only design'd an *Utopia,* an imaginary Place; and by his *Fairies,* Persons of whom he might invent any Action proper to human Kind, without being restrain'd, as he must have been, if he had chosen a real Scene and historical Characters. As for the mystical Sense, it appears both by the Work it self, and by the Author's[1] Explanation of it, that his *Fairy-Land* is *England,* and his *Fairy-Queen,* Queen *Elizabeth;* at whose Command the Adventure of every Legend is suppos'd to be undertaken.

The other Objection is, that having chosen an historical Person, Prince *Arthur,* for his principal Hero; who is no *Fairy,* yet is mingled with them: he has not however represented any part of his History. He appears here indeed only in his Minority, and performs his Exercises in *Fairy-Land,* as a private Gentleman; but we might at least have expected, that the fabulous Accounts of him, and of his Victories over the *Saxons,* shou'd have been work'd into some beautiful Vision or Prophecy: and I cannot think *Spenser* wou'd wholly omit this, but am apt to believe he had done it in some of the following Books which were lost.

In the moral Introductions to every Book, many of which have a great Propriety and Elegance, the Author has follow'd the Example of *Ariosto.* I will only beg leave to point out some of the principal Beauties in each Book, which may yet more particularly discover the Genius of the Author.

If we consider the First Book as an entire Work of it self, we shall find it to be no irregular Contrivance: There is one principal Action, which is compleated in the Twelfth Canto; and the several Incidents or Episodes are proper, as they tend either to obstruct or promote it. The same may be said of some other of the following Books, tho I think they are not so regular as this. The Author has shewn Judgment in making his Knight of the *Red Cross,* or St. *George,* no perfect Character; without which, many of the Incidents cou'd not have been represented. The Character of *Una,* or *Truth,* is very properly oppos'd by those of *Duessa,* or *Falshood,* and *Archimago,* or *Fraud. Spenser's* particular manner, which (if it may be allow'd) I wou'd call his Painter-like Genius, immediately shews it self in the Figure of *Error,* who is drawn as a Monster, and that of *Hypocrisy,* as a Hermit. The Description of the former of these, in the mix'd Shape of a Woman and a Serpent, surrounded with her Offspring, and especially that Circumstance of their creeping into her Mouth on the sudden Light which glanced upon them from the Knight's Armour, incline one to think that our Great *Milton* had it in his eye when he wrote his famous Episode of Sin and Death. The Artifices of *Archimago* and *Duessa,* to separate the Knight from *Una,* are well invented, and intermingled with beautiful Strokes of Poetry; particularly in that Episode where the Magician sends one of his Spirits to fetch a false Dream from the House of *Morpheus:*

> Amid the Bowels of the Earth full steep
> And low, where dawning Day does never peep,
> His Dwelling is ———

Mr. Rhimer, as I remember, has, by way of Comparison, collected from most of the antient and modern Poets, the finest Descriptions of the Night; among all which, he gives the Preference to the *English* Poets: This of *Morpheus,* or Sleep, being a Poetical Subject of the same kind, might be subjected to a like Trial; and the Reader may particularly compare it with that in the Eleventh Book of *Ovid's Metamorphoses;* to which, I believe, he will not think it inferior.

The miraculous Incident of a Tree shedding Drops of Blood, and a Voice speaking from the Trunk of it, is borrow'd from that of *Polidorus* in the Third Book of *Virgil's Æneis. Ariosto* and *Tasso* have both copy'd the same Story, tho in a different manner. It was impossible that the modern Poets, who have run so much into the Taste of Romance, should let a Fiction of this kind escape their Imitation.

The Adventures which befal *Una,* after she is forsaken by the Knight; her coming to the House of *Abessa,* or *Superstition;* the Consternation occasion'd by that Visit; her Reception among the Savages;

why is a great? (handwritten)

and her civilizing them, are all very fine Emblems. The Education of *Satyrane,* a young Satyr, is describ'd on this Occasion with an agreeable Wildness of Fancy.

But there is one Episode in this Book, which I cannot but particularly admire; I mean that in the Fifth Canto, where *Duessa* the Witch seeks the Assistance of *Night,* to convey the Body of the wounded *Pagan* to be cured by *Æsculapius* in the Regions below. The Author here rises above himself, and is got into a Track of imitating the Antients, different from the greatest part of his Poem. The Speech in which *Duessa* addresses *Night,* is wonderfully great, and stained with that impious Flattery, which is the Character of *Falshood,* who is the Speaker:

> O thou most antient Grandmother of all,
> More old than *Jove,* whom thou at first didst breed,
> Or that Great House of Gods Cælestial,
> Which was't begot in *Dæmogorgon's* Hall,
> And saw'st the Secrets of the World unmade!

As *Duessa* came away hastily on this Expedition, and forgot to put off the Shape of Truth, which she had assum'd a little before, *Night* does not know her: This Circumstance, and the Discovery afterwards, when she owns her for her Daughter, are finely emblematical. The Images of *Horror* are rais'd in a very masterly manner; *Night* takes the Witch into her Chariot; and being arriv'd where the Body lay, they alight.

> And all the while she stood upon the Ground,
> The wakeful Dogs did never cease to bay,
> As giving warning of th' unusual Sound
> With which her Iron Wheels did them affray,
> And her dark grisly Look them much dismay.
> The Messenger of Death, the ghastly Owl,
> With dreary Shrieks did also her bewray,
> And hungry Wolves continually did howl
> At her abhorred Face, so filthy and so foul.

They steal away the Body, and carry it down thro the Cave *Avernus,* to the Realms of *Pluto.* What Strength of Painting is there in the following Lines!

> ———On every side them stood
> The trembling Ghosts, with sad amazed Mood
> Chattring their Iron Teeth, and staring wide

> With stony Eyes; and all the hellish Brood
> Of Fiends infernal flock'd on every side
> To gaze on earthly Wight, that with the *Night* durst ride.

Longinus commending a Description in *Euripides* of *Phaeton's* Journey thro the Heavens, in which the Turnings and Windings are mark'd out in a very lively manner, says, That the Soul of the Poet seems to mount the Chariot with him, and to share all his Dangers. The Reader will find himself in a like manner transported throughout this whole Episode; which shews that it has in it the Force and Spirit of the most sublime Poetry.

The first Appearance of Prince *Arthur* in this Book is represented to great Advantage, and gives occasion to a very finish'd Description of a martial Figure. How sprightly is that Image and Simile in the following Lines!

> Upon the Top of all his lofty Crest
> A Bunch of Hairs, discolour'd diversly
> With sprinkled Pearl, and Gold full richly drest,
> Did shake, and seem'd to dance for Jollity,
> Like to an Almond-Tree ymounted high
> On Top of green *Selinis* all alone,
> With Blossoms brave bedecked daintily;
> Whose tender Locks do tremble every one
> At every little Blast that under Heav'n is blown.

I must not omit mentioning the House of *Pride,* and that of *Holiness,* which are beautiful Allegories in different Parts of this Book. In the former of these there is a minute Circumstance which is very artificial; for the Reader may observe, that the six Counsellors which attend *Pride* in her Progress, and ride on the Beasts which draw her Chariot, are plac'd in that Order in which the Vices they represent, naturally produce and follow each other. In the Dungeon among the Captives of *Pride,* the Poet has represented *Nebuchadnezzar, Cræsus, Antiochus, Alexander,* and several other eminent Persons, in Circumstances of the utmost Ignominy. The Moral is truly noble; for upon the sight of so many illustrious Slaves, the Knight hastens from the Place, and makes his Escape.

The Description of *Despair* in the Ninth Canto, is that which is said to have been taken notice of by Sir *Philip Sidney.* But I think the

Speech of *Despair,* in which the distemper'd Reasonings, that are apt to agitate the Heart of a Man abandon'd to this Passion, are so pathetically represented, is much superior to the Description.

Among the Allegories in the Tenth Canto, it is impossible not to distinguish that venerable Figure of Contemplation, in his Hermitage on the Top of a Hill, represented as an old Man almost wasted away in Study:

> With snowy Locks adown his Shoulders spread,
> As hoary Frost with Spangles doth attire
> The mossy Branches of an Oak half dead.

The Knight and his Companion enquire of him:

> **Is** not from hence the way that leadeth right
> To that most glorious House that glistereth bright
> With burning Stars, and ever-living Fire?

This is extremely noble, as well as the old Man's shewing him from the Top of the Hill, the heavenly Jerusalem; which was proper to animate the Hero against the Combat, in which he is presently after engag'd: His Success in that Combat, and his marrying Una, are a very just Conclusion of this Book, and of its chief Allegory.

It wou'd be easy to point out many Instances, besides those I have mention'd, of the Beauties in this Book; yet these few will give the Reader a Taste of that Poetical Spirit and Genius for Allegory, which every where shine in this Author. It wou'd be endless to take notice of the more minute Beauties of his Epithets, his Figures, and his Similes, which occur in almost every Page. I shall only mention one or two as a Specimen. That Image of *Strength,* in striking a Club into the Ground, which is illustrated by the following Simile, is very great.

> As when Almighty *Jove,* in wrathful Mood
> To wreak the Guilt of mortal Sins is bent,
> Hurls forth his thundring Dart with deadly Food,
> Enroll'd in Flames and smouldring Dreariment,
> Thro riven Clouds and molten Firmament
> The fierce three-forked Engine making way,
> Both lofty Tow'rs and highest Trees hath rent,
> And all that might his angry Passage stay,
> And shooting in the Earth, casts up a Mount of Clay.

> His boistrous Club so bury'd in the Ground,
> He could not rearen up again, &c.

As also that of a Giant's Fall,

> That down he tumbled as an aged Tree,
> High growing on the Top of rocky Clift;
> Whose Heart-Strings with keen Steel nigh hewen be:
> The mighty Trunk, half rent with ragged Rift,
> Doth roll adown the Rocks, and fall with fearful Drift.

These are such Passages as we may imagine our excellent *Milton* to have study'd in this Author. And here by the way it is remarkable that as *Spenser* abounds with such Thoughts as are truly sublime, so he is almost every where free from the Mixture of little Conceits, and that low Affectation of Wit which so much infected both our Verse and Prose afterwards; and from which scarce any Writer of his own Time, besides himself, was free. . . .

I have not yet said any thing concerning *Spenser's* Versification; in which, tho he is not always equal to himself, it may be affirm'd, that he is superior to all his Cotemporaries, and even to those that follow'd him for some time, except *Fairfax*, the applauded Translator of *Tasso*. In this he commendably study'd the *Italians,* and must be allow'd to have been a great Improver of our *English* Numbers: Before his time, Musick seems to have been so much a Stranger to our Poetry, that, excepting the Earl of *Surry's* Lyricks, we have very few Examples of Verses that had any tolerable Cadence. In *Chaucer* there is so little of this, that many of his Lines are not even restrain'd to a certain Number of Syllables. Instances of this loose Verse are likewise to be found in our Author, but it is only in such Places where he has purposely imitated *Chaucer,* as in the second Eclogue, and some others. This great Defect of Harmony put the Wits in Queen *Elizabeth's* Reign upon a Design of totally changing our Numbers, not only by banishing Rhime, but by new moulding our Language into the Feet and Measures of the *Latin* Poetry. Sir *Philip Sidney* was at the Head of this Project, and has accordingly given us some Hexameter and Pentameter Verses in his *Arcadia*. But the Experiment soon fail'd; and tho our Author, by some Passages in his Letters to Mr. *Harvey,* seems not to have disapprov'd it, yet it does not appear by those Poems of his, which are preserv'd, that he gave it any Authority by his Example.

As to the Stanza in which the *Fairy Queen* is written, tho the Author cannot be commended for his Choice of it, yet it is much more harmonious in its kind than the Heroick Verse of that Age. It is almost the same with what the *Italians* call their *Ottave Rime,* which is us'd both by *Ariosto* and *Tasso,* but improv'd by *Spenser,* with the Addition of a Line more in the Close, of the Length of our Alexandrines. The Defect of it, in long or narrative Poems, is apparent. The same Measure, closed always by a full Stop, in the same Place, by which every Stanza is made as it were a distinct Paragraph, grows tiresom by continual Repetition, and frequently breaks the Sense, when it ought to be carry'd on without Interruption. With this Exception, the Reader will however find it harmonious, full of well-sounding Epithets, and of such elegant Turns on the Thought and Words, that *Dryden*[2] himself owns he learn'd these Graces of Verse chiefly from our Author; and does not scruple to say, that in this Particular *only* Virgil *surpass'd him among the* Romans, *and only Mr.* Waller *among the* English.

NOTES

1. Vid. Letter to Sir W. Raleigh.
2. Dedication to Juvenal.

Remarks on the "Shepherd's Calendar," *&c.* (1715)

In the Remarks on the *Fairy Queen,* I have chiefly consider'd our Author as an Allegorical Writer; and his Poem as fram'd after a Model of a particular kind. In some of his other Writings, we find more Regularity, tho less Invention. There seems to be the same difference between the *Fairy Queen* and the *Shepherd's Calendar,* as between a Royal Palace and a little Country Seat. The first strikes the Eye with more Magnificence; but the latter may perhaps give the greatest Pleasure. In this Work the Author has not been misled by the *Italians;* tho *Tasso's Aminta* might have been at least of as good Authority to him in the Pastoral, as *Ariosto* in the greater kind of Poetry. But *Spenser* rather chose to follow Nature it self, and to paint the Life and Sentiments of Shepherds after a more simple and unaffected manner.

The two things which seem the most essential to Pastoral, are Love, and the Images of a Country Life: and to represent these, our Author had little more to do, than to examine his own Heart, and to copy the Scene about him; for at the time when he wrote the *Shepherd's Calendar,* he was a passionate Lover of his *Rosalind:* and it appears that the greatest part of it, if not the whole, was compos'd in the Country on his first leaving the University; and before he had engag'd in Business, or fill'd his Mind with the Thoughts of Preferment in a Life at Court. Perhaps too there is a certain Age most proper for Pastoral Writing; and tho the same Genius shou'd arise afterwards to greater Excellencies, it may grow less capable of this. Accordingly in the Poem call'd *Colin Clout's come home again,* which was written a considerable time after, we find him less a Shepherd than at first: He had then been drawn out of his Retirement, had appear'd at Court, and been engag'd in an Employment which brought him into a Variety of Business and Acquaintance, and gave him a quite different Sett of Ideas. And tho this Poem is not without its Beauties; yet what I wou'd here observe is, that in the Pastoral Kind it is not so simple and unmix'd, and consequently not so perfect as the *Eclogues,* of which I have perhaps given the Reason.

But I am sensible that what I have mention'd as a Beauty in *Spenser's* Pastorals, will not seem so to all Readers; and that the Simplicity which appears in them may be thought to have too much of the *Merum*

Rus. If our Author has err'd in this, he has at least err'd on the right hand. The true Model of Pastoral Writing seems indeed not to be yet fix'd by the Criticks; and there is room for the best Judges to differ in their Opinions about it: Those who wou'd argue for the Simplicity of Pastoral, may say, That the very Idea of this kind of Writing is the Representation of a Life of Retirement and Innocence, made agreeable by all those Pleasures and Amusements, which the Fields, the Woods, and the various Seasons of the Year afford to Men, who live according to the first Dictates of Nature, and without the artificial Cares and Refinements, which Wealth, Luxury, and Ambition, by multiplying both our Wants and Enjoyments, have introduc'd among the Rich and the Polite: That therefore as the Images, Similies, and Allusions are to be drawn from the Scene; so the Sentiments and Expressions ought no where to taste of the City, or the Court, but to have such a kind of plain Elegance only, as may appear proper to the Life and Characters of the Persons introduc'd in such Poems: That this Simplicity, skilfully drawn, will make the Picture more natural, and consequently more pleasing: That even the low Images in such a Representation are amusing, as they contribute to deceive the Reader, and make him fancy himself really in such a Place, and among such Persons as are describ'd; the Pleasure in this case being like that express'd by *Milton* of one walking out into the Fields:

> ———Who long in populous Cities pent,
> Where Houses thick, and Sewers annoy the Air,
> Forth issuing on a Summer's Morn to breathe
> Among the pleasant Villages and Farms
> Adjoin'd, from each thing met conceives Delight;
> The Smell of Grain, or tedded Grass, or Kine,
> Or Dairy, each rural Sight, each rural Smell.

This indeed seems to be the true Reason of the Entertainment which Pastoral Poetry gives to its Readers: for as Mankind is departed from the Simplicity, as well as the Innocence, of a State of Nature, and is immers'd in Cares and Pursuits of a very different kind; it is a wonderful Amusement to the Imagination, to be sometimes transported, as it were, out of modern Life, and to wander in these pleasant Scenes which the Pastoral Poets provide for us, and in which we are apt to fancy our selves reinstated for a time in our first Innocence and Happiness.

Those who argue against the strict Simplicity of Pastoral Writing, think there is something too low in the Characters and Sentiments of mere Shepherds, to support this kind of Poetry, if not rais'd and improv'd by the Assistance of Art; or at least that we ought to distinguish between what is simple, and what is rustick, and take care that while we represent Shepherds, we do not make them Clowns: That it is a Mistake to imagine that the Life of Shepherds is incapable of any Refinement, or that their Sentiments may not sometimes rise above the Country. To justify this, they tell us, that we conceive too low an Idea of this kind of Life, by taking it from that of modern Shepherds, who are the meanest and poorest sort of People among us. But in the first Ages of the World it was otherwise; that Persons of Rank and Dignity honour'd this Employment; that Shepherds were the Owners of their own Flocks; and that *David* was once a Shepherd, who became afterwards a King, and was himself too the most sublime of Poets. Those who argue for the first kind of Pastoral, recommend *Theocritus* as the best Model; and those who are for the latter, think that *Virgil,* by raising it to a higher Pitch, has improv'd it. I shall not determine this Controversy, but only observe, that the Pastorals of Spenser are of the former kind.

It is for the same Reason that the Language of the *Shepherd's Calendar,* which is design'd to be rural, is older than that of his other Poems. Sir *Philip Sidney* however, tho he commends this Work in his *Apology for Poetry,* censures the Rusticity of the Stile as an Affectation not to be allow'd. The Author's profess'd Veneration for *Chaucer* partly led him into this; yet there is a difference among the Pastorals, and the Reader will observe, that the Language of the Fifth and Eighth is more obsolete than that of some others; the reason of which might be, that the Design of those two Eclogues being Allegorical Satire, he chose a more antiquated Dress, as more proper to his Purpose. But however faulty he may be in the Excess of this, it is certain that a sprinkling of the rural Phrase, as it humours the Scene and Characters, has a very great Beauty in Pastoral Poetry; and of this any one may be convinc'd, by reading the Pastorals of Mr. *Philips,* which are written with great Delicacy of Taste, in the very Spirit and Manner of *Spenser.*

Having said that *Spenser* has mingled Satire in some of his Eclogues, I know not whether this may not be another Objection to them: it may be doubted whether any thing of this kind shou'd be admitted to disturb the Tranquillity and Pleasure which shou'd every where reign in Pastoral Poems; or at least nothing shou'd be introduc'd more than the light and pleasant Railleries or Contentions of Shepherds about their Flocks, their Mistresses, or their Skill in piping and singing. I cannot wholly justify my Author in this, yet must say that the Excellency of the Moral in those Pastorals does in a great measure excuse his transgressing the strict Rules of Criticism. Besides, as he design'd under an Allegory to censure the vicious Lives of bad Priests, and to expose their Usurpation of Pomp and Dominion, nothing cou'd be more proper to this purpose than the Allegory he has chosen; the Author of our Holy Religion having himself dignify'd the Parable of a *good Shepherd;* and the natural Innocence, Simplicity, Vigilance, and Freedom from Ambition, which are the Characters of that kind of Life, being a very good Contrast to the Vices and Luxury, and to that Degeneracy from their first Pattern, which the Poet wou'd there reprehend. . . .

TWO

JOSEPH SPENCE

The Defects of Our Modern Poets, in Their Allegories: Instanced from SPENSER'S Fairy Queen (1747)*

The faults of Spenser in relation to his machinery or allegories (continued Polymetis) seem to me to be all reducible to three general heads. They arise either from that poet's mixing the fables of heathenism with the truths of christianity; or from his misrepresenting the allegories of the antients; or from something that is wrong in the allegories of his own invention. As to the two former, I shall not have much to say; but shall beg leave to be a little more diffuse as to the third.

The strongest instance I can recollect of the first kind, his mixing christianity and heathenism together, is in that short view which he gives of the infernal regions in the seventh Canto of the second book. . . . The particular part I mean is where he speaks of Jupiter and Tantalus, and of Pontius Pilate and our Saviour, almost in the same breath.[1]

The instances of Spenser's misrepresenting the stories and allegorical personages of the antients are not uncommon in this poem. Thus, in a former view of hell, he speaks of Esculapius as in eternal torments.[2] In another place, he introduces a company of satyrs to save a lady from a rape, tho' their distinguishing character was lust; and makes Sylvanus the god or governor of the satyrs, a dignity which the antients never speak of for him, no more than of the ivy-girdle which he gives him round his waist.[3] It is with the same sort of liberty as I take it that he describes the day, or morning, as having purple hair;[4] the Sirens as half-fish;[5] and Bacchus as fat:[6] that he speaks of Clio as Apollo's wife;[7]

---

* This is from Dialogue XIX of *Polymetis*. Some footnotes have been omitted, others revised, and some changes in punctuation have been made.

32

and of Cupid as brother of the Graces:[8] and that he represents Orion, in one place, as flying from a snake in the heavens;[9] and, in another, as a water-god and one of the attendants of Neptune. The latter is in Spenser's account of the marriage of the Thames and Medway, in which he has greatly increased Neptune's court and added several deities as attendants to that god which were never regarded as such by any of the antients.[10]

This may be sufficient to shew that where Spenser does introduce the allegories of the antient poets, he does not always follow them so exactly as he might; and in the allegories which are purely of his own invention (tho' his invention is one of the richest and most beautiful that perhaps ever was), I am sorry to say that he does not only fall very short of that simplicity and propriety which is so remarkable in the works of the antients, but runs now and then into thoughts that are quite unworthy so great a genius. I shall mark out some of these faults to you that appear even through all his beauties; and which may, perhaps, look quite gross to you when they are thus taken from them and laid together by themselves: but if they should prejudice you at all against so fine a writer, read almost any one of his entire Cantos, and it will reconcile you to him again. The reason of my producing these instances to you is only to shew what faults the greatest allegorist may commit; whilst the manner of allegorizing is left upon so unfixed and irregular a footing as it was in his time and is still among us.

The first sort of fault I shall mention to you, from such allegories of Spenser as are purely of his own invention, is their being sometimes too complicated or over-done. Such for example are his representations of Scandal, Discord, and Pride.

Scandal is what Spenser calls the Blatant Beast, and indeed he has made a very strange beast of him. He says that his mouth was as wide as a peck, and that he had a thousand tongues in it, of dogs, cats, bears, tygers, men, and serpents.[11]

There is a duplicity in his figure of Discord which is carried on so far as to be quite preposterous. He makes her hear double and look two different ways; he splits her tongue, and even her heart, in two; and makes her act contrarily with her two hands, and walk forward with one foot and backward with the other at the same time.[12]

There is a great deal of Apparatus in Spenser's manner of introducing Pride in a personal character; and she has so many different things and attributes about her, that was this shew to be represented (in the manner of our old pageants), they would rather set one a guessing what they meant themselves than serve to point out who the principal figure should be. She makes her appearance exalted in a high chariot drawn by six different creatures: every one of them carrying a Vice, as a postilion, on his back; and all drove on by Satan as charioteer. The six Vices are Idleness, on an ass; Gluttony, on a hog; Lechery, on a goat; Avarice, on a camel laden with gold; Envy, eating a toad and riding on a wolf; and Wrath, with a firebrand in his hand, on a lion.[13] The account of each of these particular Vices in Spenser is admirable: the chief fault I find with it is that it is too complex a way of characterizing Pride in general and may possibly be as improper in some few respects, as it is redundant in others.

There is another particular in some of Spenser's allegories which I cannot but look upon as faulty, tho' it is not near so great a fault as the former. What I mean is his affixing such filthy ideas to some of his personages, or characters, that it half turns one's stomach to read his account of them. Such, for example, is the description of Error in the very first Canto of the poem;[14] of which we may very well say, in the poet's own words, on a like occasion:

Such loathly matter, were small lust to speak, or think! [15]

The third fault in the allegories of Spenser's own invention is that they are sometimes stretched to such a degree that they appear rather extravagant than great; and that he is sometimes so minute, in pointing out every particular of its vastness to you, that the object is in danger of becoming ridiculous instead of being admirable. This is not common in Spenser: the strongest instance of the few I can remember is in his description of the dragon killed by the knight of the red-cross in the last Canto of his first book. The tail of this dragon, he tells you, wanted but very little of being three furlongs in length; the blood that gushes from his wound is enough to drive a water-mill; and his roar is like that of a hundred hungry lions.[16]

The fourth class of faults in Spenser's allegories consists of such as arise from their not being well invented. You will easily, I believe, allow me here the three following postulata. That in introducing allegories, one should consider whether the thing is fit to be represented as a person or not. Secondly, that if you chuse to represent it as a human personage, it should not be represented with any thing inconsistent with the human form or nature. And thirdly, that when it is represented as a man, you should not make it perform any action which no man in his senses would do.

Spenser seems to have erred against the first of these maxims in those lines in his description of the cave of Care.

> ———They for nought would from their work refrain,
> Nor let his speeches come unto their ear;
> And eke the breathful bellows blew amain
> Like to the northern wind, that none could hear:
> Those, Pensiveness did move; and Sighs, the bellows were.[17]

Was a poet to say that sighs are "the bellows, that blow up the fire of love," that would be only a metaphor—a poor one indeed, but not at all improper—but here they are realized, or rather metamorphized into bellows, which I could never persuade myself to think any way proper. Spenser is perhaps guilty of the same sort of fault in making Gifts, or Munera, a woman, in the second Canto of the fifth book,[18] tho' that may be only a misnomer, for if he had called her Bribery, one should not have the same objection. But the grossest instance in him of this kind is in the ninth Canto of the second book, where he turns the human body into a castle; the tongue into the porter that keeps the gate; and the teeth into two and thirty warders dressed in white.[19] Spenser seems to have erred against the second of thse maxims in representing the regid execution of the laws under the character of a man all made up of iron;[20] and Bribery (or the lady Munera, before mentioned) as a woman with golden hands and silver feet;[21] and against the third, where he describes Desire as holding coals of fire in his hands and blowing them up into a flame,[22] which last particular is some degrees worse than Ariosto's bringing in Discord, in his Orlando Furioso, with a flint and steel to strike fire in the face of Pride.[23]

The fifth sort of fault is when the allegorical personages, tho' well invented, are not well marked out. There are many instances of this in Spenser which are but too apt to put one in mind of the fancifulness and whims of Ripa and Vænius that I mentioned to you this evening. Thus in one Canto, Doubt is represented as walking with a staff that shrinks under him; Hope, with an aspergoire, or the instrument the Roman catholics use for sprinkling sinners with holy-water; Dissimulation, as twisting two clews of silk together; Grief, with a pair of pincers; and Pleasure, with an humble-bee in a phial:[24] and in another (in the procession of the months and seasons), February is introduced in a waggon drawn by two fishes; May, as riding on Castor and Pollux: June is mounted on a crab; October, on a scorpion: and November comes in, on a Centaur, all in a sweat; because (as the poet observes) he had just been fatting his hogs.[25]

This might, full as well, have been ranged under my sixth and last class of faults in Spenser's allegories; consisting of such instances as, I fear, can scarce be called by any softer name than that of Ridiculous Imaginations. Such, I think, is that idea of Ignorance in the first book, where he is made to move with the back part of his head foremost;[26] and that of Danger in the fourth with Hatred, Murder, Treason, &c. in his back.[27] Such is the sorrowful lady, with a bottle for her tears and a bag to put her repentance into,[28] and both running out almost as fast as she puts them in; such the thought of a vast giant's shrinking into an empty form, like a bladder;[29] the horses of Night, foaming far;[30] Sir Guyon, putting a padlock on the tongue of Occasion;[31] and Remorse, nipping St. George's heart.[32]

Had Spenser formed his allegories on the plan of the antient poets and artists as much as he did from Ariosto and the Italian allegorists, he might have followed nature much more closely and would not have wandered so often into such strange and inconsistent imaginations. I am apt to believe that he considered the Orlando Furioso, in particular, as a poem wholly serious, tho' the author of it certainly wrote it partly in jest. There are several lines and passages in it that must have been intended for burlesque; and they surely consider that poem in the truest light, who consider it as a work of a mixed nature: as something between the professed gravity of Tasso, and the broad laugh of Berni and his followers. Perhaps Spenser's taking some things to be said seriously, which Ariosto meant for ridicule, may have led him now and then to say things that are ridiculous, where he meant to be very serious.

However that be, we may reasonably conclude from so great failures as I have been mentioning to you in so great a man (whether they arise from his too much indulging the luxuriance of his own fancy or from his copying after so irregular a pattern), that it would be extremely useful for our poets in general to follow the plan of allegory as far as it is settled to their hands by the antients: at least, till some modern may have invented and established some better plan for them to go upon; a thing which (to deal fairly with you) I do not expect to see done in our days. . . .

NOTES

1. *Faerie Queene*, II, vii, 59-62. [All subsequent references are to the *Faerie Queene* unless otherwise stated.]
2. I, v, 40-42.
3. I, vi, 6-18.
4. V, x, 16.
5. II, xii, 31.
6. III, i, 51.
7. I, xi, 5.
8. II, viii, 6.
9. II, ii, 46.
10. IV, xi, 13-15.
11. VI, xii, 26-28.
12. IV, i, 27-29.
13. I, iv, 18-35.
14. I, i, 20.
15. V, xi, 31.
16. I, xi, 11, 22, 37.
17. IV, v, 38.
18. V, ii, 9, 10.
19. II, ix, 21, 25, 26.
20. V, i, 12.
21. V, ii, 10.
22. III, xii, 9.
23. *Orlando Furioso*, Book 18, stanza 34.
24. III, xii, 10, 13, 14, 16, 18.
25. VII, vii, 43, 34, 35, 39, 40.
26. I, viii, 31.
27. IV, x, 16, 17, 20.
28. VI, viii, 24.
29. I, viii, 24.
30. I, v, 28. [Spenser's line reads: "Then foming *tarre,* their bridles they would champe."]
31. II, iv, 12.
32. I, x, 27.

THREE

JOHN UPTON

*Preface to the "Fairie Queene" (1758)**

. . . 'Tis not my intention in this place to enter into a particular criticism of any of our poet's writings, excepting the Fairy Queen; which poem seems to have been hitherto very little understood; notwithstanding he has opened, in a great measure, his design and plan in a letter to his honoured friend Sir W. R. How readily has every one acquiesced in Dryden's opinion? [1] *That the action of this poem is not one—*[2] *that there is no uniformity of design; and that he aims at the accomplishment of no action.* It might have been expected that Hughes, who printed Spenser's works, should not have joined so freely in the same censure: and yet he tells us[3] *that the several books appear rather like so many several poems, than one entire fable: each of them having its peculiar knight, and being independent of the rest.*

Just in the same manner did the critics and commentators formerly abuse old Homer; his Iliad, they said, was nothing else, but a parcel of loose songs and rhapsodies concerning the Trojan war, which he sung at festivals; and these loose ballads were first collected, and [4] stitched, as it were, together by Pisistratus; being parts without any coherence, or relation to a whole, and unity of design.

As this subject requires a particular consideration; I desire the reader will attend to the following vindication of Homer and Spenser, as they have both fallen under one common censure.

In every poem there ought to be simplicity and unity; and in the epic poem the unity of the action should never be violated by introducing any ill-joined or heterogeneous parts. This essential rule Spenser

---

*John Upton edited the *Faerie Queene* in two volumes in 1758. Reprinted from the "Preface" are pp. xx-xxvii.

seems to me strictly to have followed: for what story can well be shorter, or more simple, than the subject of his poem? A British Prince sees in a vision the Fairy Queen; he falls in love, and goes in search after this unknown fair; and at length finds her. This fable has a beginning, a middle, and an end. The beginning is, the British Prince saw in a vision the Fairy Queen, and fell in love with her: the middle, his search after her, with the adventures that he underwent: the end, his finding whom he sought.

But here our curiosity is raised, and we want a more circumstantial information of many things. Who is this British Prince? What adventures did he undergo? Who was the Fairy Queen? Where, when, and how did he find her? Thus many questions arise, that require many solutions.

The action of this poem has not only simplicity and unity, but it is great and important. The hero is no less than the British Prince, Prince Arthur (who knows not Prince Arthur?). The time when this hero commenced his adventures is marked very exactly. In the reign of Uther Pendragon, father of Prince Arthur, Octa the son of Hengist, and his kinsman Eosa, thinking themselves not bound by the treaties which they had made with Aurelius Ambrosius, began to raise disturbances, and infest his dominions. This is the historical period of time, which Spenser has chosen.

> Ye see that good King Uther now doth make
> Strong warre upon the paynim brethren, hight
> Octa and Oza, whom hee lately brake
> Beside Cayr Verolame ———
>
> B. iii. C. 3. St. 52.

Could any epic poet desire a better historical foundation to build his poem on? Hear likewise what he himself says on this subject, "I chose the history of K. Arthur, as most fit for the excellency of his person, being made famous by many mens former works, and also furthest from the danger of envy and suspicion of present time." I much question if Virgil's Æneid is grounded on facts so well supported. Beside a poet is a *Maker;* nor does he compose a poem for the sake of any one hero, but rather he makes a hero for the sake of his poem: and if he follows fame, whether from the more authentic relation of [5] old chronicles, or from the legendary tales of old romances, yet still he is at liberty to add, or to diminish: in short, to speak out, he is at liberty to *lie,* as much as he pleases, provided his lies are consistent, and he makes his tale hang well together.

Prince Arthur saw in a vision, and seeing fell in love with the Fairy Queen, just about the time that she held her annual festival, when her knights had their various adventures assigned them. From either of these periods an historian might begin his narration; but a poet must begin from neither: because 'tis his province to carry you at once into the scene of action; and to complicate and perplex his story, in order to shew his art in unravelling it. The poet therefore might have opened his poem either with Prince Arthur, now actually set out on his quest, or with one of the knights sent from the Court of the Fairy Queen: by which means the reader is introduced into the midst of things; taking it for granted, that he either knows, or some way or other will know, all that preceded. 'Tis from the latter of these periods, namely from one of the Fairy knights, who is already rode forth on his adventure, that Spenser opens his poem; and he keeps you in suspense concerning his chief hero, Prince Arthur; 'till 'tis proper to introduce him with suitable pomp and magnificence.

Homer sings the anger of Achilles and its fatal consequences to the Grecians: nor can it be fairly objected to the unity of the Iliad, that when Achilles is removed from the scene of action, you scarcely hear him mentioned in several books: one being taken up with the exploits of Agamemnon, another with Diomed, another again with the successes of Hector. For his extensive plan required his different heroes to be shown in their different characters and attitudes. What therefore you allow to the old Grecian, be not so ungracious as to deny to your own countryman.

Again, 'tis observable that Homer's poem, though he sings the anger of Achilles, is not called the Achilleid, but the Iliad; because the action was at Troy. So Spenser does not call his poem by the name of his chief hero; but because his chief hero fought for the Fairy Queen in Fairy Land, and therein performed his various adventures, therefore he intitles his poem *The Fairy Queen*. Hence it appears that the adventures of Prince Arthur are necessarily connected with the adventures of the knights of Fairy Land. This young Prince has been kept hitherto in designed ignorance of what relates to his family and real dignity: his education, under old Timon and the magician Merlin, was to prepare him for future glory; but as yet his virtues have not been called forth into action. The poet therefore by bringing you acquainted with some of the heroes of Fairy Land, at the same time that he is bringing you acquainted with his chief hero, acts agreeably to his extensive plan, without destroying the unity of the action. The only fear is, lest the underplots, and the seemingly adscititious members, should grow too large for the body of the entire action: 'tis requisite therefore that the several incidental intrigues should be unravelled, as we proceed in getting nearer and nearer to the main plot; and that we at length gain an uninterrupted view at once of the whole. And herein I cannot help admiring the resemblance between the ancient father of poets, and Spenser; who clearing the way by the solution of intermediate plots and incidents, brings you nearer to his capital piece; and then shows his hero at large: and when Achilles once enters the field, the other Greeks are lost in his splendor, as the stars at the rising of the sun. So when Prince Arthur had been perfected in heroic and moral virtues, and his fame thoroughly known and recognized in Fairy Land; Him we should have seen not only dissolving the inchantment of the witch Duessa (an adventure too hard for the single prowess of St. George), but likewise binding in adamantine chains, or delivering over to utter perdition that old wizard Archimago, the common enemy of Fairy Knights, whom no chains as yet could hold: in short, him should we have seen eclipsing all the other heroes, and in the end accompanied with the Fairy Knights making his solemn entry into the presence of Gloriana, the Fairy Queen: and thus his merits would have intitled him to that Glory, which by Magnificence, or Magnanimity, the perfection of all the rest of the virtues, he justly had acquired.

It seems, by some hints given us by the poet, that he intended likewise an Heroic Poem, whose title was to be *King Arthur;* and the chief subject of the poem, the wars of the King and Queen of Fairy Land (now governed by Arthur and Gloriana) against the Paynim King: the chief Captains employed were to be those Fairy Knights, whom already he had brought us acquainted with: and the historical allusions undoubtedly would point, in the allegorical view, at the wars that Q. Elizabeth waged with the K. of Spain; as the Fairy Knights would typically represent her warlike Courtiers. This seems plain from what St. George says to Una's parents, in B. i. C. 12. St. 18.

> I bownden am streight after this emprize ———
> Backe to retourne to that great Faery Queene,

> And her to serve sixe yeares in warlike wize
> Gainst that proud Paynim King that works her teene.

And plainer still from what the poet says in his own person, in B. i. C. 11. St. 7.

> Fayre goddesse, lay that furious fitt asyde,
> Till I of warres and bloody Mars doe sing;
> And Bryton fieldes with Sarazin blood bedyde,
> Twixt that great Faery Queen and Paynim King.

Dryden tells us in his preface to the translation of Juvenal, that he had some thoughts of making choice for the subject of an heroic poem, King Arthur's conquests over the Saxons: And hinting at the same design in the preface to his Fables says, "That it was not for this noble knight [meaning Sir R. Blackmore] that he drew the plan of an epic poem on King Arthur." Milton likewise had the same intention, as he intimates in a Latin poem to Mansus.

> Si quando indigenas revocabo in carmina reges,
> Arturumque etiam sub terris bella moventem;
> Aut dicam invictae sociali foedere mensae
> Magnanimos heroas; et, O modo spiritus adsit,
> Frangam Saxonicas Britonum Sub Marte phalanges.

We have shown that the action of the Fairy Queen is uniform, great and important; but 'tis required that the fable should be probable. A story will have probability, if it hangs well together, and is consistent: And provided the tales are speciously told, the probability of them will not be destroyed, though they are tales of wizards or witches, monstrous men and monstrous women; for who, but downright miscreants, question wonderful tales? And do you imagine that Homer, Virgil, Spenser, and Milton, ever thought of writing an epic poem for unbelievers and infidels? But if after all the reader cannot with unsuspecting credulity swallow all these marvellous tales; what should hinder the poet, but want of art, from so contriving his fable, that more might be meant, than meets the eye or ear? Cannot he say one thing in proper numbers and harmony, and yet secretly intend something else, or (to use a Greek expression) cannot he make the fable allegorical? Thus Forms and Persons might be introduced, shadowing forth, and emblematically representing the mysteries of physical and moral sciences: Virtue and Truth may appear in their original ideas and lovely forms; and even Vice might be decked out in some kind of dress, resembling beauty and truth; lest if seen without any disguise, she appear too loathsom for mortal eyes to behold her.

It must be confessed that the religion of Greece and Rome was particularly adapted to whatever figurative turn the poet intended to give it; and even philosophers mixed mythology with the gravest subjects of theology. Hesiod's Generation of the Gods, is properly the generation of the world, and a history of natural philosophy: he gives life, energy, and form to all the visible and invisible parts of the universe, and almost to all the powers and faculties of the imagination; in a word his poem is "a continued allegory." When every part therefore of the universe was thought to be under the particular care of a tutelar deity; when not only the sun, moon, and planets, but mountains, rivers, and groves; nay even virtues, vices, accidents, qualities, &c. were the objects of veneration and of religious dread; there was no violation given to public belief, if the poet changed his metaphor, or rather continued it, in an allegory. Hence Homer, instead of saying that Achilles, had not wisdom checked him, would have slain Agamemnon, continues the metaphor; and consistent with his religion, brings Minerva, the goddess of wisdom, down from heaven, on purpose to check the rage of the angry hero. On the same system is founded the well-known fable of Prodicus: and the picture of Cebes is a continued allegory, containing the most interesting truths relating to human life.

As 'tis necessary that the poet should give his work all that variety, which is consistent with its nature and design, so his allegory might be enlarged and varied by his pointing at historical events under concealed names; and while his story is told consistent, emblematically and typically, some historical characters and real transactions might be signifyed. Thus though in one sense you are in Fairy land, yet in another you may be in the British dominions. . . .

NOTES

1. Dryden's dedication of the translation of Virgil's Æneid.
2. See his dedication of the translation of Juvenal.
3. In the preface to his edition.
4. Hence called rhapsodies.
5. Our poet follows Jeffry of Monmouth, the British historian; and the old Romance intitled, The History of Prince Arthur and his Knights of the Round Table: or *La Mort d' Arthure,* as intitled at the end, and so cited by Ascham in his School-Master, pag. 87. who mentions it as a favourite author in his time. See the notes in pag. 656.

FOUR

THOMAS WARTON

*Of the Plan and Conduct of the "Fairy Queen" (1762)**

When the works of Homer and of Aristotle began to be restored and studied in Italy, when the genuine and uncorrupted sources of antient poetry and antient criticism were opened, and every species of literature at last emerged from the depths of Gothic ignorance and barbarity; it might have been expected, that, instead of the romantic manner of poetical composition introduced and established by the Provencial bards, a new and more legitimate taste of writing would have succeeded. With these advantages it was reasonable to conclude, that unnatural events, the machinations of imaginary beings, and adventures entertaining only as they were improbable, would have given place to justness of thought and design, and to that decorum which nature dictated, and which the example and the precept of antiquity had authorised. But it was a long time before such a change was effected. We find Ariosto, many years after the revival of letters, rejecting truth for magic, and preferring the ridiculous and incoherent excursions of Boyardo, to the propriety and uniformity of the Grecian and Roman models. Nor did the restoration of antient learning produce any effectual or immediate improvement in the state of criticism. Beni, one of the most celebrated critics of the sixteenth century, was still so infatuated with a fondness for the old Provencial vein, that he ventured to write a regular dissertation,[1] in which he compares Ariosto with Homer.

Trissino, who flourished a few[2] years after Ariosto, had taste and boldness enough to publish an epic poem,[3] written in professed imitation

---

* Thomas Warton's *Observations on the Fairy Queen of Spenser,* first published in 1754, was enlarged and published in two volumes in 1762. These selections are reprinted from the second edition of 1762 and include parts of Sections I, IV, and X. Some liberty has been taken in abridging certain footnotes and in omitting others.

of the Iliad. But this attempt met with little regard or applause for the reason on which its real merit was founded. It was rejected as an insipid and uninteresting performance, having few devils or enchantments to recommend it. To Trissino succeeded Tasso, who, in his Gierusaleme Liberata, took the antients for his guides; but was still too sensible of the popular prejudice in favour of ideal beings, and romantic adventures, to neglect or omit them entirely. He had studied, and acknowledged the beauties of classical purity. Yet he still kept his first and favourite acquaintance, the old Provencial poets, in his eye. Like his own Rinaldo, who after he had gazed on the diamond shield of truth, and with seeming resolution was actually departing frcm Armida and her enchanted gardens, could not help looking back upon them with some remains of fondness. Nor did Tasso's Poem, though composed in some measure on a regular plan, give its author, among the Italians at least, any greater share of esteem and reputation on that account. Ariosto, with all his extravagancies, was still preferred. The superiority of the Orlando Furioso was at length established by a formal decree of the academicians della Crusca, who, amongst other literary debates, held a solemn court of enquiry concerning the merit of both poems.

Such was the prevailing taste, when Spenser projected the Fairy Queen: a poem, which according to the practice of Ariosto, was to consist of allegories, enchantments, and romantic expeditions, conducted by knights, giants, magicians, and fictitious beings. It may be urged, that Spenser made an unfortunate choice, and discovered but little judgment, in adopting Ariosto for his example, rather than Tasso, who had so evidently exceeded his rival, at least in conduct and decorum. But our author naturally followed the poem which was most celebrated and popular. For although the French critics universally gave the preference to Tasso, yet, in Italy, the partisans on the side of Ariosto were by far the most powerful, and consequently in England: for Italy, in the age of queen Elizabeth, gave laws to our island in all matters of taste, as France has done ever since. At the same time it may be supposed, that of the two, Ariosto was Spenser's favourite; and that he was naturally biassed to prefer that plan which would admit the most extensive range for his unlimited imagination. What was Spenser's particular plan, in consequence of this choice, and how it was conducted, I now proceed to examine.

The poet supposes,[4] that the FAERIE QUEENE, according to an established annual custom, held a magnificent feast, which continued twelve days; on each of which, respectively, twelve several complaints are presented before her. Accordingly, in order to redress the injuries which were the occasion of these several complaints, she dispatches, with proper commissions, twelve different Knights, each of which, in the particular adventure allotted to him, proves an example of some particular virtue, as of holiness, temperance, justice, chastity; and has one complete book assigned to him, of which he is the hero. But besides these twelve knights, severally exemplifying twelve moral virtues, the poet has constituted one principal knight or general hero, viz. PRINCE ARTHUR. This personage represents magnificence; a virtue which is supposed to be the perfection of all the rest. He moreover assists in every book, and the end of his actions is to discover, and win, GLORIANA, or Glory. In a word, in this character the poet professes to pourtray, "THE IMAGE OF A BRAVE KNIGHT PERFECTED IN THE TWELVE PRIVATE MORAL VIRTUES."

It is evident that our author in establishing one hero, who seeking and attaining one grand end, which is GLORIANA, should exemplify one grand character, or a brave Knight perfected in the twelve private moral virtues, copied the cast and construction of the antient Epic. But sensible as he was of the importance and expediency of the unity of the hero and of his design, he does not, in the mean time, seem convinced of the necessity of that unity of action, by the means of which such a design should be properly accomplished. At least, he has not followed the method practised by Homer and Virgil, in conducting their respective heroes to the proposed end.

It may be asked with great propriety, how does ARTHUR execute the grand, simple, and ultimate design, intended by the poet? It may be answered, with some degree of plausibility, that by lending his respective assistance to each of the twelve Knights, who patronize the twelve virtues, in his allotted defence of each, ARTHUR approaches still nearer and nearer to Glory, till at last he gains a complete possession. But surely to assist is not a sufficient service. This secondary merit is inadequate to the reward. The poet ought to have made this "brave Knight" the leading adventurer. ARTHUR should have been the principal agent in vindicating the cause of Holiness, Temperance, and the rest. If our hero had thus, in his own person, exerted himself in the protection of the twelve virtues, he might have been deservedly styled the perfect Pattern of all, and consequently would have succeeded in the task assigned, the attainment of Glory. At present he is only a subordinate or accessory character. The difficulties and obstacles which we expect him to surmount, in order to accomplish his final atchievement, are removed by others. It is not he who subdues the dragon, in the first book, or quells the magician Busirane, in the third. These are the victories of St. George and of Britomart. On the whole, the twelve Knights do too much for ARTHUR to do any thing; or at least, so much as may be reasonably required from the promised plan of the poet. While we are attending to the design of the hero of the book, we forget that of the hero of the poem. Dryden remarks, "We must do Spenser that justice to observe, that magnanimity [magnificence] which is the true character of Prince Arthur, shines throughout the whole poem; and succours the rest when they are in distress." [5] If the magnanimity of Arthur did, in reality, thus shine in every part of the poem with a superior and steady lustre, our author would fairly stand acquitted. At present it bursts forth but seldom, in obscure and interrupted flashes. "To succour the rest when they are in distress," is, as I have hinted, a circumstance of too little importance in the character of this universal champion. It is a service to be performed in the cause of the hero of the Epic Poem by some dependent or inferior chief, the business of a Gyas or a Cloanthus.

On the whole, we may observe, that Spenser's adventures, separately taken as the subject of each single book, have not always a mutual dependence upon each other, and consequently do not properly contribute to constitute one legitimate poem. Hughes not considering this, has advanced a remark in commendation of Spenser's critical conduct, which is indeed one of the most blameable parts of it. "If we consider the first book as an entire work of itself, we shall find it to be no irregular contrivance. There is one principal action, which is completed in the twelfth canto, and the several incidents are proper, as they tend either to obstruct or promote it." [6]

As the heroic poem is required to be one WHOLE, compounded of many various parts, relative and dependent, it is expedient that not one of those parts should be so regularly contrived, and so completely finished, as to become a WHOLE of itself. For the mind, being once satisfied in arriving at the consummation of an orderly series of events, acquiesces in that satisfaction. Our attention and curiosity are in the midst diverted from pursuing, with due vigour, the final and general catastrophe. But while each part is left incomplete, if separated from the rest, the mind still eager to gratify its expectations, is irresistibly and imperceptibly drawn from part to part, 'till it receives a full and ultimate satisfaction from the accomplishment of one great event, which all those parts, following and illustrating each other, contributed to produce.

Our author was probably aware, that by constituting twelve several adventures for twelve several heroes, the want of a general connection would often appear. On this account, as I presume, he sometimes resumes and finishes in some distant book, a tale formerly begun and left imperfect. But as numberless interruptions necessarily intervene, this proceeding often occasions infinite perplexity to the reader. And it seems to be for the same reason, that after one of the twelve Knights has atchieved the adventure of his proper book, the poet introduces him, in the next book, acting perhaps in an inferior sphere, and degraded to some less dangerous exploit. But this conduct is highly inartificial: for it destroys that repose which the mind feels after having accompanied a hero, through manifold struggles and various distresses, to success and victory. Besides, when we perceive him entering upon any less illustrious attempt, our former admiration is in some measure diminished. Having seen him complete some memorable conquest, we become interested in his honour, and are jealous concerning his future reputation. To attempt, and even to atchieve, some petty posterior enterprise, is to derogate from his dignity, and to sully the transcendent lustre of his former victories.

Spenser perhaps would have embarassed himself and the reader less, had he made every book one entire detached poem of twelve cantos, without any reference to the rest. Thus he would have written twelve different books, in each of which he might have completed the pattern of a particular virtue in twelve Knights respectively: at present he has remarkably failed, in endeavouring to represent all the virtues exemplified in one. The poet might either have established TWELVE KNIGHTS without an ARTHUR, or an ARTHUR without TWELVE KNIGHTS. Upon supposition that Spenser was resolved to characterise the twelve moral virtues, the former plan perhaps would have been best: the latter is defective as it necessarily wants simplicity. It is an action consisting of twelve actions, all equally great and unconnected between themselves, and not compounded of one uninterrupted and coherent chain of incidents, tending to the accomplishment of one design.

I have before remarked, that Spenser intended to express the character of a hero perfected in the twelve moral virtues, by representing him as assisting in the service of all, till at last he becomes possessed of all. This plan, however injudicious, he certainly was obliged to observe. But in the third book, which is styled the Legend of Chastity, Prince Arthur does not so much as lend his assistance in the vindication of that virtue. He appears indeed; but not as an agent, or even an auxiliary, in the adventure of the book.

Yet it must be confessed, that there is something artificial in the poet's manner of varying from historical precision. This conduct is rationally illustrated by himself.[7] According to this plan, the reader would have been agreeably surprised in the last book, when he came to discover that the series of adventures, which he had just seen completed, were undertaken at the command of the FAIRY QUEEN; and that the Knights had severally set forward to the execution of them, from her annual birth-day festival. But Spenser, in most of the books, has injudiciously forestalled the first of these particulars; which certainly should have been concealed 'till the last book, not only that a needless repetition of the same thing might be prevented, but that an opportunity might be secured of striking the reader's mind with a circumstance new and unexpected.

But notwithstanding the plan and conduct of Spenser, in the poem before us, is highly exceptionable, yet we may venture to pronounce, that the scholar has more merit than his master in this respect; and that the FAIRY QUEEN is not so confused and irregular as the Orlando Furioso. There is indeed no general unity which prevails in the former: but, if we consider every book, or adventure, as a separate poem, we shall meet with so many distinct, however imperfect, unities, by which an attentive reader is less bewildered, than in the maze of indigestion and incoherence, of which the latter totally consists, where we seek in vain either for partial or universal integrity.

> ———— Cum nec pes nec caput *uni*
> Reddatur *Formæ* ————[8]

. . . . But it is absurd to think of judging either Ariosto or Spenser by precepts which they did not attend to. We who live in the days of writing by rule, are apt to try every composition by those laws which we have been taught to think the sole criterion of excellence. Critical taste is universally diffused, and we require the same order and design which every modern performance is expected to have, in poems where they never were regarded or intended. Spenser, and the same may be said of Ariosto, did not live in an age of planning. His poetry is the careless exuberance of a warm imagination and a strong sensibility. It was his business to engage the fancy, and to interest the attention by bold and striking images,[9] in the formation, and the disposition of which, little labour or art was applied. The various and the marvellous were the chief sources of delight. Hence we find our author ransacking alike the regions of reality and romance, of truth and fiction, to find the proper decorations and furniture for his fairy structure. Born in such an age, Spenser wrote rapidly from his own feelings, which at the same time were naturally noble. Exactness in his poem would have been like the cornice which a painter introduced in the grotto of Calypso. Spenser's beauties are like the flowers in Paradise.

> ———— Which not nice Art
> In beds and curious knots, but Nature boon
> Pour'd forth profuse, on hill, and dale, and plain;
> Both where the morning sun first warmly smote
> The open field, or where the unpierc'd shade
> Imbrown'd the noon-tide bowers.[10]

If the FAIRY QUEEN be destitute of that arrangement and œconomy which epic severity requires, yet we scarcely regret the loss of these while their place is so amply supplied, by something which more powerfully attracts us: something, which engages the affections [and?] the feelings of the heart, rather than the cold approbation of the head. If there be any poem, whose graces please, because they are situated beyond the reach of art, and where the force and faculties of creative imagination delight, because they are unassisted and unrestrained by those of deliberate judgment, it is this. In reading Spenser if the critic is not satisfied, yet the reader is transported.

NOTES

1. Comparazione di T. Tasso con Omero e Virgilio, insieme con la difesa dell' Ariosto paragonato ad Omero, &c.

2. He died 1550. Ariosto 1535.

3. L'Italia Liberata di Goti, 1524. It is in blank verse, which the author would have introduced instead of the *Terza* Rima of Dante, or the *Ottava* of Boccace.

4. See Spenser's Letter to Sir W. Raleigh, &c.

5. Dedication to the Translation of Juvenal.

6. Remarks on the Fairy Queen. Hughes's Edit. of Spenser, vol. I.

7. Letter to Sir W. Raleigh.

8. HOR. ART. POET. v. 8.

9. Montesquieu has partly characterised Spenser, in the judgment he has passed upon the English poets, which is not true with regard to all of them. "Leurs poetes auroient plus souvent cette rudesse originale de l'invention, qu'une certaine delicatesse que donne le gout: on y trouveroit quelque chose qui approcheroit plu de la force de M. Ange, que de la grace du Raphael." L'Esprit du Loix, liv. 19. chap. 27. The French critics are too apt to form their general notions of English poetry, from our fondness for Shakespeare.

10. Parad. Lost, b. iv. v. 241.

Of Spenser's Stanza, Versification, and Language (1762)

Although Spenser's favorite Chaucer had made use of the *ottava rima*,[1] or stanza of eight lines; yet it seems probable, that Spenser was principally induced to adopt it, with the addition of one line, from the practice of Ariosto and Tasso, the most fashionable poets of his age. But Spenser, in chusing this stanza, did not sufficiently consider the genius of the english language, which does not easily fall into a frequent repetition of the same termination; a circumstance natural to the italian, which deals largely in identical cadences.

Besides, it is to be remembered, that Tasso and Ariosto did not embarrass themselves with the necessity of finding out so many similar terminations as Spenser. Their *ottava rima* has only three similar endings, alternately rhyming. The two last lines formed a distinct rhyme. But in Spenser, the second rhyme is repeated four times, and the third three.[2]

This constraint led our author into many absurdities; the most striking and obvious of which seem to be the following.

I. It obliged him to dilate the thing to be expressed, however unimportant, with trifling and tedious circumlocutions, viz.

> Now hath fair Phœbe, with her silver face,
> Thrice seen the shadows of this nether world,
> Sith last I left that honourable place,
> In which her royal presence is enroll'd.
>
> 2. 2. 44.

That is, "it is three months since I left her palace."

II. It necessitated him, when matter failed towards the close of a stanza, to run into a ridiculous redundancy and repetition of words, viz.

> In which was nothing pourtrahed nor wrought,
> Nor wrought nor pourtrahed, but easie to be thought.
>
> 2. 9. 33.

III. It forced him, that he might make out his complement of rhymes, to introduce a puerile or impertinent idea, viz.

> Not that proud towre of Troy, though richly GILT.
>
> 2. 9. 45.

Being here laid under the compulsion of producing a consonant word to *spilt* and *built,* which are preceding rhymes, he has mechanically given us an image at once little and improper.

To the difficulty of a stanza so injudiciously chosen, I think we may properly impute the great number of his elleipses, some of which will be pointed out at large in another place;* and it may be easily conceived, how that constraint which occasioned superfluity, should at the same time be the cause of omission.

Notwithstanding these inconveniencies flow from Spenser's measure, it must yet be owned, that some advantages arise from it; and we may venture to affirm, that the fullness and significancy of Spenser's descriptions, is often owing to the prolixity of his stanza, and the multitude of his rhymes. The discerning reader is desired to consider the following stanza, as an instance of what is here advanced. Guyon is binding FUROR.

> With hundred iron chaines he did him bind
> And hundred knots, which did him sore constraine;
> Yet his great iron teeth he still did grind,
> And grimly gnash, threatening revenge in vaine:
> His burning eyen, whom bloudie strakes did staine,
> Stared full wide, and threw forth sparks of fire;
> And more for ranke despight, than for great paine,
> Shakt his long locks colour'd like copper wire,
> And bit his tawny beard, to shew his raging ire.
>
> 2. 4. 15.

In the subsequent stanza there are some images, which perhaps were produced by a multiplicity of rhymes.

> He all that night, that too long night did passe,
> And now the day out of the ocean-maine
> Began to peep above this earthly masse,
> With pearly dew sprinkling the morning grasse;
> Then up he rose like heavy lump of leade,
> That in his face, as in a looking glasse,
> The signs of anguish one might plainly reade.
>
> 4. 5. 45.

Dryden, I think, somewhere remarks, that rhyme often helped him

---

* See Vol. II, pp. 4-12.

to a thought; an observation, which, probably, Spenser's experience had likewise supplied him with. Spenser, however, must have found more assistance in this respect, from writing in rhyme, than Dryden, in proportion as his stanza obliged him to a more repeated use of it.

In speaking of Spenser's rhyme, it ought to be remarked, that he often new-spells a word to make it rhyme more precisely.

Take these specimens.

> And of her own foule entrailes makes her *meat,*
> Meat fit for such a monster's monsterous DIEAT.
> > 5. 12. 31.

> Timely to joy, and carry comely *cheare,*
> For though this clowd have now me overcast,
> Yet do I not of better times DESPEARE.
> > 5. 5. 38.

> Though when the term is full ACCOMPLISHID,
> Then shall a sparke of fire which hath long while
> Bene in his ashes raked up and *hid.*
> > 3. 3. 48.

> Then all the rest into their coches CLIM,
> And through, &c.
> Upon great Neptune's necke they softly *swim.*
> > 3. 4. 42.

> ———Mightily *amate,*
> As fast as forward earst, now backward to RETRATE.
> > 4. 3. 26.

> Shall have that golden girdle for *reward,*
> And of, &c.
> Shall to the fairest lady be PREFAR'D.
> > 4. 2. 27.

> ———Into the hardest *stone,*
> Such as behind their backes, &c.
> Were thrown by Pyrrha, and DEUCALIONE.
> > 5. Introd. 2.

And, to be short, we meet with *ycled* for yclad, *darre* for dare, *prejudize* for prejudice, *sam* for same, *lam* for lamb, *denay* for deny, *pervart* for pervert, *heare* for hair, and numberless other instances of orthography destroyed for the sake of rhyme. This was a liberty which Chaucer, Gower, and Lydgate frequently made use of; and it may not be improper in this place, to exhibit the sentiments of a critic in queen Elizabeth's age upon it. "Now there cannot be in a MAKER a fowler fault than to falsifie his accent to serve his cadence; or by untrue orthograghy [*sic*] to wrench his words to help his rhyme; for it is a sign that such a maker is not copious in his own language." However he seems afterwards to allow the deviation from true spelling, in some measure. "It is somewhat more tollerable to help the rhyme by false orthographie, than to leave an unpleasant dissonance to the eare, by keeping trewe orthographie and losing the rime; as for example, it is better to rime *dore* with *restore*, than in his true orthographie which is *doore*. Such men were in effect the most part of all your old rimers, and 'specially Gower, who to make up his rime, would for the most part write his terminant syllable with false orthographie; and many times not sticke to put a plaine french word for an english; and so by your leave do many of our common rimers at this day." *

. . . It is indeed surprising upon the whole, that Spenser should execute a poem of uncommon length, with so much spirit and ease, laden as he was with so many shackles, and embarrassed with so complicated a BONDAGE of RIMING. Nor can I recollect, that he has been so careless as to suffer the same word to be repeated as a rhyme to itself, in more than four or five instances; a fault, which if he had more frequently committed, his manifold beauties of versification would have obliged us to overlook; and which Harrington should have avoided more scrupulously, to compensate, in some degree, for the tameness and prosaic mediocrity of his numbers. . . .

Our author's *Pastorals* are written in professed imitation of Chaucer's style. This he tells us expressly in the beginning of *Colin Clouts come home again*.

> The shepherd's boy, best knowen by that name,
> That after TITYRUS [3] first sung his lay.

---

*This quotation is from George Puttenham's *The Arte of English Poesie,* Book II, Chapter IX, printed in G. Gregory Smith, *Elizabethan Critical Essays,* Oxford University Press, 1904, II, 84-85.

And the tale of the *Oak* and *Brier,* in the Eclogue of *Februarie,* is more peculiarly modelled after Chaucer's manner, and is accordingly thus introduced.

————A tale of truth
Which I cond of TITYRUS in my youth.

And in another pastoral he hints at his having copied Chaucer.

That *Colin* hight which well could pipe and sing,
For he of TITYRUS his song did lere.

In the *Pastorals* he likewise appears to have attempted an imitation of the *Visions* of *Pierce Plowman;* for after exhorting his muse not to contend with Chaucer, he adds,

Nor with the PLOWMAN that the pilgrim playde awhile.[4]

And besides, that his *Pastorals* might, in every respect, have the air of a work in old english, he has adopted and given them the title of an old book, called the SHEPHEARD'S KALENDER,[5] first printed by Wynkin de Worde, and reprinted about twenty years before he published these Pastorals, viz. 1559. This is what E. K. means, where he says in his epistle prefixed, "He tearmeth it the SHEPHERD'S KALENDER, applying an *old name* to a *new* work." One of Spenser's reasons for using so much antient phraseology in these Pastorals, was undoubtedly the obvious one of cloathing rural characters in the dress of doric simplicity, but the principal reason is most probably, that which is delivered by his friend and commentator, E. K.[6] who was "privie to all his designs": "In myne opinion, it is one especial prayse of many which are due to this poet, that he hath laboured to restore, as to their rightful heritage, such good and natural english words, as have been long time out of use, and almost cleane disherited; which is the only cause that our mother-tongue, which truly of itselfe is both *full enough for prose,* and *stately enough for verse,* hath long time beene counted most bare and barren of both; which default, when as some have endeavoured to salve and recure, they patched up the holes with peeces and ragges of other languages; borrowing here of the french, there of the italian, and every where of the latine; not weighing how ill those tongues accord with themselves, but much worse with ours; so now they have made our englishe tongue a gallimaufrey, or hodgepodge of all other speeches." Thus that which induced Spenser to adopt so much

obsolete language in the Pastorals, induced him likewise to do the same
in the FAIRY QUEEN. Hence too it appears, that he was disgusted
with the practice of his cotemporary writers, who had adulterated, according to his judgment, the purity of the english tongue by various
innovations from the spanish, french, latin, and italian. . . .

Our author's disapprobation of this practice appears more fully
from his own words, where he expressly hints that Chaucer's language,
which he so closely copied, was the pure English.

————Dan Chaucer WELL OF ENGLISH UNDEFILDE.
4. 2. 32.

But although Spenser disapproved of this corrupt adulteration of
style, so fashionable in his age, yet we find him notwithstanding, frequently introducing words from a foreign tongue, such as, *visnomie,
amenance, arret, mesprise, sovenance, afrap, aguise, amenage, obase,*
and the like; but these words the frequent return of his rhyme obliged
him to introduce, and accordingly they will generally be found at the
end of his lines. The poverty of our tongue, or rather the unfrequency of
it's identical terminations, compelled him likewise, for the sake of rhyme,
perpetually to coin new english words, such as *damnify'd, unmercify'd,
wonderment, warriment, unruliment, habitaunce, hazardrie,* &c. &c. To
this cause his many latinisms also may be attributed, which, like all the
rest, are substituted to make out the necessary jingle.

The censure of Jonson, upon our author's style, is perhaps un-
reasonable: "Spenser, in affecting the antients, writ no language." The
ground work and substance of his style is the language of his age. This
indeed is seasoned with various expressions, adopted from the elder
poets; but in such a manner, that the language of his age was rather
strengthened and dignified, than debased or disguised, by such a practice. In truth, the affectation of Spenser in this point, is by no means so
striking and visible, as Jonson has insinuated; nor is his phraseology so
difficult and obsolete, as it is generally supposed to be. For many stanzas
together, we may frequently read him with as much facility, as we can
the same number of lines in Shakespeare.

But although I cannot subscribe to Jonson's opinion concerning
Spenser's language, I must confess that the following sentiments of that
critic, concerning the use of old words in poetry, are admirable. "Words
borrowed of antiquity do lend a kind of majesty to style, and are not

without their delight sometimes. For they have the authority of yeares, and out of their intermission do lend a kind of grace-like newnesse. BUT THE ELDEST OF THE PRESENT, AND THE NEWEST OF THE PAST LANGUAGE IS THE BEST." But Jonson has literally translated the latter part of the paragraph, from Quintilian, without acknowledgment. "ERGO UT NOVORUM OPTIMA ERUNT MAXIME VETERA, ITA VETERUM MAXIME NOVA." [7]

I conclude this Section with a passage from the nervous, poetical, and witty Satires of bishop Hall; who having censured the petty poets of his age, for their various corruptions, and licentious abuses, of the english language, makes this compliment to Spenser.

> But lett no rebel satyr dare traduce
> Th' eternall Legends of thy FAERIE MUSE,
> Renowned SPENSER! whom no earthly wight
> Dares once to emulate, much less despight.
> *Salust* of France, and Tuscan *Ariost!*
> Yield up the lawrel-girlond ye have lost:
> And lett all others willows wear with mee,
> Or lett their undeserving temples bared bee.[8]

NOTES

1. Chaucer's stanza is not *strictly* so. Betussi in his Life of Boccace, acquaints us, that Boccace was the inventor of the OTTAVA RIMA, and that the *Theseide* of that author was the first poem in which it was ever applied.

2. See examples of the measures of the Provencial poets, in Petrarch. Spenser forms a compound of many of these.

3. Milton, in imitation of our author, styles Chaucer TITYRUS, where he hints at Chaucer's having travelled into Italy.

Quin et in has quondam pervenit TITYRUS oras.

Mansus, v. 34.

4. EPILOGUE to *Shep. Kalend.*

5. Hearne calls this piece, "a comical odd book, of which I have an imperfect copy, and look upon it as a GREAT CURIOSITY." Not. ad Gul. Neubrig. vol. 3. pag. 749.

6. Some have thought that his Name was Kerke. I suppose, because Spenser, in his letters to Harvey, mentions his lodging with one Mrs. Kerke, and, in the same, sends E. K.'s compliments to Harvey.

7. Instit. Or. l. I. cap. 6.

8. B. I. s. 4.

Of Spenser's Allegorical Character (1762)

In reading the works of a poet who lived in a remote age, it is necessary that we should look back upon the customs and manners which prevailed in that age. We should endeavour to place ourselves in the writer's situation and circumstances. Hence we shall become better enabled to discover, how his turn of thinking, and manner of composing, were influenced by familiar appearances and established objects, which are utterly different from those with which we are at present surrounded. For want of this caution, too many readers view the knights and damsels, the tournaments and enchantments, of Spenser, with modern eyes; never considering that the encounters of chivalry subsisted in our author's age; that romances were then most eagerly and universally studied; and that consequently Spenser, from the fashion of the times, was induced to undertake a recital of chivalrous atchievements, and to become, in short, a ROMANTIC Poet.

Spenser, in this respect, copied real manners, no less than Homer. A sensible historian observes, that "Homer copied true natural manners, which, however rough and uncultivated, will always form an agreeable and interesting picture: But the pencil of the english poet [Spenser] was employed in drawing the affectations, and conceits, and fopperies of chivalry." [1] This however, was nothing more than an imitation of real life; as much, at least, as the plain descriptions in Homer, which corresponded to the simplicity of manners then subsisting in Greece. Spenser, in the address of the *Shepherd's Kalendar,* to Sir Philip Sidney, couples his patron's learning with his skill in chivalry; a topic of panegyric, which would sound very odd in a modern dedication, especially before a sett of pastorals. *"To the noble and virtuous* gentleman, most worthy *of all titles, both of Learning and* CHIVALRIE, *Master Philip Sidney,"*

> Go little booke; thyself present,
> As child whose parent is unkent,
> To him that is the president
> Of noblenesse and CHIVALRIE.[2]

Nor is it sufficiently considered, that a popular practice of Spenser's

age, contributed, in a considerable degree, to make him an ALLEGOR-
ICAL Poet. We should remember, that in this age, allegory was applied
as the subject and foundation of public shews and spectacles, which
were exhibited with a magnificence superior to that of former times. The
virtues and vices, distinguished by their respective emblematical types,
were frequently personified, and represented by living actors. These figures bore a chief part in furnishing what they called PAGEAUNTS;[3]
which were then the principal species of entertainment, and were shewn,
not only in private, or upon the stage, but very often in the open streets
for solemnising public occasions, or celebrating any grand event. As a
proof of what is here mentioned, I refer the reader to Hollingshed's[4]
Description of the SHEW OF MANHOOD AND DESERT, exhibited
at Norwich, before queen Elizabeth; and more particularly to that historian's account of a TURNEY[5] performed by Fulke Grevile, the lords
Arundell and Windsor, and Sir Philip Sydney, who are feigned to be
the children of DESIRE, attempting to win the FORTRESS of
BEAUTY. In the composition of the last spectacle, no small share of
poetical invention appears.

In the mean time, I do not deny that Spenser was, in great measure, tempted by the *Orlando Furioso,* to write an allegorical poem. Yet
it must still be acknowledged, that Spenser's peculiar mode of allegorising seems to have been dictated by those spectacles, rather than by the
fictions of Ariosto. In fact, Ariosto's species of allegory does not so
properly consist in impersonating the virtues, vices, and affections of the
mind, as in the adumbration of moral doctrine,[6] under the actions of
men and women. On this plan Spenser's allegories are sometimes
formed: as in the first book, where the Red-crosse Knight or a TRUE
CHRISTIAN, defeats the wiles of Archimago, or the DEVIL, &c. &c.
These indeed are fictitious personages; but he proves himself a much
more ingenious allegorist, where his imagination BODIES forth unsubstantial things, TURNS THEM TO SHAPE, and marks out the nature,
powers, and effects, of that which is ideal and abstracted, by visible and
external symbols; as in his delineations of FEAR, DESPAIR, FANCY,
ENVY, and the like. Ariosto gives us but few symbolical beings of this
sort; for a picturesque invention was by no means his talent: while those
few which we find in his poem, are seldom drawn with that character-
istical fullness, and significant expression, so striking in the fantastic
portraits of Spenser. And that Spenser painted these figures in so distinct

and animated a style, may we not partly account for it from this cause: that he had been long habituated to the sight of these emblematical personages, visibly decorated with their proper attributes, and actually endued with speech, motion, and life?

As a more convincing argument in favour of this hypothesis, I shall remark, that Spenser expressly denominates his most exquisite groupe of allegorical figures, the MASKE of CUPID. Thus, without recurring to conjecture, his own words[7] evidently demonstrate that he sometimes had representations of this sort in his eye. He tells us moreover, that these figures were,

————A jolly company,
In manner of a maske enranged orderly.
3. 12. 5.

In his introduction to this groupe, it is manifest that he drew from another allegoric spectacle of that age, called the DUMB SHEW, which was wont to be exhibited before every act of a tragedy. st. 3.

And forth issewd, as on the ready flore
Of some theatre, a grave personage,
That in his hand a branch of laurel bore,
With comely haveour, and countnance sage,
Yclad in costly garments, fit for tragicke stage.

iv.

Proceeding to the midst he still did stand,
As if in mind he somewhat had to say;
And to the vulgar beckning with his hand,
In sign of silence, as to hear a play,
By lively actions he gan bewray
Some argument of matter passioned;
Which doen, he backe retyred soft away;
And passing by, his name discovered,
EASE on his robe in golden letters cyphered.

He afterwards styles these figures MASKERS. st. 6.

The whiles the MASKERS marched forth in trim array.

vii.

The first was FANCY, like a lovely boy,
Of rare aspect. ————

From what has been said, I would not have it objected, that I have intended to arraign the powers of our author's invention; or insinuated, that he servilely copied such representations. All I have endeavoured to prove is, that Spenser was not only better qualified to delineate fictions of this sort, because they were the real objects of his sight; but, as all men are influenced by what they see, that he was prompted and induced to delineate them, because he saw them, especially as they were so much the delight of his age.

Instead of entering into a critical examination of Spenser's manner of allegorising, and of the poetical conduct of his allegories, which has been done with an equally judicious and ingenious discernment by Mr. Spence,[s] I shall observe, that our author frequently introduces an allegory, under which no meaning is couched; viz. 2. 9. 21. ALMA is the mind, and her CASTLE the body. The tongue is the porter of this castle, the nose the portcullis, and the mouth the porch, about the inside of which are placed twice sixteen warders clad in white, which are the teeth; these ALMA passes by, who rise up, and do obeisance to her, st. 26. But how can the teeth be said to rise up and bow to the mind? Spenser here forgot, that he was allegorising, and speaks as if he was describing, without any latent meaning, a real queen, with twice sixteen real warders, who, as such, might, with no impropriety, be said to rise and bow to their queen. Many instances of his confounding allegory with reality, occur through this whole canto, and the two next; particularly, where he is describing the kitchen of this castle, which is the belly, he gives us a formal description of such a kitchen, as was to be seen in his time in castles, and great houses, by no means expressive of the thing intended. Again, the occult meaning of his bringing Scudamore to the house of CARE, 4. 5. 32. clashes with what he had before told us. By this allegory of Scudamore coming to CARE'S house, it should be UNDERSTOOD, that "Scudamore, from a happy, passed into a miserable state." For we may reasonably suppose, that before he came to CARE'S house, he was unacquainted with CARE; whereas the poet had before represented him as involved in extreme misery. It would be tedious, by an allegation of particular examples, to demonstrate how frequently his allegories are mere descriptions; and that taken in their literal sense, they contain an improper, or no signification. I shall, however, mention one. The BLATANT BEAST is said to break into the monasteries, to rob their chancels, cast down the desks of the monks, deface the altars, and destroy the images found in their churches. By the BLATANT BEAST is understood Scandal, and by the havock just mentioned as effected by it, is implied the suppression of religious houses and popish superstition. But how can this be properly said to have been brought about by scandal? And how could Spenser in particular, with any consistency say this, who was, as appears by his pastorals, a friend to the reformation, as was his heroine Elizabeth?

But there is another capital fault in our author's allegories, which does not immediately fall under the stated rules of criticism. "Painters, says a French writer, ought to employ their allegories in religious pictures, with much greater reserve than in profane pieces. They may, indeed, in such subjects as do not represent the mysteries and miracles of our religion, make use of an allegorical composition, the action whereof shall be expressive of some truth, that cannot be represented otherwise, either in painting or sculpture. I agree therefore to let them draw FAITH and HOPE supporting a dying person, and RELIGION in deep affliction at the feet of a deceased prelate. But I am of opinion, that artists who treat of the miracles and dogmas of our religion, are allowed no kind of allegorical composition. . . . The facts whereon our religion is built, and the doctrine it delivers, are subjects in which the painter's imagination has no liberty to sport." [9] The conduct which this author blames, is practised by Spenser, with this difference only; that the painters here condemned are supposed to adapt human allegory to divine mystery, whereas Spenser has mingled divine mystery with human allegory. Such a practice as this, tends not only to confound sacred and profane subjects, but to place the licentious sallies of imagination upon a level with the dictates of divine inspiration; to debase the truth and dignity of heavenly things, by making Christian allegory subservient to the purposes of Romantic fiction.

This fault our author, through a defect of judgement rather than a contempt of religion, has most glaringly committed throughout his whole first book, where the imaginary instruments and expedients of romance, are perpetually interwoven with the mysteries contained in the BOOK of REVELATIONS. Duessa, who is formed upon the idea of a romantic enchantress, is gorgeously arrayed in gold and purple, presented with a triple[10] crown by the giant Orgoglio, and seated by him on a monstrous seven-headed dragon (1. 7. 16.), whose tail reaches to the skies, and throws down the stars (s. 18.), she bearing a golden cup

in her hand(1. 8. 25.). This is the SCARLET WHORE, and the RED
DRAGON in the REVELATIONS. "Behold a great red dragon, having seven heads, and ten horns, and seven crowns upon his heads; and
his tail drew the third part of the stars of heaven, and did cast them to
earth." [11] Again, "I saw a woman sit upon a scarlet-coloured beast, full
of names of blasphemy, having seven heads, and ten horns; and the
woman was arrayed in purple and scarlet colour, and decked with gold,
and precious stones, and pearls, having a golden cup in her hands, full
of abomination, and filthiness of her fornication." [12]

In Orgoglio's castle, which is described as very magnificent, Prince
Arthur discovers,

> An altar carv'd with cunning imagery,
> On which true Christians blood was often spilt,
> And holy martyrs often doen to die,
> With cruel malice and strong tyranny;
> Whose blessed sprites, from underneath the stone,
> To God for vengeance cride continually.
>
> 1. 8. 36.

The inspired author of the above-named book mentions the same of
what he saw in heaven. "I saw under the altar the souls of them that
were slain for the word of God, and for the testimony which they held;
and they cried with a loud voice, how long, O Lord, holy and true, dost
thou not judge, and avenge our blood on them that dwell on earth?" [13]

A hermit points out to the RED-CROSSE knight the New Jerusalem (1. 10. 53.), which an angel discovers to St. John (c. 21. 10.
&c.). This prospect is taken, says the poet, from a mountain more lofty
than either the mount of Olives or Parnassus. These two comparisons
thus impertinently linked together, strongly remind us of the absurdity
now spoken of, the mixture of divine truth, and profane invention; and
naturally lead us to reflect on the difference between the oracles uttered
from the former, and the fictions of those who dreamed on the latter.

Spenser, in the visionary dominions of Una's father, has planted
the TREE of LIFE, and of KNOWLEDGE: from the first of the trees,
he says, a well flowed, whose waters contained a most salutary virtue,
and which the dragon could not approach. Thus in the same scripture,
"He shewed me a pure river of water of life, clear as crystal, proceeding
out of the throne of God, and of the lamb. In the midst of the street of

it, and on either side of the river, was there the TREE of LIFE." [14] The circumstance, in particular, of the dragon not being able to approach this water, is literally adopted from romance, as has been before observed.[15] Thus also by the steps and fictions of romance, we are conducted to the death of the dragon who besieged the parents of Una, by which is figured the destruction of the old serpent mentioned in the *Apocalypse.*

The extravagancies of pagan mythology are not improperly introduced into a poem of this sort, as they are acknowledged falsities; or at best, if expressive of any moral truth, no more than the inventions of men. But the poet that applies the VISIONS of God in such a manner is guilty of an impropriety, which, I fear, amounts to an impiety. . . .

NOTES

1. Hume's Hist. of Engl. TUDOR, vol. 2. 1759. p. 739.
2. Before the *Shepherd's Kalendar.* The GALLANTRIES of civilised chivalry, in particular, were never carried to a higher pitch than in the queen's Court: of which, says our author, describing the MANNERS of that court.

> Ne any there doth *brave* or *valiant* seeme,
> Unless that some *gay mistresse badge he weare.*
> *Colin Clouts come home.*

3. Spenser himself wrote a sett of PAGEAUNTS, which were descriptions of these feigned representations.
4. "And to keep that shew companie, (but yet furre off) stoode the SHEWE OF MANHODE and DESART; as first to be presented: and that shewe was as well furnished as the other: men all, saving one boy called BEAUTIE, for which MANHOOD, FAVOUR, and DESART, did strive (or should have contended), but GOOD FORTUNE (as victor of all conquests) was to come in and overthrow MANHOOD, &c."

> *Hollinshed's Chron.* v. 3. p. 1297.

5. Exhibited before the queen at Westminster, ibid. p. 1317. et seq.
6. It is observed by Plutarch, that "Allegory is that, in which one thing is *related* and another *understood.*" Thus Ariosto RELATES the adventures of Orlando, Rogero, Bradamante, &c. by which is UNDERSTOOD the conquest of the passions, the importance of virtue, and other moral doctrines; on which account we may call the ORLANDO a MORAL poem; but can we call the FAIRY QUEEN, upon the whole, a MORAL POEM? Is it not equally an HISTORICAL or POLITICAL poem? For though it be, according to it's [sic] author's words, an ALLEGORY or DARK CONCEIT, yet that which is couched or understood under this allegory is the history, and intrigues, of queen Elizabeth's courtiers; which however are introduced with a Moral design.
7. Thus also, in the *Ruines of Time,* he calls his noble allegoric representations of *Empire, Pleasure, Strength,* &c. TRAGICKE PAGEAUNTS.

> Before mine eyes *strange sights* presented were
> Like TRAGICKE PAGEAUNTS seeming to appeare.

8. Polymet. b. 10. d. 4.
9. Abbe du Bos, *Reflexions,* &c. tom. i. c. xxiv.
10. By the triple crown he plainly glances at popery.

11. Ch. 12. ver. 3. 4.
12. Ch. 17. ver. 3. 4.
13. Ch. 6. ver. 9. 10.
14. Ch. 22. ver. 1. 2.
15. Sect. ii. supra.

FIVE

RICHARD HURD

*LETTER VIII (1762)**

I spoke "of criticizing Spenser's poem, under the idea, not of a classical but Gothic composition."

It is certain much light might be thrown on that singular work, were an able critic to consider it in this view. For instance, he might go some way towards explaining, perhaps justifying, the general plan and *conduct* of the Faery Queen, which, to classical readers has appeared indefensible.

I have taken the fancy, with your leave, to try my hand on this curious subject.

When an architect examines a Gothic structure by Grecian rules, he finds nothing but deformity. But the Gothic architecture has it's own rules, by which when it comes to be examined, it is seen to have it's merit, as well as the Grecian. The question is not, which of the two is conducted in the simplest or truest taste: but, whether there be not sense and design in both, when scrutinized by the laws on which each is projected.

The same observation holds of the two sorts of poetry. Judge of the *Faery Queen* by the classic models, and you are shocked with it's disorder: consider it with an eye to it's Gothic original, and you find it regular. The unity and simplicity of the former are more complete: but the latter has that sort of unity and simplicity, which results from it's nature.

The Faery Queen then, as a Gothic poem, derives it's METHOD, as well as the other characters of it's composition, from the established modes and ideas of chivalry.

---

*From *Letters on Chivalry and Romance.*

It was usual, in the days of knight-errantry, at the holding of any great feast, for Knights to appear before the Prince, who presided at it, and claim the privilege of being sent on any adventure, to which the solemnity might give occasion. For it was supposed that, when such a *throng of knights and barons bold,* as Milton speaks of, were got together, the distressed would flock in from all quarters, as to a place where they knew they might find and claim redress for all their grievances.

This was the real practice, in the days of pure and antient chivalry. And an image of this practice was afterwards kept up in the castles of the great, on any extraordinary festival or solemnity: of which, if you want an instance, I refer you to the description of a feast made at Lisle in 1453, in the court of Philip the Good, Duke of Burgundy, for a crusade against the Turks: As you may find it given at large in the memoirs of *Matthieu de Conci, Olivier de la Marche,* and *Monstrelet.*

That feast was held for *twelve* days: and each day was distinguished by the claim and allowance of some adventure.

Now laying down this practice, as a foundation for the poet's design, you will see how properly the *Faery Queen* is conducted.

"I devise, says the poet himself in his Letter to Sir W. Raleigh, that the Faery Queen kept her annual feaste xii days: upon which xii several days, the occasions of the xii several adventures hapened; which being undertaken by xii several knights, are in these xii books severally handled."

Here you have the poet delivering his own method, and the reason of it. It arose out of the order of his subject. And would you desire a better reason for his choice?

Yes; you will say, a poet's method is not that of his subject. I grant you, as to the order of *time,* in which the recital is made; for here, as Spenser observes (and his own practice agrees to the Rule) lies the main difference between *the poet historical, and the historiographer:* The reason of which is drawn from the nature of Epic composition itself, and holds equally, let the subject be what it will, and whatever the system of manners be, on which it is conducted. Gothic or Classic makes no difference in this respect.

But the case is not the same with regard to the general plan of a work, or what may be called the order of *distribution,* which is and must be governed by the subject-matter itself. It was as requisite for the Faery

Queen to consist of the adventures of twelve knights, as for the Odyssey
to be confined to the adventures of one Hero: Justice had otherwise not
been done to his subject.

So that if you will say any thing against the poet's method, you must
say that he should not have chosen this subject. But this objection arises
from your classic ideas of Unity, which have no place here; and are in
every view foreign to the purpose, if the poet has found means to give
his work, tho' consisting of many parts, the advantage of Unity. For in
some reasonable sense or other, it is agreed, every work of art must be
one, the very idea of a work requiring it.

If you ask then, what is this *Unity* of Spenser's Poem? I say, it consists in the relation of it's several adventures to one common *original,*
the appointment of the Faery Queen; and to one common *end,* the completion of the Faery Queen's injunctions. The knights issued forth on
their adventures on the breaking up of this annual feast; and the next
annual feast, we are to suppose, is to bring them together again from the
atchievement of their several charges.

This, it is true, is not the classic Unity, which consists in the representation of one entire action: but it is an Unity of another sort, an unity
resulting from the respect which a number of related actions have to one
common purpose. In other words, It is an unity of *design,* and not of
action.

This Gothic method of design in poetry may be, in some sort, illustrated by what is called the Gothic method of design in Gardening. A
wood or grove cut out into many separate avenues or glades was amongst
the most favourite of the works of art, which our fathers attempted in
this species of cultivation. These walks were distinct from each other,
had, each, their several destination, and terminated on their own proper
objects. Yet the whole was brought together and considered under one
view by the relation which these various openings had, not to each other,
but to their common and concurrent center. You and I are, perhaps,
agreed that this sort of gardening is not of so true a taste as that which
Kent and Nature have brought us acquainted with; where the supreme
art of the Designer consists in disposing his ground and objects into an
entire landskip; and grouping them, if I may use the term, in so easy a
manner, that the careless observer, tho' he be taken with the symmetry
of the whole, discovers no art in the combination:

> In lieto aspetto il bel giardin s'aperse,
> Acque stagnanti, mobili cristalli,
> Fior vari, e varie piante, herbe diverse,
> Apriche Collinette, ombrose valli,
> Selve, e spelunche in UNA VISTA offerse:
> E quel, che'l bello, e'l caro accresce à l'opre,
> L'Arte, che tutto fà, nulla si scopre.
>   TASSO. C. xvi. S. ix.

This, I say, may be the truest taste in gardening, because the simplest: Yet there is a manifest regard to unity in the other method; which has had it's admirers, as it may have again, and is certainly not without it's *design* and beauty.

But to return to our poet. Thus far he drew from Gothic ideas, and these ideas, I think, would lead him no farther. But, as Spenser knew what belonged to classic composition, he was tempted to tie his subject still closer together by *one* expedient of his own, and by *another* taken from his classic models.

His *own* was to interrupt the proper story of each book, by dispersing it into several; involving by this means, and as it were intertwisting the several actions together, in order to give something like the appearance of one action to his twelve adventures. And for this conduct, as absurd as it seems, he had some great examples in the Italian poets, tho' I believe, they were led into it by different motives.

The *other* expedient which he borrowed from the classics, was by adopting one superior character, which should be seen throughout. Prince Arthur, who had a separate adventure of his own, was to have his part in each of the other; and thus several actions were to be embodied by the interest which one principal Hero had in them all. It is even observable, that Spenser gives this adventure of Prince Arthur, in quest of Gloriana, as the proper subject of his poem. And upon this idea the late learned editor* of the Faery Queen has attempted, but I think without success, to defend the Unity and simplicity of it's fable. The truth was, the violence of classic prejudices forced the poet to affect this appearance of unity, tho' in contradiction to his gothic system. And, as far as we can judge of the tenour of the whole work from the finished half of it, the adventure of Prince Arthur, whatever the author pretended, and his

---

*Hurd refers to John Upton.

critic too easily believed, was but an after thought; and at least with regard to the *historical fable,* which we are now considering, was only one of the expedients by which he would conceal the disorder of his Gothic plan.

And if this was his design, I will venture to say that both his expedients were injudicious. Their purpose was to ally two things, in nature incompatible, the Gothic, and the classic unity; the effect of which misalliance was to discover and expose the nakedness of the Gothic.

I am of opinion then, considering the Faery Queen as an epic or *narrative* poem constructed on Gothic ideas, that the Poet had done well to affect no other unity than that of *design,* by which his subject was connected. But his poem is not simply narrative; it is throughout *Allegorical:* he calls it *a perpetual allegory or dark conceit:* and this character, for reasons I may have occasion to observe hereafter, was even predominant in the Faery Queen. His narration is subservient to his moral, and but serves to colour it. This he tells us himself at setting out.

Fierce wars and faithful loves shall *moralize* my song,

that is, shall serve for a vehicle, or instrument to convey the moral.

Now under this idea, the *Unity* of the Faery Queen is more apparent. His twelve knights are to exemplify as many virtues, out of which one illustrious character is to be composed. And in this view the part of Prince Arthur in each book becomes *essential,* and yet not *principal;* exactly, as the poet has contrived it. They who rest in the literal story, that is, who criticize it on the footing of a narrative poem, have constantly objected to this management. They say, it necessarily breaks the unity of design. Prince Arthur, they affirm, should either have had no part in the other adventures, or he should have had the chief part. He should either have done nothing, or more. And the objection is unanswerable; at least I know of nothing that can be said to remove it but what I have supposed above might be the purpose of the poet, and which I myself have rejected as insufficient.

But how faulty soever this conduct be in the literal story, it is perfectly right in the *moral:* and that for an obvious reason, tho' his critics seem not to have been aware of it. His chief hero was not to have the twelve virtues in the *degree* in which the knights had, each of them, their own; (such a character would be a monster) but he was to have so much of each as was requisite to form his superior character. Each virtue, in it's perfection, is exemplified in it's own knight: they are all, in a due degree, concenter'd in Prince Arthur.

This was the poet's *moral:* And what way of expressing this moral in the *history,* but by making Prince Arthur appear in each adventure, and in a manner subordinate to it's proper hero? Thus, tho' inferior to each in his own specific virtue, he is superior to all by uniting the whole circle of their virtues in himself: And thus he arrives, at length, at the possession of that bright form of *Glory,* whose ravishing beauty, as seen in a dream or vision, had led him out into these miraculous adventures in the land of Faery.

The conclusion is, that, as an *allegorical* poem, the method of the Faery Queen is governed by the justness of the *moral:* As a *narrative* poem, it is conducted on the ideas and usages of *chivalry.* In either view, if taken by itself, the plan is defensible. But from the union of the two designs there arises a perplexity and confusion, which is the proper, and only considerable, defect of this extraordinary poem.

SIX

WILLIAM HAZLITT

*On Chaucer and Spenser (1818)**

Spenser, as well as Chaucer, was engaged in active life; but the genius of his poetry was not active: it is inspired by the love of ease, and relaxation from all the cares and business of life. Of all the poets, he is the most poetical. Though much later than Chaucer, his obligations to preceding writers were less. He has in some measure borrowed the plan of his poem (as a number of distinct narratives) from Ariosto; but he has engrafted upon it an exuberance of fancy, and an endless voluptuousness of sentiment, which are not to be found in the Italian writer. Further, Spenser is even more of an inventor in the subject-matter. There is an originality, richness, and variety in his allegorical personages and fictions, which almost vies with the splendor of the ancient mythology. If Ariosto transports us into the regions of romance, Spenser's poetry is all fairy-land. In Ariosto, we walk upon the ground, in a company, gay, fantastic, and adventurous enough. In Spenser, we wander in another world, among ideal beings. The poet takes and lays us in the lap of a lovelier nature, by the sound of softer streams, among greener hills and fairer valleys. He paints nature, not as we find it, but as we expected to find it; and fulfils the delightful promise of our youth. He waves his wand of enchantment—and at once embodies airy beings, and throws a delicious veil over all actual objects. The two worlds of reality and of fiction are poised on the wings of his imagination. His ideas, indeed, seem more distinct than his perceptions. He is the painter of abstractions, and describes them with dazzling minuteness. In the Mask

---

*William Hazlitt's "On Chaucer and Spenser" appears in his *Lectures on the English Poets*. I have reprinted that part of the essay which discusses Spenser.

of Cupid he makes the God of Love "clap on high his coloured winges *twain:*" and it is said of Gluttony, in the Procession of the Passions,

> In green vine leaves he was right fitly clad.

At times he becomes picturesque from his intense love of beauty; as where he compares Prince Arthur's crest to the appearance of the almond tree:

> Upon the top of all his lofty crest,
>   A bunch of hairs discolour'd diversely
> With sprinkled pearl and gold full richly drest
>   Did shake and seem'd to daunce for jollity;
> Like to an almond tree ymounted high
>   On top of green Selinis all alone,
> With blossoms brave bedecked daintily;
>   Her tender locks do tremble every one
> At every little breath that under heav'n is blown.

The love of beauty, however, and not of truth, is the moving principle of his mind; and he is guided in his fantastic delineations by no rule but the impulse of an inexhaustible imagination. He luxuriates equally in scenes of Eastern magnificence; or the still solitude of a hermit's cell—in the extremes of sensuality or refinement.

In reading the Faery Queen, you see a little withered old man by a wood-side opening a wicket, a giant, and a dwarf lagging far behind, a damsel in a boat upon an enchanted lake, wood-nymphs, and satyrs; and all of a sudden you are transported into a lofty palace, with tapers burning, amidst knights and ladies, with dance and revelry, and song, "and mask, and antique pageantry." What can be more solitary, more shut up in itself, than his description of the house of Sleep, to which Archimago sends for a dream:

> And more to lull him in his slumber soft
>   A trickling stream from high rock tumbling down,
> And ever-drizzling rain upon the loft,
>   Mix'd with a murmuring wind, much like the sound
> Of swarming Bees, did cast him in a swound.
>   No other noise, nor people's troublous cries
> That still are wont t' annoy the walled town
>   Might there be heard; but careless Quiet lies
> Wrapt in eternal silence, far from enemies.

It is as if "the honey-heavy dew of slumber" had settled on his pen in writing these lines. How different in the subject (and yet how like in beauty) is the following description of the Bower of Bliss:

> Eftsoones they heard a most melodious sound
>   Of all that mote delight a dainty ear;
> Such as at once might not on living ground,
>   Save in this Paradise, be heard elsewhere:
> Right hard it was for wight which did it hear,
>   To tell what manner musicke that mote be;
> For all that pleasing is to living eare
>   Was there consorted in one harmonee:
> Birds, voices, instruments, windes, waters, all agree.
>
> The joyous birdes shrouded in chearefull shade
>   Their notes unto the voice attempred sweet:
> The angelical soft trembling voices made
>   To th' instruments divine respondence meet.
> The silver sounding instruments did meet
>   With the base murmur of the water's fall;
> The water's fall with difference discreet,
>   Now soft, now loud, unto the wind did call;
> The gentle warbling wind low answered to all.

The remainder of the passage has all that voluptuous pathos, and languid brilliancy of fancy, in which this writer excelled:

[Hazlitt quotes II, xii, 74-78.]

The finest things in Spenser are, the character of Una, in the first book; the House of Pride; the Cave of Mammon, and the Cave of Despair; the account of Memory, of whom it is said, among other things,

> The wars he well remember'd of King Nine,
> Of old Assaracus and Inachus divine;

the description of Belphœbe; the story of Florimel and the Witch's son; the Gardens of Adonis, and the Bower of Bliss; the Mask of Cupid; and Colin Clout's vision, in the last book. But some people will say that all this may be very fine, but that they cannot understand it on account of the allegory. They are afraid of the allegory, as if they thought it would bite them: they look at it as a child looks at a painted dragon, and think it will strangle them in its shining folds. This is very idle. If they do not meddle with the allegory, the allegory will not meddle with them. Without minding it at all, the whole is as plain as a pike-staff. It might as well be pretended that we cannot see Poussin's pictures for the allegory, as that the allegory prevents us from understanding Spenser. For instance, when Britomart, seated amidst the young warriors, lets fall her hair and discovers her sex, is it necessary to know the part she plays in the allegory, to understand the beauty of the following stanza?

> And eke that stranger knight amongst the rest
> Was for like need enforc'd to disarray.
> Tho when as vailed was her lofty crest,
> Her golden locks that were in trammels gay
> Upbounden, did themselves adown display,
> And raught unto her heels like sunny beams
> That in a cloud their light did long time stay;
> Their vapour faded, shew their golden gleams,
> And through the persant air shoot forth their azure streams.

Or is there any mystery in what is said of Belphœbe, that her hair was sprinkled with flowers and blossoms which had been entangled in it as she fled through the woods? Or is it necessary to have a more distinct idea of Proteus, than that which is given of him in his boat, with the frighted Florimel at his feet, while

> ———the cold icicles from his rough beard
> Dropped adown upon her snowy breast!

Or is it not a sufficient account of one of the sea-gods that pass by them, to say:

> That was Arion crowned: ———
> So went he playing on the watery plain.

Or to take the Procession of the Passions that draw the coach of Pride, in which the figures of Idleness, of Gluttony, of Lechery, of Avarice, of Envy, and of Wrath speak, one should think, plain enough for themselves; such as this of Gluttony:

> And by his side rode loathsome Gluttony,
> Deformed creature, on a filthy swine;
> His belly was up blown with luxury;
> And eke with fatness swollen were his eyne;
> And like a crane his neck was long and fine,

With which he swallowed up excessive feast,
For want whereof poor people oft did pine.

In green vine leaves he was right fitly clad;
 For other clothes he could not wear for heat:
And on his head an ivy garland had,
 From under which fast trickled down the sweat:
Still as he rode, he somewhat still did eat.
 And in his hand did bear a bouzing can,
Of which he supt so oft, that on his seat
 His drunken corse he scarce upholden can;
In shape and size more like a monster than a man.

Or this of Lechery:

And next to him rode lustfull Lechery
 Upon a bearded goat, whose rugged hair
And whaly eyes (the sign of jealousy)
 Was like the person's self whom he did bear:
Who rough and black, and filthy did appear.
 Unseemly man to please fair lady's eye:
Yet he of ladies oft was loved dear,
 When fairer faces were bid standen by:
O! who does know the bent of women's fantasy?

In a green gown he clothed was full fair,
 Which underneath did hide his filthiness;
And in his hand a burning heart he bare,
 Full of vain follies and new fangleness;
For he was false and fraught with fickleness;
 And learned had to love with secret looks;
And well could dance; and sing with ruefullness;
 And fortunes tell; and read in loving books;
And thousand other ways to bait his fleshly hooks.

Inconstant man that loved all he saw,
 And lusted after all that he did love;
Ne would his looser life be tied to law;
 But joyed weak women's hearts to tempt and prove,
If from their loyal loves he might them move.

This is pretty plain-spoken. Mr. Southey says of Spenser:

————Yet not more sweet
Than pure was he, and not more pure than wise;
High priest of all the Muses' mysteries!

On the contrary, no one was more apt to pry into mysteries which do not strictly belong to the Muses.

Of the same kind with the Procession of the Passions, as little obscure, and still more beautiful, is the Mask of Cupid, with his train of votaries:

The first was Fancy, like a lovely boy
Of rare aspect, and beauty without peer;

His garment neither was of silk nor say,
But painted plumes in goodly order dight,
Like as the sun-burnt Indians do array
Their tawny bodies in their proudest plight:
As those same plumes, so seem'd he vain and light,
That by his gait might easily appear;
For still he far'd as dancing in delight,
And in his hands a windy fan did bear
That in the idle air he mov'd still here and there.

[Hazlitt quotes III, xii, 9-13, 22-23.]

The description of Hope, in this series of historical portraits, is one of the most beautiful in Spenser; and the triumph of Cupid at the mischief he has made, is worthy of the malicious urchin deity. In reading these descriptions, one can hardly avoid being reminded of Rubens's allegorical pictures; but the account of Satyrane taming the lion's whelps and lugging the bear's cubs along in his arms while yet an infant, whom his mother so naturally advises to "go seek some other play-fellows," has even more of this high picturesque character. Nobody but Rubens could have painted the fancy of Spenser; and he could not have given the sentiment, the airy dream that hovers over it!

With all this, Spenser neither makes us laugh nor weep. The only jest in his poem is an allegorical play upon words, where he describes Malbecco as escaping in the herd of goats, "by the help of his fayre horns on hight." But he has been unjustly charged with a want of passion and of strength. He has both in an immense degree. He has not indeed the pathos of immediate action or suffering, which is more prop-

erly the dramatic; but he has all the pathos of sentiment and romance—
all that belongs to distant objects of terror, and uncertain, imaginary
distress. His strength, in like manner, is not strength of will or action, of
bone and muscle, nor is it coarse and palpable—but it assumes a character of vastness and sublimity seen through the same visionary medium,
and blended with the appalling associations of preternatural agency. We
need only turn, in proof of this, to the Cave of Despair, or the Cave of
Mammon, or to the account of the change of Malbecco into Jealousy.
The following stanzas, in the description of the Cave of Mammon, the
grisly house of Plutus, are unrivalled for the portentous massiness of the
forms, the splendid chiaro-scuro, and shadowy horror.

> That house's form within was rude and strong,
>   Like an huge cave hewn out of rocky clift,
> From whose rough vault the ragged breaches hung,
>   Embossed with massy gold of glorious gift,
> And with rich metal loaded every rift,
>   That heavy ruin they did seem to threat:
> And over them Arachne high did lift
>   Her cunning web, and spread her subtle net,
> Enwrapped in foul smoke, and clouds more black than jet.
>
> Both roof and floor, and walls were all of gold,
>   But overgrown with dust and old decay,[1]
> And hid in darkness that none could behold
>   The hue thereof: for view of cheerful day
> Did never in that house itself display,
>   But a faint shadow of uncertain light;
> Such as a lamp whose life doth fade away;
>   Or as the moon clothed with cloudy night
> Does shew to him that walks in fear and sad affright.

* * *

> And over all sad Horror with grim hue
>   Did always soar, beating his iron wings;
> And after him owls and night-ravens flew,
>   The hateful messengers of heavy things,
> Of death and dolour telling sad tidings;
>   Whiles sad Celleno, sitting on a clift,
> A song of bitter bale and sorrow sings,

> That heart of flint asunder could have rift;
> Which having ended, after him she flieth swift.

The Cave of Despair is described with equal gloominess and power of
fancy; and the fine moral declamation of the owner of it, on the evils of
life, almost makes one in love with death. In the story of Malbecco, who
is haunted by jealousy, and in vain strives to run away from his own
thoughts—

> High over hill and over dale he flies—

the truth of human passion and the preternatural ending are equally
striking. It is not fair to compare Spenser with Shakspeare, in point of
interest. A fairer comparison would be with Comus; and the result
would not be unfavourable to Spenser. There is only one work of the
same allegorical kind, which has more interest than Spenser (with
scarcely less imagination): and that is the Pilgrim's Progress. The three
first books of the Faery Queen are very superior to the three last. One
would think that Pope, who used to ask if any one had ever read the
Faery Queen through, had only dipped into these last. The only things
in them equal to the former, are the account of Talus, the Iron Man,
and the delightful episode of Pastorella.

The language of Spenser is full, and copious, to overflowing: it is
less pure and idiomatic than Chaucer's, and is enriched and adorned
with phrases borrowed from the different languages of Europe, both
ancient and modern. He was, probably, seduced into a certain license of
expression by the difficulty of filling up the moulds of his complicated
rhymed stanza from the limited resources of his native language. This
stanza, with alternate and repeatedly recurring rhymes, is borrowed
from the Italians. It was peculiarly fitted to their language, which
abounds in similar vowel terminations, and is as little adapted to ours,
from the stubborn, unaccommodating resistance which the consonant
endings of the northern languages make to this sort of endless sing-
song.—Not that I would, on that account, part with the stanza of Spenser. We are, perhaps, indebted to this very necessity of finding out new
forms of expression, and to the occasional faults to which it led, for a
poetical language rich and varied and magnificent beyond all former,
and almost all later example. His versification is, at once, the most
smooth and the most sounding in the language. It is a labyrinth of sweet
sounds, "in many a winding bout of linked sweetness long drawn out"

—that would cloy by their very sweetness, but that the ear is constantly relieved and enchanted by their continued variety of modulation—lingering on the pauses of the action, or flowing on in a fuller tide of harmony with the movement of the sentiment. It has not the bold dramatic transitions of Shakspeare's blank verse, nor the high-raised tone of Milton's; but it is the perfection of melting harmony, dissolving the soul in pleasure, or holding it captive in the chains of suspense. Spenser was the poet of our waking dreams; and he has invented not only a language, but a music of his own for them. The undulations are infinite, like those of the waves of the sea: but the effect is still the same, lulling the senses into a deep oblivion of the jarring noises of the world, from which we have no wish to be ever recalled.

NOTES

1. That all with one consent praise new-born gauds,
   Tho' they are made and moulded of things past,
   And give to Dust, that is a little gilt,
   More laud than gold o'er-dusted.

   Troilus and Cressida

SEVEN

JAMES RUSSELL LOWELL

*Spenser (1875)**

. . . The publication of his "Shepherd's Calendar" in 1579 (though the poem itself be of little interest) is one of the epochs in our literature. Spenser had at least the originality to see clearly and to feel keenly that it was essential to bring poetry back again to some kind of understanding with nature. His immediate predecessors seem to have conceived of it as a kind of bird of paradise, born to float somewhere between heaven and earth, with no very well defined relation to either. It is true that the nearest approach they were able to make to this airy ideal was a shuttlecock, winged with a bright plume or so from Italy, but, after all, nothing but cork and feathers, which they bandied back and forth from one stanza to another, with the useful ambition of *keeping it up* as long as they could. To my mind the old comedy of "Gammer Gurton's Needle" is worth the whole of them. It may be coarse, earthy, but in reading it one feels that he is at least a man among men, and not a humbug among humbugs.

The form of Spenser's "Shepherd's Calendar," it is true, is artificial, absurdly so if you look at it merely from the outside—not, perhaps, the wisest way to look at anything, unless it be a jail or a volume of the "Congressional Globe"—but the spirit of it is fresh and original. We have at last got over the superstition that shepherds and shepherdesses are any wiser or simpler than other people. We know that wisdom can be won only by wide commerce with men and books, and that simplicity,

*This essay was first published in the *North American Review,* CXX (April, 1875), 334-394, and reappeared with minor revisions in *The Writings of James Russell Lowell* (Riverside Edition, Houghton Mifflin Company, c1890-c1901), IV 265-353. About two-fifths of the essay has been reprinted from the Riverside Edition.

whether of manners or style, is the crowning result of the highest culture. But the pastorals of Spenser were very different things, different both in the moving spirit and the resultant form from the later ones of Browne or the "Piscatory Eclogues" of Phineas Fletcher. And why? Browne and Fletcher wrote because Spenser had written, but Spenser wrote from a strong inward impulse—an instinct it might be called—to escape at all risks into the fresh air from that horrible atmosphere into which rhymer after rhymer had been pumping carbonic-acid gas with the full force of his lungs, and in which all sincerity was on the edge of suffocation. His longing for something truer and better was as honest as that which led Tacitus so long before to idealize the Germans, and Rousseau so long after to make an angel of the savage.

Spenser himself supremely overlooks the whole chasm between himself and Chaucer, as Dante between himself and Virgil. He called Chaucer master, as Milton was afterwards to call *him*. And, even while he chose the most artificial of all forms, his aim—that of getting back to nature and life—was conscious, I have no doubt, to himself, and must be obvious to whoever reads with anything but the ends of his fingers. It is true that Sannazzaro had brought the pastoral into fashion again, and that two of Spenser's are little more than translations from Marot; but for manner he instinctively turned back to Chaucer, the first and then only great English poet. He has given common instead of classic names to his personages, for characters they can hardly be called. Above all, he has gone to the provincial dialects for words wherewith to enlarge and freshen his poetical vocabulary.[1] I look upon the "Shepherd's Calendar" as being no less a conscious and deliberate attempt at reform than Thomson's "Seasons" were in the topics, and Wordsworth's "Lyrical Ballads" in the language of poetry. But the great merit of these pastorals was not so much in their matter as their manner. They show a sense of style in its larger meaning hitherto displayed by no English poet since Chaucer. Surrey had brought back from Italy a certain inkling of it, so far as it is contained in decorum. But here was a new language, a choice and arrangement of words, a variety, elasticity, and harmony of verse most grateful to the ears of men. If not passion, there was fervor, which was perhaps as near it as the somewhat stately movement of Spenser's mind would allow him to come. Sidney had tried many experiments in versification, which are curious and interesting, especially his attempts to naturalize the *sliding* rhymes of Sannazzaro in English. But there is everywhere the uncertainty of a 'prentice hand. Spenser shows himself already a master, at least in verse, and we can trace the studies of Milton, a yet greater master, in the "Shepherd's Calendar" as well as in the "Faery Queen." We have seen that Spenser, under the misleading influence of Sidney[2] and Harvey, tried his hand at English hexameters. But his great glory is that he taught his own language to sing and move to measures harmonious and noble. Chaucer had done much to vocalize it, as I have tried to show elsewhere,[3] but Spenser was to prove

> That no tongue hath the muse's utterance heired
> For verse, and that sweet music to the ear
> Struck out of rhyme, so naturally as this.

The "Shepherd's Calendar" contains perhaps the most picturesquely imaginative verse which Spenser has written. It is in the eclogue for February, where he tells us of the

> Faded oak
> Whose body is sere, whose branches broke,
> Whose naked arms stretch unto the fire.

It is one of those verses that Joseph Warton would have liked in secret, that Dr. Johnson would have proved to be untranslatable into reasonable prose, and which the imagination welcomes at once without caring whether it be exactly conformable to *barbara* or *celarent*. Another pretty verse in the same eclogue,

> But gently took that ungently came,

pleased Coleridge so greatly that he thought it was his own. But in general it is not so much the sentiments and images that are new as the modulation of the verses in which they float. The cold obstruction of two centuries thaws, and the stream of speech once more let loose, seeks out its old windings, or overflows musically in unpractised channels. The service which Spenser did to our literature by this exquisite sense of harmony is incalculable. His fine ear, abhorrent of barbarous dissonance, his dainty tongue that loves to prolong the relish of a musical phrase, made possible the transition from the cast-iron stiffness of "Ferrex and Porrex" to the Damascus pliancy of Fletcher and Shakespeare. It was he that

> Taught the dumb on high to sing,
> And heavy ignorance aloft to fly:

> That added feathers to the learned's wing,
> And gave to grace a double majesty.

I do not mean that in the "Shepherd's Calendar" he had already achieved that transmutation of language and metre by which he was afterwards to endow English verse with the most varied and majestic of stanzas, in which the droning old alexandrine, awakened for the first time to a feeling of the poetry that was in him, was to wonder, like M. Jourdain, that he had been talking prose all his life—but already he gave clear indications of the tendency and premonitions of the power which were to carry it forward to ultimate perfection. . . .

It was this instantly felt if not easily definable charm that forthwith won for Spenser his never-disputed rank as the chief English poet of that age, and gave him a popularity which, during his life and in the following generation, was, in its select quality, without a competitor. It may be thought that I lay too much stress on this single attribute of diction. But apart from its importance in his case as showing their way to the poets who were just then learning the accidence of their art, and leaving them a material to work in already mellowed to their hands, it should be remembered that it is subtle perfection of phrase and that happy coalescence of music and meaning, where each reinforces the other, that define a man as poet and make all ears converts and partisans. Spenser was an epicure in language. He loved "seld-seen costly" words perhaps too well, and did not always distinguish between mere strangeness and that novelty which is so agreeable as to cheat us with some charm of seeming association. He had not the concentrated power which can sometimes pack infinite riches in the little room of a single epithet, for his genius is rather for dilation than compression.[4] But he was, with the exception of Milton and possibly Gray, the most learned of our poets. His familiarity with ancient and modern literature was easy and intimate, and as he perfected himself in his art, he caught the grand manner and high-bred ways of the society he frequented. But even to the last he did not quite shake off the blunt rusticity of phrase that was habitual with the generation that preceded him. In the fifth book of the "Faery Queen," where he is describing the passion of Britomart at the supposed infidelity of Arthegall, he descends to a Teniers-like realism[5]— he whose verses generally remind us of the dancing Hours of Guido, where we catch but a glimpse of the real earth and that far away beneath. But his habitual style is that of gracious loftiness and refined luxury. . . .

. . . the commentators, who seem never willing to let their poet be a poet pure and simple, though, had he not been so, they would have lost their only hold upon life, try to make out from his "Mother Hubberd's Tale" that he might have been a very sensible matter-of-fact man if he would. For my own part, I am quite willing to confess that I like him none the worse for being *un*practical, and that my reading has convinced me that being too poetical is the rarest fault of poets. Practical men are not so scarce, one would think, and I am not sure that the tree was a gainer when the hamadryad flitted and left it nothing but shiptimber. Such men as Spenser are not sent into the world to be part of its motive power. The blind old engine would not know the difference though we got up its steam with attar of roses, nor make one revolution more to the minute for it. What practical man ever left such an heirloom to his countrymen as the "Faery Queen"?

Undoubtedly Spenser wished to be useful and in the highest vocation of all, that of teacher, and Milton calls him "our sage and serious poet, whom I dare be known to think a better teacher than Scotus or Aquinas." And good Dr. Henry More was of the same mind. I fear he makes his vices so beautiful now and then that we should not be very much afraid of them if we chanced to meet them; for he could not escape from his genius, which, if it led him as philosopher to the abstract contemplation of the beautiful, left him as poet open to every impression of sensuous delight. When he wrote the "Shepherd's Calendar" he was certainly a Puritan, and probably so by conviction rather than from any social influences or thought of personal interests. There is a verse, it is true, in the second of the two detached cantos of "Mutability,"

Like that ungracious crew which feigns demurest grace,

which is supposed to glance at the straiter religionists, and from which it has been inferred that he drew away from them as he grew older. It is very likely that years and widened experience of men may have produced in him their natural result of tolerant wisdom which revolts at the hasty destructiveness of inconsiderate zeal. But with the more generous side of Puritanism I think he sympathized to the last. His rebukes of clerical worldliness are in the Puritan tone, and as severe a one as any is in "Mother Hubberd's Tale," published in 1591.[6] There is an iconoclas-

tic relish in his account of Sir Guyon's demolishing the Bower of Bliss
that makes us think he would not have regretted the plundered abbeys
as perhaps Shakespeare did when he speaks of the winter woods as "bare
ruined choirs where late the sweet birds sang":

> But all those pleasant bowers and palace brave
> Guyon broke down with rigor pitiless,
> Ne ought their goodly workmanship might save
> Them from the tempest of his wrathfulness,
> But that their bliss he turned to balefulness;
> Their groves he felled, their gardens did deface,
> Their arbors spoil, their cabinets suppress,
> Their banquet-houses burn, their buildings rase,
> And of the fairest late now made the foulest place.

But whatever may have been Spenser's religious opinions (which
do not nearly concern us here), the bent of his mind was toward a Platonic mysticism, a supramundane sphere where it could shape universal
forms out of the primal elements of things, instead of being forced to
put up with their fortuitous combinations in the unwilling material of
mortal clay. He who, when his singing robes were on, could never be
tempted nearer to the real world than under some subterfuge of pastoral
or allegory, expatiates joyously in this untrammelled ether:

> Lifting himself out of the lowly dust
> On golden plumes up to the purest sky.

Nowhere does his genius soar and sing with such continuous aspiration,
nowhere is his phrase so decorously stately, though rising to an enthusiasm which reaches intensity while it stops short of vehemence, as in his
Hymns to Love and Beauty, especially the latter. There is an exulting
spurn of earth in it, as of a soul just loosed from its cage. I shall make
no extracts from it, for it is one of those intimately coherent and tran-
scendentally logical poems that "moveth altogether if it move at all,"
the breaking off a fragment from which would maim it as it would a
perfect group of crystals. Whatever there is of sentiment and passion is
for the most part purely disembodied and without sex, like that of angels
—a kind of poetry which has of late gone out of fashion, whether to our
gain or not may be questioned. Perhaps one may venture to hint that
the animal instincts are those that stand in least need of stimulation.
Spenser's notions of love were so nobly pure, so far from those of our

common ancestor who could hang by his tail, as not to disqualify him
for achieving the quest of the Holy Grail, and accordingly it is not un-
instructive to remember that he had drunk, among others, at French
sources not yet deboshed with *absinthe.*[7] Yet, with a purity like that of
thrice-bolted snow, he had none of its coldness. He is, of all our poets,
the most truly sensuous, using the word as Milton probably meant it
when he said that poetry should be "simple, sensuous, and passionate."
A poet is innocently sensuous when his mind permeates and illumines
his senses; when they, on the other hand, muddy the mind, he becomes
sensual. Every one of Spenser's senses was as exquisitely alive to the impressions of material, as every organ of his soul was to those of spiritual
beauty. Accordingly, if he painted the weeds of sensuality at all, he could
not help making them "of glorious feature." It was this, it may be sus-
pected, rather than his "praising love," that made Lord Burleigh shake
his "rugged forehead." Spenser's gamut, indeed, is a wide one, ranging
from a purely corporeal delight in "precious odors fetched from far
away" upward to such refinement as

> Upon her eyelids many graces sate
> Under the shadow of her even brows,

where the eye shares its pleasure with the mind. He is court-painter in
ordinary to each of the senses in turn, and idealizes these frail favorites
of his majesty King Lusty Juventus, till they half believe themselves the
innocent shepherdesses into which he travesties them.[8]

In his great poem he had two objects in view: first, the ephemeral
one of pleasing the court, and then that of recommending himself to the
permanent approval of his own and following ages as a poet, and especially as a moral poet. To meet the first demand, he lays the scene of his
poem in contemporary England, and brings in all the leading personages
of the day under the thin disguise of his knights and their squires and
lady-loves. He says this expressly in the prologue to the second book:

> Of Faery Land yet if he more inquire,
> By certain signs, here set in sundry place,
> He may it find; . . .
> And thou, O fairest princess under sky,
> In this fair mirror mayst behold thy face
> And thine own realms in land of Faery.

Many of his personages we can still identify, and all of them were once as easily recognizable as those of Mademoiselle de Scudéry. This, no doubt, added greatly to the immediate piquancy of the allusions. The interest they would excite may be inferred from the fact that King James, in 1596, wished to have the author prosecuted and punished for his indecent handling of his mother, Mary Queen of Scots, under the name of Duessa.[9] To suit the wider application of his plan's other and more important half, Spenser made all his characters double their parts, and appear in his allegory as the impersonations of abstract moral qualities. When the cardinal and theological virtues tell Dante,

> Noi siam qui ninfe e in ciel siamo stelle,

the sweetness of the verse enables the fancy, by a slight gulp, to swallow without solution the problem of being in two places at the same time. But there is something fairly ludicrous in such a duality as that of Prince Arthur and the Earl of Leicester, Arthegall and Lord Grey, and Belphœbe and Elizabeth.

> In this same interlude it doth befall
> That I, one Snout by name, present a wall.

The reality seems to heighten the improbability, already hard enough to manage. But Spenser had fortunately almost as little sense of humor as Wordsworth,[10] or he could never have carried his poem on with enthusiastic good faith so far as he did. It is evident that to him the Land of Faery was an unreal world of picture and illusion,

> The world's sweet inn from pain and wearisome turmoil,

in which he could shut himself up from the actual, with its shortcomings and failures.

> The ways through which my weary steps I guide
>   In this delightful land of Faery
> Are so exceeding spacious and wide,
>   And sprinkled with such sweet variety
>   Of all that pleasant is to ear and eye,
> That I, nigh ravisht with rare thoughts' delight,
>   My tedious travail do forget thereby,
> And, when I 'gin to feel decay of might,
> It strength to me supplies, and cheers my dullèd spright.

Spenser seems here to confess a little weariness; but the alacrity of his mind is so great that, even where his invention fails a little, we do not share his feeling nor suspect it, charmed as we are by the variety and sweep of his measure, the beauty or vigor of his similes, the musical felicity of his diction, and the mellow versatility of his pictures. In this last quality Ariosto, whose emulous pupil he was, is as Bologna to Venice in the comparison. That, when the personal allusions have lost their meaning and the allegory has become a burden, the book should continue to be read with delight, is proof enough, were any wanting, how full of life and light and the other-worldliness of poetry it must be. As a narrative it has, I think, every fault of which that kind of writing is capable. The characters are vague, and, even were they not, they drop out of the story so often and remain out of it so long, that we have forgotten who they are when we meet them again; the episodes hinder the advance of the action instead of relieving it with variety of incident or novelty of situation; the plot, if plot it may be called,

> That shape has none
> Distinguishable in member, joint, or limb,

recalls drearily our ancient enemy, the Metrical Romance; while the fighting, which in those old poems was tediously sincere, is between shadow and shadow, where we know that neither can harm the other, though we are tempted to wish he might. Hazlitt bids us not mind the allegory, and says that it won't bite us nor meddle with us if we do not meddle with it. But how if it bore us, which after all is the fatal question? The truth is that it is too often forced upon us against our will, as people were formerly driven to church till they began to look on a day of rest as a penal institution, and to transfer to the Scriptures that suspicion of defective inspiration which was awakened in them by the preaching. The true type of the allegory is the Odyssey, which we read without suspicion as pure poem, and then find a new pleasure in divining its double meaning, as if we somehow got a better bargain of our author than he meant to give us. But this complex feeling must not be so exacting as to prevent our lapsing into the old Arabian Nights simplicity of interest again. The moral of a poem should be suggested, as when in some mediæval church we cast down our eyes to muse over a fresco of Giotto, and are reminded of the transitoriness of life by the mortuary tablets under our feet. The vast superiority of Bunyan over Spenser lies in the fact that we help make his allegory out of our own experience. Instead of striving to embody abstract passions and temptations, he has given us his own in all their pathetic simplicity. He is the Ulysses of his own prose-epic. This is the secret of his power and his charm, that, while the representation of what *may* happen to all men comes home to none of us in particular, the story of any one man's real experience finds its startling parallel in that of every one of us. The very homeliness of Bunyan's names and the everydayness of his scenery, too, put us off our guard, and we soon find ourselves on as easy a footing with his allegorical beings as we might be with Adam or Socrates in a dream. Indeed, he has prepared us for such incongruities by telling us at setting out that the story was of a dream. The long nights of Bedford jail had so intensified his imagination, and made the figures with which it peopled his solitude so real to him, that the creatures of his mind become *things,* as clear to the memory as if we had seen them. But Spenser's are too often mere names, with no bodies to back them, entered on the Muses' muster-roll by the specious trick of personification. There is, likewise, in Bunyan, a childlike simplicity and taking-for-granted which win our confidence. His Giant Despair,[11] for example, is by no means the Ossianic figure into which artists who mistake the vague for the sublime have misconceived it. He is the ogre of the fairy-tales, with his malicious wife; and he comes forth to us from those regions of early faith and wonder as something beforehand accepted by the imagination. These figures of Bunyan's are already familiar inmates of the mind, and, if there be any sublimity in him, it is the daring frankness of his verisimilitude. Spenser's giants are those of the later romances, except that grand figure with the balances in the second Canto of Book V., the most original of all his conceptions, yet no real giant, but a pure eidolon of the mind. As Bunyan rises not seldom to a natural poetry, so Spenser sinks now and then, through the fault of his topics, to unmistakable prose. Take his description of the House of Alma,[12] for instance:

> The master cook was cald Concoctiön,
> A careful man, and full of comely guise;
> The kitchen-clerk, that hight Digestiön,
> Did order all the achates in seemly wise.

And so on through all the organs of the body. The author of Ecclesiastes understood these matters better in that last pathetic chapter of his, blunderingly translated as it apparently is. This, I admit, is the worst failure of Spenser in this kind; though, even here, when he gets on to the organs of the mind, the enchantments of his fancy and style come to the rescue and put us in good-humor again, hard as it is to conceive of armed knights entering the chamber of the mind, and talking with such visionary damsels as Ambition and Shamefastness. Nay, even in the most prosy parts, unless my partiality deceive me, there is an infantile confidence in the magical powers of Prosopopœia which half beguiles us, as of children who *play* that everything is something else, and are quite satisfied with the transformation.

The problem for Spenser was a double one: how to commend poetry at all to a generation which thought it effeminate trifling,[13] and how he, Master Edmund Spenser, of imagination all compact, could commend *his* poetry to Master John Bull, the most practical of mankind in his habitual mood, but at that moment in a passion of religious anxiety about his soul. *Omne tulit punctum qui miscuit utile dulci* was not only an irrefragable axiom because a Latin poet had said it, but it exactly met the case in point. He would convince the scorners that poetry might be seriously useful, and show Master Bull his new way of making fine words butter parsnips, in a rhymed moral primer. Allegory, as then practised, was imagination adapted for beginners, in words of one syllable and illustrated with cuts, and would thus serve both his ethical and pictorial purpose. Such a primer, or a first instalment of it, he proceeded to put forth; but he so bordered it with bright-colored fancies, he so often filled whole pages and crowded the text hard in others with the gay frolics of his pencil, that, as in the Grimani missal, the holy function of the book is forgotten in the ecstasy of its adornment. Worse than all, does not his brush linger more lovingly along the rosy contours of his sirens than on the modest wimples of the Wise Virgins? "The general end of the book," he tells us in his Dedication to Sir Walter Raleigh, "is to fashion a gentleman of noble person in virtuous and gentle discipline." But a little further on he evidently has a qualm, as he thinks how generously he had interpreted his promise of cuts: "To some I know this method will seem displeasant, which had rather have good discipline delivered plainly in way of precepts or sermoned at large,[14] as they use, than thus cloudily enwrapped in allegorical devices." Lord

Burleigh was of this way of thinking, undoubtedly, but how could poor
Clarion help it? Has he not said,

> And whatso else *of virtue good or ill,*
>   Grew in this garden, fetcht from far away,
> Of every one he takes and tastes at will,
>   And on their pleasures greedily doth prey?

One sometimes feels in reading him as if he were the pure sense of the
beautiful incarnated to the one end that he might interpret it to our
duller perceptions. So exquisite was his sensibility,[15] that with him sensation and intellection seem identical, and we "can almost say his body
thought." This subtle interfusion of sense with spirit it is that gives his
poetry a crystalline purity without lack of warmth. He is full of feeling,
and yet of such a kind that we can neither say it is mere intellectual per-
ception of what is fair and good, nor yet associate it with that throbbing
fervor which leads us to call sensibility by the physical name of heart.

Charles Lamb made the most pithy criticism of Spenser when he
called him the poet's poet. We may fairly leave the allegory on one side,
for perhaps, after all, he adopted it only for the reason that it was in
fashion, and put it on as he did his ruff, not because it was becoming,
but because it was the only wear. The true use of him is as a gallery of
pictures which we visit as the mood takes us, and where we spend an
hour or two at a time, long enough to sweeten our perceptions, not so
long as to cloy them. He makes one think always of Venice; for not only
is his style Venetian,[16] but as the gallery there is housed in the shell of an
abandoned convent, so his in that of a deserted allegory. And again, as
at Venice you swim in a gondola from Gian Bellini to Titian, and from
Titian to Tintoret, so in him, where other cheer is wanting, the gentle
sway of his measure, like the rhythmical impulse of the oar, floats you
lullingly along from picture to picture.

> If all the pens that ever poet held
> Had fed the feeling of their master's thoughts,
> And every sweetness that inspired their hearts
> Their minds and muses on admirèd themes,
> If all the heavenly quintessence they still
> From their immortal flowers of poesy,
> If these had made one poem's period,

And all combined in beauty's worthiness;
Yet should there hover in their restless heads
One thought, one grace, one wonder at the best,
Which into words no virtue can digest.[17]

Spenser at his best, has come as near to expressing this unattainable something as any other poet. He is so purely poet that with him the meaning does not so often modulate the music of the verse as the music makes great part of the meaning and leads the thought along its pleasant paths. No poet is so splendidly superfluous as he; none knows so well that in poetry enough is not only not so good as a feast, but is a beggarly parsimony. He spends himself in a careless abundance only to be justified by incomes of immortal youth.

Pensier canuto nè molto nè poco
Si può quivi albergare in alcun cuore;
Non entra quivi disagio nè inopia,
Ma vi sta ogn'or col corno pien la Copia.[18]

This delicious abundance and overrunning luxury of Spenser appear in the very structure of his verse. He found the *ottava rima* too monotonously iterative; so, by changing the order of his rhymes, he shifted the couplet from the end of the stave, where it always seems to put on the brakes with a jar, to the middle, where it may serve at will as a brace or a bridge; he found it not roomy enough, so first ran it over into another line, and then ran that added line over into an alexandrine, in which the melody of one stanza seems forever longing and feeling forward after that which is to follow. There is no ebb and flow in his metre more than on the shores of the Adriatic, but wave follows wave with equable gainings and recessions, the one sliding back in fluent music to be mingled with and carried forward by the next. In all this there is soothingness indeed, but no slumberous monotony; for Spenser was no mere metrist, but a great composer. By the variety of his pauses— now at the close of the first or second foot, now of the third, and again of the fourth—he gives spirit and energy to a measure whose tendency it certainly is to become languorous. He knew how to make it rapid and passionate at need, as in such verses as,

But he, my lion, and my noble lord,
How does he find in cruel heart to hate

> Her that him loved and ever most adored
> As the God of my life? Why hath he me abhorred? [19]

or this,

> Come hither, come hither, O, come hastily! [20]

Joseph Warton objects to Spenser's stanza, that its "constraint led him into many absurdities." Of these he instances three, of which I shall notice only one, since the two others (which suppose him at a loss for words and rhymes) will hardly seem valid to any one who knows the poet. It is that it "obliged him to dilate the thing to be expressed, however unimportant, with trifling and tedious circumlocutions, namely, Faery Queen, II. ii. 44:

> Now hath fair Phœbe with her silver face
> Thrice seen the shadows of this nether world,
> Sith last I left that honorable place,
> In which her royal presence is enrolled.

That is, it is three months since I left her palace." [21] But Dr. Warton should have remembered (what he too often forgets in his own verses) that, in spite of Dr. Johnson's dictum, poetry is not prose, and that verse only loses its advantage over the latter by invading its province. [22] Verse itself is an absurdity except as an expression of some higher movement of the mind, or as an expedient to lift other minds to the same ideal level. It is the cothurnus which gives language an heroic stature. I have said that one leading characteristic of Spenser's style was its spaciousness, that he habitually dilates rather than compresses. But his way of measuring time was perfectly natural in an age when everybody did not carry a dial in his poke as now. He is the last of the poets, who went (without affectation) by the great clock of the firmament. Dante, the miser of words, who goes by the same timepiece, is full of these roundabout ways of telling us the hour. It had nothing to do with Spenser's stanza, and I for one should be sorry to lose these stately revolutions of the *superne ruote*. Time itself becomes more noble when so measured; we never knew before of how precious a commodity we had the wasting. Who would prefer the plain time of day to this?

> Now when Aldebaran was mounted high
> Above the starry Cassiopeia's chair;

or this?

> By this the northern wagoner had set
> His seven-fold team behind the steadfast star
> That was in ocean's waves yet never wet,
> But firm is fixt and sendeth light from far
> To all that in the wide deep wandering are;

or this?

> At last the golden oriental gate
> Of greatest heaven gan to open fair,
> And Phœbus, fresh as bridegroom to his mate,
> Came dancing forth, shaking his dewy hair
> And hurls his glistening beams through dewy air.

The generous indefiniteness, which treats an hour more or less as of no account, is in keeping with that sense of endless leisures which it is one chief merit of the poem to suggest. . . .

. . . His natural tendency is to shun whatever is sharp and abrupt. He loves to prolong emotion, and lingers in his honeyed sensations like a bee in the translucent cup of a lily. So entirely are beauty and delight in it the native element of Spenser, that, whenever in the "Faery Queen" you come suddenly on the moral, it gives you a shock of unpleasant surprise, a kind of grit, as when one's teeth close on a bit of gravel in a dish of strawberries and cream. He is the most fluent of our poets. Sensation passing through emotion into revery is a prime quality of his manner. And to read him puts one in the condition of revery, a state of mind in which our thoughts and feelings float motionless, as one sees fish do in a gentle stream, with just enough vibration of their fins to keep themselves from going down with the current, while their bodies yield indolently to all its soothing curves. He chooses his language for its rich canorousness rather than for intensity of meaning. To characterize his style in a single word, I should call it *costly*. None but the daintiest and nicest phrases will serve him, and he allures us from one to the other with such cunning baits of alliteration, and such sweet lapses of verse, that never any word seems more eminent than the rest, nor detains the feeling to eddy around it, but you must go on to the end before you have time to stop and muse over the wealth that has been lavished on you. But he has characterized and exemplified his own style better than any description could do:

> For round about the walls yclothed were
> With goodly arras of great majesty,

Woven with gold and silk so close and near
That the rich metal lurked privily
As faining to be hid from envious eye;
Yet here and there and everywhere, unwares
It showed itself and shone unwillingly
Like to a discolored snake whose hidden snares
Through the green grass his long bright-burnished back declares.[23]

And of the lulling quality of his verse take this as a sample:

And, more to lull him in his slumber soft,
A trickling stream from high rock tumbling down
And ever drizzling rain upon the loft,
Mixt with the murmuring wind much like the soun
Of swarming bees did cast him in a swoon.
No other noise, nor peoples' troublous cries,
As still are wont to annoy the wallëd town,
Might there be heard: but careless quiet lies
Wrapt in eternal silence far from enemies.[24]

In the world into which Spenser carries us there is neither time nor space, or rather it is outside of and independent of them both, and so is purely ideal, or, more truly, imaginary; yet it is full of form, color, and all earthly luxury, and so far, if not real, yet apprehensible by the senses. There are no men and women in it, yet it throngs with airy and immortal shapes that have the likeness of men and women, and hint at some kind of foregone reality. Now this place, somewhere between mind and matter, between soul and sense, between the actual and the possible, is precisely the region which Spenser assigns (if I have rightly divined him) to the poetic susceptibility of impression,

To reign in the air from the earth to highest sky.

Underneath every one of the senses lies the soul and spirit of it, dormant till they are magnetized by some powerful emotion. Then whatever is imperishable in us recognizes for an instant and claims kindred with something outside and distinct from it, yet in some inconceivable way a part of it, that flashes back on it an ideal beauty which impoverishes all other companionship. This exaltation with which love sometimes subtilizes the nerves of coarsest men so that they feel and see, not the thing as it seems to others, but the beauty of it, the joy of it, the soul of eternal youth that is in it, would appear to have been the normal condition of

Spenser. While the senses of most men live in the cellar, his "were laid in a large upper chamber which opened toward the sunrise."

> His birth was of the womb of morning dew,
> And his conception of the joyous prime.

The very greatest poets (and is there, after all, more than one of them?) have a way, I admit, of getting within our inmost consciousness and in a manner betraying us to ourselves. There is in Spenser a remoteness very different from this, but it is also a seclusion, and quite as agreeable, perhaps quite as wholesome in certain moods when we are glad to get away from ourselves and those importunate trifles which we gravely call the realities of life. In the warm Mediterranean of his mind everything

> Suffers a sea-change
> Into something rich and strange.

He lifts everything, not beyond recognition, but to an ideal distance where no mortal, I had almost said human, fleck is visible. Instead of the ordinary bridal gifts, he hallows his wife with an Epithalamion fit for a conscious goddess, and the "savage soil" [25] of Ireland becomes a turf of Arcady under her feet, where the merchants' daughters of the town are no more at home than the angels and the fair shapes of pagan mythology whom they meet there. He seems to have had a common-sense side to him, and could look at things (if we may judge by his tract on Irish affairs) in a practical and even hard way; but the moment he turned toward poetry he fulfilled the condition which his teacher Plato imposes on poets, and had not a particle of prosaic understanding left. His fancy, habitually moving about in worlds not realized, unrealizes everything at a touch. The critics blame him because in his Prothalamion the subjects of it enter on the Thames as swans and leave it at Temple Gardens as noble damsels; but to those who are grown familiar with his imaginary world such a transformation seems as natural as in the old legend of the Knight of the Swan.

> Come now ye damsels, daughters of Delight,
>   Help quickly her to dight:
> But first come ye, fair Hours, which were begot
> In Jove's sweet paradise of Day and Night, . . .
> And ye three handmaids of the Cyprian Queen,
> The which do still adorn her beauty's pride,

Help to adorn my beautifulest bride.

. . . .

Crown ye god Bacchus with a coronal,
And Hymen also crown with wreaths of vine,
And let the Graces dance unto the rest,———
    For they can do it best.
The whiles the maidens do their carols sing,
To which the woods shall answer and their echo ring.

The whole Epithalamion is very noble, with an organ-like roll and majesty of numbers, while it is instinct with the same joyousness which must have been the familiar mood of Spenser. It is no superficial and tiresome merriment, but a profound delight in the beauty of the universe and in that delicately surfaced nature of his which was its mirror and counterpart. Sadness was alien to him, and at funerals he was, to be sure, a decorous mourner, as could not fail with so sympathetic a temperament; but his condolences are graduated to the unimpassioned scale of social requirement. Even for Sir Philip Sidney his sighs are regulated by the official standard. It was in an unreal world that his affections found their true object and vent, and it is in an elegy of a lady whom he had never known that he puts into the mouth of a husband whom he has evaporated into a shepherd the two most naturally pathetic verses he ever penned:

I hate the day because it lendeth light
To see all things, but not my love to see.[26]

In the Epithalamion there is an epithet which has been much admired for its felicitous tenderness:

Behold, whiles she before the altar stands,
Hearing the holy priest that to her speakes
And blesseth her with his two *happy* hands.

But the purely impersonal passion of the artist had already guided him to this lucky phrase. It is addressed by Holiness—a dame surely as far abstracted from the enthusiasms of love as we can readily conceive of— to Una, who, like the visionary Helen of Dr. Faustus, has every charm of womanhood except that of being alive, as Juliet and Beatrice are.

O happy earth,
Whereon thy innocent feet do ever tread! [27]

Can we conceive of Una, the fall of whose foot would be as soft as that of a rose-leaf upon its mates already fallen—can we conceive of her treading anything so sordid? No; it is only on some unsubstantial floor of dream that she walks securely, herself a dream. And it is only when Spenser has escaped thither, only when this glamour of fancy has rarefied his wife till she is grown almost as purely a creature of the imagination as the other ideal images with which he converses, that his feeling becomes as nearly passionate—as nearly human, I was on the point of saying—as with him is possible. I am so far from blaming this idealizing property of his mind that I find it admirable in him. It is his quality, not his defect. Without some touch of it life would be unendurable prose. If I have called the world to which he transports us a world of unreality, I have wronged him. It is only a world of unrealism. It is from pots and pans and stocks and futile gossip and inch-long politics that he emancipates us, and makes us free of that to-morrow, always coming and never come, where ideas shall reign supreme.[28] . . .

Spenser, in one of his letters to Harvey, had said, "Why, a God's name, may not we, as else the Greeks, have the kingdom of our own language?" This is in the tone of Bellay, as is also a great deal of what is said in the epistle prefixed to the "Shepherd's Calendar." He would have been wiser had he followed more closely Bellay's advice about the introduction of novel words: "Fear not, then, to innovate somewhat, particularly in a long poem, with modesty, however, with analogy, and judgment of ear; and trouble not thyself as to who may think it good or bad, hoping that posterity will approve it—she who gives faith to doubtful, light to obscure, novelty to antique, usage to unaccustomed, and sweetness to harsh and rude things." Spenser's innovations were by no means always happy, as not always according with the genius of the language, and they have therefore not prevailed. He forms English words out of French or Italian ones, sometimes, I think, on a misapprehension of their true meaning; nay, he sometimes makes new ones by unlawfully grafting a scion of Romance on a Teutonic root. His theory, caught from Bellay, of rescuing good archaisms from unwarranted oblivion, was excellent; not so his practice of being archaic for the mere sake of escaping from the common and familiar. A permissible archaism is a word or phrase that has been supplanted by something less apt, but has not become unintelligible; and Spenser's often needed a glossary, even in his own day.[29] But he never endangers his finest passages by any experiments of this kind. There his language is living, if ever any, and of one substance with the splendor of his fancy. Like all masters of speech, he is fond of toying with and teasing it a little; and it may readily be granted that he sometimes "hunted the letter," as it was called, out of all cry. But even where his alliteration is tempted to an excess, its prolonged echoes caress the ear like the fading and gathering reverberations of an Alpine horn, and one can find in his heart to forgive even such a debauch of initial assonances as

> Eftsoones her shallow ship away did slide,
> More swift than swallow shears the liquid sky.

Generally, he scatters them at adroit intervals, reminding us of the arrangement of voices in an ancient catch, where one voice takes up the phrase another has dropped, and thus seems to give the web of harmony a firmer and more continuous texture.

Other poets have held their mirrors up to nature, mirrors that differ very widely in the truth and beauty of the images they reflect; but Spenser's is a magic glass in which we see few shadows cast back from actual life, but visionary shapes conjured up by the wizard's art from some confusedly remembered past or some impossible future; it is like one of those still pools of mediæval legend which covers some sunken city of the antique world; a reservoir in which all our dreams seem to have been gathered. As we float upon it, we see that it pictures faithfully enough the summer-clouds that drift over it, the trees that grow about its margin, but in the midst of these shadowy echoes of actuality we catch faint tones of bells that seem blown to us from beyond the horizon of time, and looking down into the clear depths, catch glimpses of towers and far-shining knights and peerless dames that waver and are gone. Is it a world that ever was, or shall be, or can be, or but a delusion? Spenser's world, real to him, is real enough for us to take a holiday in, and we may well be content with it when the earth we dwell on is so often too real to allow of such vacations. It is the same kind of world that Petrarca's Laura has walked in for five centuries with all ears listening for the music of her footfall.

The land of Spenser is the land of Dream, but it is also the land of Rest. To read him is like dreaming awake, without even the trouble of doing it yourself, but letting it be done for you by the finest dreamer that ever lived, who knows how to color his dreams like life and make

them move before you in music. They seem singing to you as the sirens
to Guyon, and we linger like him:

> O, thou son of gentle Faery
> That art in mighty arms most magnified
> Above all knights that ever battle tried,
> O, turn thy rudder hitherward awhile,
> Here may thy storm-beat vessel safely ride,
> This is the port of rest from troublous toil,
> The world's sweet inn from pain and wearisome turmoil.[30]
> With that the rolling sea, resounding swift
> In his big bass, them fitly answerëd,
> And on the rock the waves, breaking aloft,
> A solemn mean unto them measurëd,
> The whiles sweet Zephyrus loud whistelëd
> His treble, a strange kind of harmony
> Which Guyon's senses softly tickelëd
> That he the boatman bade row easily
> And let him hear some part of their rare melody.

Despite Spenser's instinctive tendency to idealize, and his habit of
distilling out of the actual an ethereal essence in which very little of the
possible seems left, yet his mind, as is generally true of great poets, was
founded on a solid basis of good sense. I do not know where to look for
a more cogent and at the same time picturesque confutation of Socialism
than in the Second Canto of the Fifth Book. If I apprehend rightly his
words and images, there is not only subtle but profound thinking here.
The French Revolution is prefigured in the well-meaning but too theo-
retic giant, and Rousseau's fallacies exposed two centuries in advance.
Spenser was a conscious Englishman to his inmost fibre, and did not
lack the sound judgment in politics which belongs to his race. He was
the more English for living in Ireland, and there is something that moves
us deeply in the exile's passionate cry:

> Dear Country! O how dearly dear
> Ought thy remembrance and perpetual band
> Be to thy foster-child that from thy hand
> Did common breath and nouriture receive!
> How brutish is it not to understand
> How much to her we owe that all us gave,
> That gave unto us all whatever good we have!

His race shows itself also where he tells us that

> Chiefly skill to ride seems a science
> Proper to gentle blood,

which reminds one of Lord Herbert of Cherbury's saying that the finest sight God looked down on was a fine man on a fine horse.

Wordsworth, in the supplement to his preface, tells us that the "Faery Queen" "faded before" Sylvester's translation of Du Bartas. But Wordsworth held a brief for himself in this case, and is no exception to the proverb about men who are their own attorneys. His statement is wholly unfounded. Both poems, no doubt, so far as popularity is concerned, yielded to the graver interests of the Civil War. But there is an appreciation much weightier than any that is implied in mere popularity, and the vitality of a poem is to be measured by the kind as well as the amount of influence it exerts. Spenser has *coached* more poets and more eminent ones than any other writer of English verse. I need say nothing of Milton, nor of professed disciples like Browne, the two Fletchers, and More. Cowley tells us that he became "irrecoverably a poet" by reading the "Faery Queen" when a boy. Dryden, whose case is particularly in point because he confesses having been seduced by Du Bartas, tells us that Spenser had been his master in English. He regrets, indeed, comically enough, that Spenser could not have read the rules of Bossu, but adds that "no man was ever born with a greater genius or more knowledge to support it." Pope says, "There is something in Spenser that pleases one as strongly in one's old age as it did in one's youth. I read the *Faery Queen* when I was about twelve with a vast deal of delight; and I think it gave me as much when I read it over about a year or two ago." Thomson wrote the most delightful of his poems in the measure of Spenser; Collins, Gray, and Akenside show traces of him; and in our own day his influence reappears in Wordsworth, Byron, Shelley, and Keats. Landor is, I believe, the only poet who ever found him tedious. Spenser's mere manner has not had so many imitators as Milton's, but no other of our poets has given an impulse, and in the right direction also, to so many and so diverse minds; above all, no other has given to so many young souls a consciousness of their wings and a delight in the use of them. He is a standing protest against the tyranny of Commonplace, and sows the seeds of a noble discontent with prosaic views of life and the dull uses to which it may be put.

Three of Spenser's own verses best characterize the feeling his poetry gives us:

Among wide waves set like a little nest,

Wrapt in eternal silence far from enemies,

The world's sweet inn from pain and wearisome turmoil.

We are wont to apologize for the grossness of our favorite authors sometimes by saying that their age was to blame and not they; and the excuse is a good one, for often it is the frank word that shocks us while we tolerate the thing. Spenser needs no such extenuations. No man can read the "Faery Queen" and be anything but the better for it. Through that rude age, when Maids of Honor drank beer for breakfast and Hamlet could say a gross thing to Ophelia, he passes serenely abstracted and high, the Don Quixote of poets. Whoever can endure unmixed delight, whoever can tolerate music and painting and poetry all in one, whoever wishes to be rid of thought and to let the busy anvils of the brain be silent for a time, let him read in the "Faery Queen." There is the land of pure heart's ease, where no ache or sorrow of spirit can enter.

NOTES

1. Sir Philip Sidney did not approve of this. "That same framing of his style to an old rustic language I dare not allow, since neither Theocritus in Greek, Virgil in Latin, nor Sannazzaro in Italian did affect it," *(Defence of Poesy.)* Ben Jonson, on the other hand, said that Guarini "kept not decorum in making shepherds speak as well as himself could." *(Conversations with Drummond.)* I think Sidney was right, for the poets' Arcadia is a purely ideal world, and should be treated accordingly. But whoever looks into the glossary appended to the *Calendar* by E. K., will be satisfied that Spenser's object was to find unhackneyed and poetical words rather than such as should seem more on a level with the speakers. See also the *Epistle Dedicatory.* I cannot help thinking that E. K. was Spenser himself, with occasional interjections of Harvey. Who else could have written such English as many passages in this *Epistle?*

2. It was at Penshurst that he wrote the only specimen that has come down to us, and bad enough it is. I have said that some of Sidney's are pleasing.

3. See *Literary Essays,* iii. 338 *seqq.*

4. Perhaps his most striking single epithet is the "sea-shouldering whales," B. II. 12, xxiii. His ear seems to delight in prolongations. For example, he makes such words as *glorious, gratious, joyeous, havior, chapelet* dactyls, and that, not at the end of verses, where it would not have been unusual, but in the first half of them. Milton contrives a break (a kind of heave, as it were) in the uniformity of his verse by a practice exactly the opposite of this. He also shuns a *hiatus* which does

not seem to have been generally displeasing to Spenser's ear, though perhaps in the compound epithet *bees-alluring* he intentionally avoids it by the plural form.

5.   Like as a wayward child, whose sounder sleep
    Is broken with some fearful dream's affright,
    With froward will doth set himself to weep
    Ne can be stilled for all his nurse's might,
    But kicks and squalls and shrieks for fell despight,
    Now scratching her and her loose locks misusing,
    Now seeking darkness and now seeking light,
    Then craving suck, and then the suck refusing.

He would doubtless have justified himself by the familiar example of Homer's comparing Ajax to a donkey in the eleventh book of the *Iliad*. So also in the *Epithalamion* it grates our nerves to hear,

    Pour not by cups, but by the bellyful,
    Pour out to all that wull.

Such examples serve to show how strong a dose of Spenser's *aurum potabile* the language needed.

6. Ben Jonson told Drummond "that in that paper Sir W. Raleigh had of the allegories of his *Faery Queen,* by the Blatant Beast the Puritans were understood." But this is certainly wrong. There were very different shades of Puritanism, according to individual temperament. That of Winthrop and Higginson had a mellowness of which Endicott and Standish were incapable. The gradual change of Milton's opinions was similar to that which I suppose in Spenser. The passage in *Mother Hubberd* may have been aimed at the Protestant clergy of Ireland (for he says much the same thing in his *View of the State of Ireland*), but it is general in its terms.

7. Two of his eclogues, as I have said, are from Marot, and his earliest known verses are translations from Bellay, a poet who was charming whenever he had the courage to play truant from a bad school. We must not suppose that an analysis of the literature of the *demi-monde* will give us all the elements of the French character. It has been both grave and profound; nay, it has even contrived to be wise and lively at the same time, a combination so incomprehensible by the Teutonic races that they have labelled it levity. It puts them out as Nature did Fuseli.

8. Taste must be partially excepted. It is remarkable how little eating and drinking there is in the *Faery Queen*. The only time he fairly sets a table is in the house of Malbecco, where it is necessary to the conduct of the story. Yet taste is not wholly forgotten:

    In her left hand a cup of gold she held,
    And with her right the riper fruit did reach,
    Whose sappy liquor, that with fulness sweld,
    Into her cup she scruzed with dainty breach
    Of her fine fingers without foul impeach,
    That so fair wine-press made the wine more sweet.
            (B. II. c. xii. 56.)

Taste can hardly complain of unhandsome treatment!

9. Had the poet lived longer, he might perhaps have verified his friend Raleigh's saying, that "whosoever in writing modern history shall follow truth too near the heels, it may haply strike out his teeth." The passage is one of the very few disgusting ones in the *Faery Queen*. Spenser was copying Ariosto; but the Italian poet, with the discreeter taste of his race, keeps to generalities. Spenser goes into particulars which can only be called nasty. He did this, no doubt, to pleasure his mistress, Mary's rival; and this gives us a measure of the brutal coarseness of contemporary manners. It becomes only the more marvellous that the fine flower of his genius could have transmuted the juices of such a soil into the purity and sweetness which are its own peculiar properties.

10. There is a gleam of humor in one of the couplets of *Mother Hubberd's Tale,* where the Fox, persuading the Ape that they should disguise themselves as discharged soldiers in order to beg the more successfully, says,

> Be you the soldier, for you likest are
> For manly semblance *and small skill in war.*

11. Bunyan probably took the hint of the Giant's suicidal offer of "knife, halter, or poison," from Spenser's "swords, ropes, poison," in *Faery Queen,* B. I. c. ix. I.

12. Book II. c. 9.

13. See Sidney's *Defence,* and Puttenham's *Art of English Poesy,* Book I. c. 8.

14. We can fancy how he would have done this by Jeremy Taylor, who was a kind of Spenser in a cassock.

15. Of this he himself gives a striking hint, where speaking in his own person he suddenly breaks in on his narrative with the passionate cry,

> Ah, dearest God, me grant I dead be not defouled.
>   (*Faery Queen,* B. I. c. x. 43.)

16. Was not this picture painted by Paul Veronese, for example?

> Arachne figured how Jove did abuse
> Europa like a bull, and on his back
> Her through the sea did bear: . . .
> She seemed still back unto the land to look,
> And her playfellows' aid to call, and fear
> The dashing of the waves, that up she took
> Her dainty feet, and garments gathered near. . . .
> Before the Bull she pictured wingèd Love,
> With his young brother Sport, . . .
> Any many nymphs about them flocking round,
> Any many Tritons which their horns did sound.
>   (*Muiopotmos,* 281-296.)

Spenser begins a complimentary sonnet prefixed to the *Commonwealth and Government of Venice* (1599) with this beautiful verse,

> Fair Venice, flower of the last world's delight.

Perhaps we should read "lost"?

17. Marlowe's *Tamburlaine,* Part I. Act V. 2.

18.   Grayheaded Thought, nor much nor little, may
> Take up its lodging here in any heart;
> Unease nor Lack can enter at this door;
> But here dwells full-horned Plenty evermore.
>   (*Orl. Fur.,* c. vi. 73.)

19. *Faery Queen,* I. c. iii. 7. Leigh Hunt, one of the most sympathetic of critics, has remarked the passionate change from the third to the first person in the last two verses.

20. *Faery Queen,* II. c. viii. 3.

21. *Observations on Faery Queen,* vol. i. pp. 158, 159. Mr. Hughes also objects to Spenser's measure, that it is "closed always by a full-stop, in the same place, by which every stanza is made as it were a distinct paragraph." (Todd's *Spenser,* II. xli.) But he could hardly have read the poem attentively, for there are numerous instances to the contrary. Spenser was a consummate master of versification, and not only did Marlowe and Shakespeare learn of him, but I have little doubt that, but for the *Faery Queen,* we should never have had the varied majesty of Milton's blank verse.

22. As where Dr. Warton himself says:

> How nearly had my spirit past,
> Till stopt by Metcalf's skilful hand,
> To death's dark regions wide and waste

> And the black river's mournful strand,
> Or to, . . .

to the end of the next stanza. That is, I had died but for Dr. Metcalf's boluses.

23. *Faery Queen,* III. c. xi. 28.

24. *Ibid.* I. c. i. 41.

25. This phrase occurs in the sonnet addressed to the Earl of Ormond and in that to Lord Grey de Wilton in the series prefixed to the *Faery Queen.* These sonnets are of a much stronger build than the *Amoretti,* and some of them (especially that to Sir John Norris) recall the firm tread of Milton's, though differing in structure.

26. *Daphnaida,* 407, 408.

27. *Faery Queen,* I. c. x. 9.

28. Strictly taken, perhaps his world is not *much* more imaginary than that of other epic poets, Homer (in the *Iliad*) included. He who is familiar with mediæval epics will be extremely cautious in drawing inferences as to contemporary manners from Homer. He evidently *archaizes* like the rest.

29. I find a goodly number of Yankeeisms in him, such as *idee* (not as a rhyme); but the oddest is his twice spelling *dew deow,* which is just as one would spell it who wished to phonetize its sound in rural New England.

30. This song recalls that in Dante's *Purgatorio* (XIX. 19-24), in which the Italian tongue puts forth all its siren allurements. Browne's beautiful verses ("Turn, hither turn your wingèd pines") were suggested by these of Spenser. It might almost seem as if Spenser had here, in his usual way, expanded the sweet old verses:

> Merry sungen the monks binnen Ely
> When Knut king rew thereby;
> "Roweth knightës near the lond,
> That I may hear these monkës song."

EIGHT

EDWARD DOWDEN

Spenser, the Poet and Teacher (1884)*

In England of the age of Elizabeth what place is filled by the poetry of Spenser? What blank would be made by its disappearance? In what, for each of us who love that poetry, resides its special virtue? Shall we say in answer to these questions that Spenser is the weaver of spells, the creator of illusions, the enchanter of the Elizabethan age; and that his name is to us a word of magic by which we conjure away the pain of actual life, and obtain entrance into a world of faery? Was Spenser, as a poet of our own time names himself, "the idle singer" of his day—that day not indeed "an empty day," but one filled with heroic daring and achievement? While Raleigh was exploring strange streams of the New World, while Drake was chasing the Spaniard, while Bacon was seeking for the principles of a philosophy which should enrich man's life, while Hooker, with the care of a wise master-builder, was laying the foundation of polity in the national Church, where was Spenser? Was he forgetful of England, forgetful of earth, lulled and lying in some bower of fantasy, or moving in a dream among imaginary champions of chivalry, distressed damsels, giants and dragons and satyrs and savage men, or shepherds who pipe and shepherdesses who dance for ever in a serene Arcady?

Assuredly it was not thus that a great Englishman of a later age thought of Spenser. When Milton entered upon his manhood, he entered upon a warfare; the peaceful Horton days, days of happy ingathering of varied culture, days of sweet repose amid rural beauty, were past

---

*This essay appeared in *The Complete Works in Verse and Prose of Edmund Spenser,* ed. Alexander B. Grosart, I. 304-339. Reprinted are pp. 304-306, 313-339.

and gone; and he stood with loins girt, prepared for battle on behalf of liberty. And then, in London, when London was a vast arsenal in which weapons were forging for the defence of truth and freedom, Milton in his moment of highest and most masculine ardour, as he wrote his speech on behalf of unlicensed printing, thought of Spenser. It was not as a dreamer that Milton thought of him. Spenser had been a power with himself in youth, when he, "the lady of his college," but such a lady as we read of in *Comus,* grew in virginal beauty and virginal strength. He had listened to Spenser's "sage and solemn tunes,"

> Of turneys and of trophies hung;
> Of forests and enchantments drear,
> Where more is meant than meets the ear.

And now, in his manhood, when all of life has grown for him so grave, so glorious with heroic effort, Milton looks back and remembers his master, and he remembers him not as an idle singer, not as a dreamer of dreams, but as "our sage and serious Spenser, whom I dare to name a better teacher than Scotus or Aquinas."

A teacher—what is the import of this? "The true use of Spenser," says a poet of our own day, Mr. J. R. Lowell, "is as a gallery of pictures which we visit as the mood takes us, and where we spend an hour or two at a time, long enough to sweeten our perceptions, not so long as to cloy them." And again: "Whenever in the *Faery Queen* you come suddenly on the moral, it gives you a shock of unpleasant surprise, a kind of grit, as when one's teeth close on a bit of gravel in a dish of strawberries and cream." This, then, is the *Faery Queen*—a dish of strawberries and cream mixed up unfortunately with a good deal of grit. And as for the allegory, we may "fairly leave it on one side";[1] Spenser employed it to "convince the scorners that poetry might be seriously useful, and show Master Bull his new way of making fine words butter parsnips, in a rhymed moral primer." Shall we accept this view, or that of Milton— "a better teacher than Scotus or Aquinas"? Was Spenser such a teacher "sage and serious" to his own age? If so, does he remain such a teacher for this age of ours? . . .

In the *Shepherd's Calendar* we discern much of the future writer of the *Faery Queen*. It contains the poetical record of his personal griefs as a lover; it expresses his enthusiasm for his art as a poet; his loyalty to the crown as a servant of the Queen; his loyalty to the Reformation as an English churchman; his delight in natural beauty, and in the fairness of woman. It is now gay and sportive, now staid and serious; sensuous ardour and moral wisdom are united in it; the allegorical form in miniature is already employed; it exhibits a mode of idealized treatment of contemporary public affairs not dissimilar in essentials from that afterwards put to use in his romantic epic. The pastoral, with its ideals of peace and simplicity, possessed a singular charm for Europe in the highwrought and artificial age of the Renaissance. It had a charm for Spenser; but his is not the Arcadian pastoral of Sannazaro and Sidney. Colin and Cuddie keep their flocks upon the hills of Kent; the disdainful Rosalinde, "the widow's daughter of the glen," is a North-country lass. Spenser's power of taking up real objects, persons and incidents, of plunging these in some solvent of the imagination, and then of recreating them— the same and not the same—is manifest throughout. Everything has been submitted to the shaping power of the imagination; everything has been idealised; yet Spenser does not remove from real life, does not forsake his own country and his own time; he does not shrink from taking a side in controversies then troubling the English Church; he is primarily a poet, but while a poet, he also aspires to be what Milton named him— a teacher. In these poems the little archer, Love, shoots his roguish shafts; Pan is the patron of shepherds; Cynthia sits crowned upon the grassy green. The poet freely appropriates what pleases his fancy in classical or neo-classical mythology; yet at heart he is almost Puritan. Not indeed Puritan in any turning away from innocent delights; not Puritan in casting dishonour on our earthly life, its beauty, its splendour, its joy, its passion; but Puritan as Milton was when he wrote *Lycidas,* in his weight of moral purpose, in his love of a grave plainness in religion and of humble laboriousness in those who are shepherds under Christ.

    The tenth eclogue of the *Calendar,* that for the month of October, is especially characteristic of its author. In it, as stated in the argument, is set out "the perfect pattern of a poet." In what way does Spenser conceive of poetry? We know how in periods which are not creative, periods which are not breathed upon by new divine ideas, which are not driven by the urge of strong emotions, poetry comes to be looked on as primarily an art, or even as an accomplishment, and it is treated as if its function were to decorate life much as the artistic upholsterer decorates our houses. At such a time great regard is had to the workmanship of verse exclusive of the burden and inspiration of the song, and elegant little specimens of mosaic or of enamelling are turned out of the workshops of skilled artists; until the thing descends into a trade. In the creative periods there is not less devotion to form and workmanship; but the devotion is of a less self-conscious kind, because generative powers work in the poet with a rapturous blindness of love, and he thinks of himself less as a master of technique (though he is also this) than as a man possessed by some influence out of and beyond himself, some dominant energy of Nature or of God, to which it is his part to submit, which he cannot lay claim to as if it were an attainment of skill, and which he dare not call his own. At such times poetry aims at something more than to decorate life; it is spoken of as if it possessed some imperial authority, a power to bind and to loose, to sway man's total nature, to calm, to regulate and restrain, and also to free, to arouse, to dilate the spirit—power not to titillate a particular sense, but to discipline the will and mould a character. In such a tone of high assumption Spenser speaks of poetry. About this time he heard much of experiments in new and ingenious forms of English verse. Sidney and Dyer, Drant and Gabriel Harvey, were full of a scheme for introducing classical metres into our poetry, and Spenser was for a while taken by the scheme. He could not at such a time, he did not ever, despise the craftsman's part of poetry; yet while he thinks of poetry as an art, in the same moment it appears to him to be "no art, but a divine gift and heavenly instinct not to be gotten by labour and learning, but adorned with both; and poured into the wit by a certain 'Ενθουσιασμος and celestial inspiration." When in the eclogue the needy poet complains that Apollo is a poor paymaster, Piers replies in the spirit of Sidney when he maintains that the highest end of literature is to instruct and incite men to virtuous action:

> Cuddie, the prayse is better than the price,
> The glory eke much greater than the gayne;
> O! what an honor it is to restraine
> The lust of lawless youth with good advice,
> Or pricke them forth with pleasaunce of thy vaine,
> Whereto thou list their trayned wills entice.

> Soon as thou gynst to set thy notes in frame,
> O, how the rurall routes to thee doe cleave!
> Seemeth thou dost their soule of sense bereave;
> All as the shepheard that did fetch his dame

> From Plutoes balefull bowre withouten leave,
> His musicks might the hellish hound did tame.

From the eclogue which contains this pronouncement as to the end of poetry, it appears that Spenser already was meditating verse of a loftier kind, and was even now aware that he should before long change his "oaten reeds" for trumpets:

> Abandon, then, the base and viler clowne;
> Lift up thy self out of the lowly dust,
> And sing of bloody Mars, of wars, of giusts;
> Turne thee to those that weld the awful crowne,
> To doubted knights, whose woundlesse armour rusts,
> And helmes unbruzed wexen daily browne.

The *Faery Queen* is here almost promised. Was this to be a mere romance of adventures, like Ariosto's *Orlando*, but unsupported by the wit and worldly wisdom of an Ariosto? Or did Spenser conceive his great poem as something more than a play of fancy? Did he conceive it as capable of winning that praise which he declares in the *Shepherd's Calendar* to be the true glory of art?

The *Shepherd's Calendar* was dedicated

> To him who is the president
> Of Noblesse and of chevalree,

to Philip Sidney, "the noble and virtuous Gentleman, most worthy of all titles both of learning and chevalrie." It was possibly on the enforcement of Sidney that Spenser undertook his task "to sing of knights and ladies gentle deeds." Now, although we have to regret the loss of the work entitled *The English Poet,* in which Spenser treated of his own art, there remains to us the admirable essay by Sidney written in defence of poetry against the well-meant but ill-considered attack of the playwright-turned-precisian, Stephen Gosson. The delight and pride of the Queen, the court, and indeed of all cultivated England, in Sidney, the deep and universal sorrow for his early death, can be accounted for only by some extraordinary personal noblenesses over and above those which dignify the passionate story of the *Astrophel and Stella,* and redeem from mannered sentimentality the endless pages of the *Arcadia.* Sidney, the radiant "Hesper-Phosphor" of the time of Elizabeth, fades in the brightness of that great morning, yet no radiance that follows is quite so clear and keen. He charmed by a sweet youthful gravity underlying a sweet youthful joyousness of nature. To Spenser doubtless he appeared to be the realized ideal of what Spenser admired more than any other earthly thing—the chivalric English gentleman. Sidney belonged to both the great movements of his century, and he felt them to be in harmony one with the other. He belonged heartily to the Reformation; he had the courage to appear prominently as an opponent of the French marriage; he translated Philip of Mornay's treatise on the *Trueness of the Christian Religion*. He belonged heartily to the Renaissance, introducing into our prose literature the chivalric-pastoral romance, and engaging eagerly in the reform of versification and in the criticism of poetry. "The Muses met him," says Matthew Roydon, "every day upon Mount Parthenie," and taught him to say and sing; there was in his face, says the same writer, "the lineaments of Gospel books." Sidney could perceive no feud between culture and religion, between the genius of art and the moral temper, between the Muses on "Mount Parthenie" and the Christian Evangelists.

In Sidney's reply to Gosson's attack on poetry he inquires what is the end or object of the life of man, and he answers—as Aristotle had answered in the *Nicomachean Ethics*—it is virtuous action. He compares, with reference to their tendency to lead men to an active virtue, three branches of human learning—philosophy, history, poetry; and his contention is that to poetry must be assigned the highest place. Philosophy enlightens the intellect, but does not move the will; it is weak in its influence on conduct because it deals too exclusively with abstract truth; it lays down the rule, but omits to give the example. History fails for an opposite reason: it deals too exclusively with concrete fact; it gives the example, but the example unilluminated by its principle. Poetry excels them both, giving as it does neither precept apart from example, nor the example apart from the precept or principle, but both together; and thus it not only enlightens the intellect, but vivifies the emotions and moves the will.

In the spirit of Sidney's *Apologie for Poetry* Spenser conceived and wrote the *Faery Queen*. It is an attempt to harmonize the three divisions of learning discussed by Sidney—history, moral philosophy, poetry; and to make the first and second of these subserve the greatest of the three. The end of the whole is virtuous action; Spenser would set forth an ideal of human character, and incite men to its attainment. He thought of his poem, while never ceasing to be a true poem, as if it were, in a certain sense, a study in ethics. One day Spenser's friend Bryskett in his cottage near Dublin gathered about him a circle of distinguished acquaintances, and conversing on the subject of ethics, which he wished were worthily handled in English, "whereby our youth might speedily enter into the right course of vertuous life," he turned to Spenser with an embarrassing request—that Spenser should forthwith proceed to deliver a discourse on the virtues and vices, and give the company a taste of true moral philosophy. Spenser naturally excused himself, and pleaded on his own behalf that, though he could not improvise a lecture on ethics, he had actually in hand a work which might in some sort satisfy his friend's desire: "For sure I am, that it is not unknowne unto you, that I have already undertaken a work tending to the same effect, which is in heroical verse under the title of a *Faerie Queene* to represent all the moral vertues, assigning to every vertue a Knight to be the patron and defender of the same, in whose actions and feats of arms and chivalry the operations of that vertue, whereof he is the protector, are to be expressed, and the vices and unruly appetites that oppose themselves against the same, to be beaten down and overcome."

"A poet at that time," says the Dean of St. Paul's, commenting on this passage, "still had to justify his employment by presenting himself in the character of a professed teacher of morality." But this is hardly in accordance with the facts. It was not as a professed teacher of morality that Chaucer had told his *Canterbury Tales;* it was not as a professed teacher of morality that Marlowe wrote his *Hero and Leander,* or Shakespeare his *Venus and Adonis.* "Every great poet," said Wordsworth, "is a teacher: I wish either to be considered as a teacher, or as nothing." May it not be that Spenser had higher thoughts than of justifying his employment? May not he, like Wordsworth, but unlike Chaucer and Marlowe, have really aimed at edification—such edification as is proper to a poet? "You have given me praise," Wordsworth wrote to John Wilson, "for having reflected faithfully in my poems the feelings of human nature. I would fain hope that I have done so. But a great poet ought to do more than this: he ought, to a certain degree, to rectify men's feelings, to give them new compositions of feeling, to render their feelings more sane, pure, and permanent, in short, more consonant to nature and the great moving spirit of things." To render men's feelings more sane, pure, and permanent—this surely was included in the great design of the *Faery Queen;* it was deliberately kept before him as an object by Spenser—"our sage and serious Spenser, whom I dare to name a better teacher than Scotus or Aquinas."

How, then, should we read the *Faery Queen?* Is it poetry? Or is it philosophy? Are we merely to gaze on with wide-eyed expectancy as at a marvellous pageant or procession, in which knights and ladies, Saracens and wizards, anticks and wild men pass before our eyes? Or are these visible shows only a rind or shell, which we must break or strip away in order to get at that hidden wisdom which feeds the spirit? Neither of these things are we to do. The mere visible shows of Spenser's poem are indeed goodly enough to beguile a summer's day in some old wood, and to hold us from morning to evening in a waking dream. The ethical teaching of Spenser extracted from his poetry is worthy a careful study. Raphael drew his fainting Virgin Mother as a skeleton in his preparatory study, and the student of Raphael may well consider the anatomy of the figure, because whatever an artist has put into his work, that a critic may try to discover in it. So the moral philosophy of Spenser even apart from his poetry may rightly form a subject of study. But the special virtue of the *Faery Queen* will be found only by one who receives it neither as pageantry nor as philosophy, but in the way in which Spenser meant that it should be received—as a living creature of the imagination, a spirit incarnate, "one altogether," "of a reasonable soul and human flesh subsisting."

There are, indeed, portions of the *Faery Queen* which are not vital —which are, so to speak, excrementitious. In a short poem—the expression of a moment of lyrical excitement—a single line, a single word which is not vital, destroys the integrity of the piece. But a poem which has taken into itself the writer's entire mind during long years cannot but be like a wide landscape that includes level with rise, and sandy patches with verdurous tracts. It seems inevitable that in such comprehensive works as the *Divine Comedy,* the *Paradise Lost,* the two parts of *Faust,* the *Faery Queen,* the stream of pure imagination should sometimes well out of rocky masses of intellectual argument or didactic meditation. The dullest portions of Spenser's poem are those in which he works with most self-consciousness, piecing together definite meanings to definite symbols; where his love of beauty slumbers and his spirit of ingenuity awakes; where his ideas do not play and part and gather themselves together and deploy themselves abroad, like the shifting and shredding of clouds blown by soft upper airs, but are rather cut out with hard edges by some process of mechanism. When in the "Legende of Temperance" the poet allegorizes Aristotle's doctrine that virtue is a mean betwixt the extremes of excess and of defect, our distaste for Elissa and Perissa would surely content the moralist, were it not that our feeling towards their virtuous sister is hardly less unfriendly. From the "Castle of Alma" we should not be ill-pleased if the master-cook, Concoction, and the kitchen-clerk, Digestion, were themselves ignobly conveyed away (if allegory would permit such a departure) by that nether gate, the Port Esquiline.

These lapses and declensions we may pardon and forget. Upon the whole the *Faery Queen,* if nothing else, is at least a labyrinth of beauty, a forest of old romance in which it is possible to lose oneself more irrecoverably amid the tangled luxury of loveliness than elsewhere in English poetry. Spenser's delight in the beauty of external nature is often of a high-wrought and elaborated kind, and yet no poet has written a line of more faultless simplicity than that which tells how Calepine when recovered from his wound goes forth "to take the air and hear the thrush's song." But Spenser's rare sensibility to beauty would have found itself ill content if he had merely solitudes of nature, however fair, to contemplate. In his perfect joy in the presence of human beauty he is thoroughly a man of the Renaissance. The visions which he creates of man and woman cast a spell over their creator; they subdue and they exalt him; he cannot withdraw his gaze from the creatures of his imagination; he must satiate his senses with their loveliness; all his being is thrilled with a pure ecstasy as he continues to gaze. And what form of human beauty is there to which Spenser does not pay a poet's homage? Is it infancy? There is the babe rescued by Calepine from the bear's jaws. Spenser speaks of it as the knight's "lovely little spoil." Calepine takes it up in his two arms, and can hardly endure to hear its gentle moaning; he wipes away its tears, and cleanses its face, and searches every little limb, and every part under the swathe-bands, to be assured that the tender flesh is unhurt. Is it old age? There is that goodly sire who, blind himself, granted to Saint George a prospect of the New Jerusalem from his delectable mountain; keen of inward vision is the old man, though his earthly eyes are dim; he is bright in his extreme age with a visionary glory:

With snowy locks adown his shoulders shed;
As hoary frost with spangles doth attire
The mossy branches of an oak half dead.

Is it manhood in all the superb vitality and grandeur of early adult
years? There is Arthur as first seen by Una, riding towards her in re-
splendent armour, or Artegall as shown in the magic globe of glass to
Britomart:

Eftsoones there was presented to her eye
A comely knight, all armed in complete wise,
Through whose bright ventayle, lifted up on high,
His manly face that did his foes agrise,
And friends to terms of gentle truce entice,
Lookt forth, as Phœbus face out of the East
Betwixt two shady mountains doth arise,
Portly his person was and much increast
Through his heroic grace and honourable gest.

Or, if we look for a more youthful type of manly strength and grace,
there is Calidore, knightliest of shepherds and milkmen, devoted to the
service of Pastorella, Spenser's "shepherdess queen of curds and cream,"
his bright arms exchanged for a rustic weed, and his spear for a shepherd's hook:

So being clad, into the fields he went
With the faire Pastorella every day,
And kept her sheepe with diligent attent,
Watching to drive the ravenous wolfe away,
And every evening helping them to fold;
The whylest at pleasure she mote sport and play;
And otherwhiles for need he did assay
In his strong hand their rugged teats to hold,
And out of them to presse the milke: Love so much could.

But more than any other form of beauty that of womanhood charms
Spenser, renders his imagination (to use a favourite word of his own)
"empassioned," or calms and completely satisfies it. There is Una, with
face sad under her wimpled veil, yet, however sad, luminous like an
angel's, and making, when stole and fillet have been laid aside, "a sun-
shine in the shady place." There is Belphœbe, no lily but a rose of chas-

tity, the ideal of virginal freedom, vigour, health, and hardihood, her
face clear as the sky, with the glow in it of the quickened blood, her eyes
two living lamps, her broad ivory forehead a table for love to engrave
his triumphs on, her voice resonant like silver, her moving fleet and firm,
a boar-spear in her hand, her brown hair the lovelier for flowers and
leaves of the forest which she has borne away in her speed. There is
Britomart, of sterner virginal force, yet made for the love of Artegall,
tall and large of limb, a martial maid. Let us remember Britomart as
she appears when, roused from quiet sleep by the treachery of Malecasta
—now standing for a moment in snow-white smock, with locks un-
bound, her advanced sword in her hand, and now flying with the flame
of wronged and insulted maidenhood in her heart at the dastard knights
who would do her shame. And there is Amoret, the type of perfect
womanhood, as Belphœbe is of maidenhood; Amoret, brought up by
Psyche in the garden of Adonis—

> To be the ensample of true love alone
> And loadstar of all chaste affection;

Amoret, the most tried and true of wives, whom I like best to remember
as pictured in the first form of the legend, rescued from the snares and
tortures of the enchanter Busirane, and now lost in the happy secrecy of
one long embrace:

> Lightly he clipt her in his armès twaine,
> And straitly did embrace her body bright,
> Her body, late the prison of sad pain,
> Now the sweet lodge of love and dear delight.
>
> But the fair lady, overcomen quite
> Of huge affection, did in pleasure melt,
> And in sweet ravishment poured forth her spright.
> No word they spake, nor earthly thing they felt,
> But like two senseless stocks in long embracements melt.

And there is Florimell, who seems like the spirit of some inland stream,
but irresistibly drawn seaward by her bold lover, Marinell. And there is
Serena, scarcely seen in her loveliness by the light of stars, unclothed
upon the woodland altar and prepared for death. And there is Calidore's
shepherdess maiden gathering strawberries in the greenwood—a sister of
Shakspeare's Perdita. And there is Charissa, the fruitful mother, hung

upon by her multitude of babes. And there is Dame Celia, the reverend lady of the "House of Holiness," who bows over Una, and embraces her with the protectiveness of age and experience towards youth. And there is Spenser's own Elizabeth, whom Sir Calidore espies encircled by the Graces, and danced around by the hundred naked maidens, lily white.

Now, this sensibility to beauty—the beauty of earth and sky, the beauty of man and woman—does it bring with it any peculiar dangers, any temptations and seductions? Every noble sensibility, every high faculty of man, it may be answered, brings with it some peculiar danger. Spenser certainly was conscious of risks attending this sensibility to beauty. Puritanism was also aware of these risks; and Puritanism, when it had attained to full strength, said, "Lest thy right eye offend thee straightway pluck it out." Spenser said, "See that it offend thee not." Ascetic in the best sense of that word Spenser assuredly was: he desired to strengthen every part of our nature by heroic discipline, and to subordinate the lower parts to the higher, so that, if strong, they might be strong for service, not for mastery. But Spenser was almost as free as Wordsworth from asceticism in its evil sense, and for the same reason as Wordsworth. To Spenser and to Wordsworth it could not seem desirable to put out the right eye, because to both the eye was an inlet of divine things for the uses of the spirit. With respect to beauty, Spenser's teaching is that true beauty is always sacred, always ennobling to the spirit which is itself sane and pure, but the sensual mind will put even beauty to sensual uses. And he declares further that there is a forged or feigned beauty, which is no more than a fair illusion covering inward foulness and shame. The true beauty, according to Spenser, may be recognized by a certain illuminating quality; it is not mere pasture for the eye; rather it smites the gazer, long accustomed to the dimness of common things, as if with sudden and exquisite light; it is indeed a ray derived from God, the central Luminary of the universe.

But neither the Aristotelian doctrine of the mean, nor Platonic conceptions of love and beauty, serve best to protect and deliver us from the temptations of sense as set forth in Spenser's poetry. By his enthusiasm on behalf of the noblest moral qualities, by his strenuous joy in presence of the noblest human creatures—man and woman—Spenser breathes into us a breath of life, which has an antiseptic power, which kills the germs of disease, and is antagonistic to the relaxed fibre, the lethargy, the dissolution, or disintegrating life-in-death of sensuality. Any heroism of man or woman is like wine to gladden Spenser's heart; we see through the verse how it quickens the motion of his blood. A swift, clear flame of sympathy, like an answering beacon lit upon the high places of his soul, leaps up in response to the beacon-fire of chivalric virtue in another soul, even though it be an imagined one, summoning his own. The enchantress Acrasia in her rosy bower is so bewitchingly fair and soft that it goes hard with us to see her garden defaced and herself rudely taken captive. Or it would go hard with us did we not know the faithfulness and soft invincibility of Amoret, the virgin joy and vigour of Belphœbe, the steadfastness and animating trust in Una's eyes—or had we not beheld the face of Britomart shining beneath her umbriere like daydawn to a belated wanderer, and then all that is vain and false and sensual becomes to us what those ignoble knights of Malecasta were to the warrior virgin—no more than shadows:

> All were faire knights and goodly well beseene,
> But to faire Britomart they all but shadows beene.

We have no need to inspect the rout of monsters degraded from manhood by Acrasia's witchcraft. Britomart has clean delivered us from Acrasia.

And so we are brought back to the statement that the high distinction of Spenser's poetry is to be found in the rare degree in which it unites sense and soul, moral seriousness and the Renaissance appetite for beauty. Herein lay his chief lesson for men of his own time. To incite and to conduct men to an active virtue is not only the express purpose of the *Faery Queen,* but as far as a poem can render such service, the *Faery Queen* doubtless has actually served to train knights of holiness, knights of temperance, knights of courtesy. Spenser, although an ardent patriot of the time of Elizabeth, or rather because he was an ardent patriot, did not flatter his own age. He believed that the world had declined from its high estate, and fearing that things might tend to worse, he observed anxiously the wrong-doings of the time. He speaks very plainly in *Mother Hubberd's Tale* of vices in the court, the church, the army. He desired to serve his country and his age, as other great Englishmen were doing, and yet in his own proper way. Now, Spenser expected little—perhaps even less than Shakespeare—from the people; the doctrine of equality he held, as Shakespeare also held, to be a dangerous and misleading cry of demagogues; Spenser expressly argues against that idea in his "Legend of Justice." Liberty he held to consist in obedience to highest law; that people, he thought, is wise and happy which follows its appointed leaders. What Spenser's political faith would be, if he were now living, we may surmise, but cannot assert. Living in the age of great monarchies, he was monarchical and aristocratic. He admired heroic personalities, and he found some of these among the gentle and noble persons of England. He had known Sidney; he served under Lord Grey. When he conceived and planned this vast poem, of which only six out of the twenty-four contemplated books were written, it was with a design which doubtless seemed to Spenser the best suited and the most needful to his own time; his end, as he declared to Raleigh, was "to fashion a gentleman or noble person in vertuous and gentle discipline." He desired to see at the head of affairs in England a company of noble Englishmen serving for no selfish ends, but following honour in the highest sense of that word—the "Gloriana" of the *Faery Queen.*

Thus, with all its opulence of colour and melody, with all its imagery of delight, the *Faery Queen* has primarily a moral or spiritual intention. While Spenser sees the abundant beauty of the world, and the splendour of man and of the life of man, his vision of human life is grave and even stern. For life he regards as a warfare, a warfare needing all our foresight, strength, and skill. Thus to a certain point Spenser's conception of life may be said to be the Puritan conception; it is certainly the reverse of the Epicurean conception. Nor is the combat between good and evil in Spenser's poem one in which victory is lightly or speedily attainable; the sustaining thought is that victory is possible. There is a well-known painting by Raphael of the Archangel Michael slaying the Dragon; the heavenly avenger descends like a young Apollo, with light yet insupportable advance, and in a moment the evil thing must be abolished. There is a little engraving by Albert Dürer which contrasts strangely with that famous picture. It represents the moment of St. George's victory; the monster, very hideous and ignoble, has bitten the dust and lies impotent. But is the victor elated? He is too weary for much elation, too thankful that the struggle is ended; he rests for a short space, still mounted on his heavy German stallion; we can perceive that other combats await him, and that the battle with evil is a battle that lasts a lifetime. Spenser's conception of the strife with wrong comes nearer to that of Dürer than to that of Raphael.

Among the elements of character which Spenser's ideal noble or

gentle person must possess, he places godliness first—the religious spirit;
and the religious spirit honoured by Spenser is not cloistered or contem-
plative; he does, indeed, assign a place to contemplation in the discipline
of the soul, but the Knight of the Red-cross is, like other knights, sent
forth by his mistress, the inspirer and prompter of honourable deeds, to
achieve knightly victory over a monstrous evil. Man in relation to God
being first studied, Spenser then proceeds to consider man in relation, so
to speak, to himself; and the subject of the second book is temperance,
or, as we might say, self-control. "Incontinence in anger," says Aristotle
(*Nic. Eth.*, B. VII., chap. v.), "is less disgraceful than incontinence in
appetite." And Spenser, following Aristotle, deals first with the less de-
praved form of incontinence. "People are called incontinent," says Aristotle, making a distinction between the scientific and the metaphorical
use of the word, "even with respect to honour and gain." Spenser, again
following Aristotle, leads his Knight of Temperance into the delve where
Mammon lurks, sunning his treasure, and to Pluto's realm, where Queen
Philotime, the patroness of worldly honour, as Gloriana is of divine
honour, sits enthroned in glistering splendour. From temptations of the
pride of life Sir Guyon passes on to temptations of the lust of the flesh—
Phædria, mere wanton frivolity, a bubble on the Idle Lake, leading on
to the enchantress Acrasia, subduer of so many stout hearts. With a
tragic incident the second book of the *Faery Queen* opens—an incident
which presents in all its breadth the moral theme of the legend. After his
first error through anger—being angry, as Aristotle would say, with the
wrong person (for he is on the point of setting his lance in rest against
his fellow-servant St. George)—Guyon, accompanied by the Palmer,
hears the piercing cries of a woman in distress, and discovers the hapless
Amavia lying upon the dead body of her husband, and bleeding to death
from the stroke of her own hand. It is all the work of Acrasia. Mordant,
the dead knight, had been the victim of her sensual snares; through his
wife's devotion he had been delivered from them, and restored to his
better self; but the witch had pronounced a spell:

> Sad Verse, give death to him that death does give,
> And losse of love to her that loves to live
> So soone as Bacchus with the Nymphe does linck.

Coming to a well, Mordant stooped and drank; the charm found its
fulfilment, and of a sudden he sank down to die. "Probably," says the

ingenious Boyd, "by the mortal sentence being executed 'when Bacchus with the Nymph does link,' may be meant one very common effect of intemperance, viz., dropsical complaints." O foolish commentator and slow of heart, has not Spenser himself explained that this is no mere stream of water, but a metamorphosed virgin, who, flying from the lust of Faunus, was changed by Diana into a fountain? Mordant, although he has escaped from the garden of Acrasia, still bears the sinful taint in his veins, and he is slain by the sudden shock of purity. So awful is innocence; so sure to work out their mischief, soon or late, are Acrasia's spells. Mordant, the strong man, lies a ruin of manhood because he could not resist pleasure; his gentle wife perishes because she cannot with womanly fortitude endure pain. Both are the victims of intemperance; both die because they lack that self-control which forms the subject of the entire legend:

The strong through pleasure soonest falles, the weake through smart.

Guyon, with such piteous examples in view, must learn to resist alike the temptations of pleasure and of pain.

From a man's relation to God (Book I) and a man's relation to himself (Book II), the poem passes to his relations to his fellows. Chief among these is that between the sexes, the law of which is chastity. The representative of that virtue, the Knight of Chastity, is rightly a woman, and the name Britomart is chosen partly because this was a Cretan name for Diana. But by chastity Spenser means no cloistered virtue, and this Diana is the lover of Artegall. There is no chastity, Spenser would assure us, so incapable of stain as the heroic love of a magnanimous woman. Next follows the love of man for man—friendship. "Friendship," says Aristotle, "is the bond that holds states together, and lawgivers are even more eager to secure it than justice." Spenser accordingly gives friendship the precedence of the sterner virtue. We love one another, says Aristotle, either because we are useful to one another; or because we provide pleasure each for the other; or, finally, because "we wish well to one another as good men." "The perfect kind of friendship is that of good men who resemble one another in virtue" (*Nic. Eth.*, Book VIII, chap. iii, § 6). Spenser makes Aristotle's distinctions his own. Sir Blandamour and Paridell lay aside their wrath, and are accorded as friends for sake of mutual aid against the rival claimants of the false Florimell; it is an example of Aristotle's "accidental" friendship, founded on motives of utility; under it, says Spenser, lay hidden hate and hollow guile; nor can such friendship last long—

> For virtue is the band that bindeth hearts most sure.

The second kind of friendship described by Aristotle—that founded on motives of pleasure—is of a higher nature; yet even this is not the ideal friendship. Scudamour finds in the gardens of the Temple of Venus "thousand payres of lovers" (that is, of friends), who walk

> Praysing their God, and yeelding him great thankes,
> Ne ever ought but of their true loves talkt,
> Ne ever for rebuke or blame of any balkt.

> All these together by themselves did sport
> Their spotless pleasures and sweet loves content.
> But, farre away from these, another sort
> Of lovers linckèd in true harts consent;
> Which lovèd not as these for like intent,
> But on chaste vertue grounded their desire,
> Far from all fraud or faynèd blandishment,
> Which, in their spirits kindling zealous fire,
> Brave thoughts and noble deeds did evermore aspire.

It was the fashion of Spenser's time to do high honour to friendship. But doubtless one reason why he assigns it so important a place in his poem was that he had himself known the worth of friendship and tasted its delight. In one of the few letters of his which are extant, he writes, when about, as he supposed, to leave England for the Continent: "With you I end my last Farewell, not thinking any more to write unto you before I go; and withal committing to your faithful credence the eternal memorie of our everlasting friendship, the inviolable memorie of our unspotted friendship, the sacred memorie of our vowed friendship." Having assigned its place to love, Spenser proceeds to determine the sphere and exhibit the action of justice. The sternness of Spenser in this fifth Book is remarkable. It may be a difficulty with some readers to bring into harmony with their conception of Spenser his emphatic approval of the terrible policy of Lord Grey, the hero of this book, towards the Irish people. Spenser was no dreamer; his *View of the State of Ireland* is full of precise information and practical suggestion. But towards the Irish people Spenser felt as an old Anglo-Indian might feel towards

Sepoys in time of mutiny. Last of the existing Books of the *Faery Queen* is the legend of the courteous knight, Sir Calidore. And Spenser's chief thought on this subject is that true courtesy is not an accomplishment or an acquirement, but grows out of character, and is indeed the delicate flowering of a beautiful nature.

All these virtues are summed up in the one central virtue of High-mindedness (μεγαλοψνχία), or, as Spenser names it, Magnificence. "Indeed, greatness in every virtue or excellence," says Aristotle, "would seem to be necessarily implied in being a high-souled or great-souled man." But there is one thing, Aristotle goes on, about which the high-souled man is especially concerned: "For desert has reference to external good things. Now, the greatest of external good things we may assume to be that which we render to the gods as their due, and that which people in high stations most desire, and which is the prize appointed for the noblest deeds. But the thing which answers to this description is honour, which, we may safely say, is the greatest of all external goods. Honours and dishonours, therefore, are the field in which the high-minded man behaves as he ought." And again: "High-mindedness, as we have said, has to do with honour on a large scale." Or, as Spenser puts it, Prince Arthur, his ideal of "Magnificence," is the lover of Gloriana.

Spenser's conception of life was Puritan in its seriousness; yet we think with wonder of the wide space that lies between the *Faery Queen* and our other great allegory, the *Pilgrim's Progress*. To escape from the City of Destruction and to reach the Celestial City is Christian's one concern; all his recompense for the countless trials of the way lies upon the other side of the river of death. His consuming thought is this: "What must I do to be saved?" Spenser is spiritual, but he is also mundane; he thinks of the uses of noble human creatures to this world in which we move. His general end in the poem is "to fashion a gentleman or noble person in vertuous and gentle discipline." "A grand self-culture," I have elsewhere said, "is that about which Spenser is concerned; not, as with Bunyan, the escape of the soul to heaven; not the attainment of supernatural grace through a point of mystical contact, like the vision which was granted to the virgin knight, Galahad, in the mediæval allegory. Self-culture, the formation of a complete character for the uses of earth, and afterwards, if need be, for the uses of heaven—this was subject sufficient for the twenty-four books designed to form the epic of the age of Elizabeth. And the means of that self-culture are of an active kind—namely, warfare—warfare, not for its own sake, but for the generous accomplishment of unselfish ends." Bunyan, with whom the visionary power was often involuntary, who would live for a day and a night in some metaphor that had attacked his imagination, transcribed into allegory his own wonderful experience of terrors and of comfort. Spenser is more impersonal: he can refashion Aristotle in a dream. But behind him lies all the sentiment of Christian chivalry, and around him all the life of Elizabethan England; and from these diverse elements arises a rich and manifold creation, which, if it lacks the personal, spiritual passion of Bunyan's allegory, compensates by its moral breadth, its noble sanity, its conciliation of what is earthly and what is divine. "A better teacher than Scotus or Aquinas." We have seen to some small extent what Spenser sought to impress upon the mind of his own age. He strove, in his own way as poet, to make the national life of England a great unity—spiritual, yet not disdaining earth or the things of earth. He strove, as far as in him lay, to breed a race of high-souled English gentlemen, who should have none of the meanness of the libertine, none of the meanness of the precisian. But the contending parties of the English nation went their ways—one party to moral licentiousness and political servility, the other to religious intolerance and the coarse extravagances of the sectaries. Each extreme ran its course. And when the Puritan excess and the Cavalier excess had alike exhausted themselves, and England once more recovered a portion of her wisdom and her calm, it had become impossible to revert to the ideals of Spenser. Enthusiasm had been discredited by the sectaries until it had grown to be a byword of reproach. The orgies of the Restoration had served to elevate common decency into something like high virtue. After the Puritan excess and the Cavalier excess, England recovered herself not by moral ardour or imaginative reason, but by good sense, by a prosaic but practical respect for the respectable, and by a utilitarian conviction that honesty is the best policy.

"A better teacher than Scotus or Aquinas." Yet we are told by the Dean of St. Paul's, that in giving himself credit for a direct purpose to instruct, Spenser "only conformed to the curiously utilitarian spirit which pervaded the literature of the time." It is the heresy of modern art that only useless things should be made beautiful. We want beauty only in playthings. In elder days the armour of a knight was as beautiful as sunlight, or as flowers. "In unaffected, unconscious, artistic excellence of invention," says one of our chief living painters,[2] "approaching more nearly to the strange beauty of nature, especially in vegetation, mediæval armour perhaps surpasses any other effort of human ingenuity." What if Spenser wrought armour for the soul, and, because it was precious and of finest temper, made it fair to look upon? That which gleams as bright as the waters of a sunlit lake is perhaps a breastplate to protect the heart; that which appears pliant as the blades of summer grass may prove at our need to be a sword of steel.

NOTES

1. With which contrast Coleridge's words, "No one can appreciate Spenser without some reflection on the nature of allegorical writing"; and Mr. Ruskin's painstaking attempt in *Stones of Venice* to interpret the allegory of Book I.

2. Mr. G. F. Watts.

NINE

EDWIN A. GREENLAW

*Spenser and British Imperialism (1912)**

In the preceding articles in this series[1] it has been my endeavor to show that Spenser, like the other men of the brilliant circle with which he was connected, sought to win glory through political service. At first, he seems to have hoped to take an active part, for he wrote to Harvey in October, 1579, that he was about to be sent abroad in Leicester's service, that he had no time to think on such toys as verses, and that he looked forward to corresponding with Sidney. This hope, however, was soon dispelled, probably because of his speaking too plainly, in *Mother Hubberds Tale,* about the plot to make Alençon the king consort. At about the same time, the *Shepheards Calender* was published, and in it was a carefully constructed and cumulative argument warning Leicester and the Queen that the activities of the papal propaganda in England and Ireland, together with factional troubles in the government, would lead to Catholic supremacy and perhaps the overthrow of Elizabeth. As a result of these publications by a man not yet powerful enough to venture on such boldness, he was shipped to Ireland as secretary to Lord Grey.

Moreover, Spenser was from the first a student of theories of government. Harvey writes: "What though Il Magnifico Segnior Immerito Benivolo hath noted this amongst his politique discourses and matters of

---

*This essay was first published in *Modern Philology,* IX (January, 1912), 347-370, and reappeared with minor revisions under the title "Spenser and the 'Party in Progress' " in the late Professor Greenlaw's *Studies in Spenser's Historical Allegory* (The Johns Hopkins Press, 1932), pp. 133-166. Pages 347-360 and 364-370 have been reprinted from *Modern Philology.*

state and governmente that the most courageous and valorous minds have evermore bene where was most furniture of eloquence and greatest stoare of notable orators and famous poets," etc.,[2] a statement which not only recalls Sidney's theories as to the value of poetry to the state and Spenser's own lost work on the *English Poet,* but also suggests the fact that in the circle in which Spenser moved literature was an avocation, not a trade. Again, in the *Faerie Queene* is found abundant evidence that he carefully studied the chronicles of past history and that he made use of current politics for purposes of his allegory. In the *Veue of the Present State of Ireland* he showed thorough acquaintance with Machiavelli and proved that he understood the real meaning of *Il principe* far better than most of his contemporaries.

There is at first sight nothing remarkable in Spenser's allegorical treatment of national dangers in *Mother Hubberds Tale* and in the *Calender.* Such early dramas as *Gorboduc* and *Kynge Johann* contain similar warnings; Lyly's *Sapho and Phao* is another allegory of the Alencon matter, as is also his *Endimion,*[3] though from a viewpoint hostile to Leicester, as might be expected from a poet whose patrons were Burghley and Oxford. Gascoigne in 1575 wrote a masque for the use of Leicester in entertaining the Queen at Kenilworth, which was designed to further the ambition of the earl to gain her hand.[4] But most examples of this kind of work are isolated, mere attempts to gain the favor of some powerful personage or works written at the behest of some patron. Spenser differed from all other literary men of his time in that he persistently clung to that conception of a poet's function that made him a *vates,* a "seer," a man who should warn and advise, directly or through cloudy allegories, those who ruled England. Every important production of his pen, with the exception of his *Amoretti* and the *Hymnes,* is an illustration of this statement. Moreover, a study of these works in chronological order proves that he was not merely a dreamer, an idle singer in an empty day, a poet's poet, but a farsighted student of government who saw clearly the great destiny of his nation. How this element in his work persists and enlarges it is my purpose in the present paper to point out.

I

What the feelings of Spenser were when he learned that he was to go to Ireland instead of to the Continent it is impossible to say. He may

not have relished the change in plan, though his objection could not
have been due to his desire to remain in London. It must be remembered
that he belonged to the circle which included Sidney, Raleigh, and Fulke
Greville, and that these men were not town gallants but adventurous
spirits who despised the vices and effeminacy of the courtier class. There
are in Spenser's works, in the *Mother Hubberds Tale*, in *Colin Clout*, in
the *Faerie Queene*, too many passages that pour contempt on those who
loafed about the court, making a living by their wits, aping the gallantries and affectations of the French and Italians, to make it conceivable
that he wished to be of their number. No small part of the task that confronted Elizabeth was the government of restless and eager men like
Drake, Gilbert, Raleigh, Sidney, who felt the intoxication of England's
dawning greatness and like Tamburlaine sought to add new realms to
its domain. In 1576 Gilbert wrote the tract which first suggested the
duty of England to seize and colonize the lands across the seas; two
years later he received a charter authorizing him to fit out an expedition
to carry his project into execution: in 1583 he sailed with five ships to
plant a colony in Newfoundland. Raleigh was forbidden to accompany
him on this expedition, but in 1584 Virginia was named by him and in
the next few years he was ceaselessly employed in furthering the project
of colonization. Sidney was sent to the Low Countries to prevent him
from carrying out his project to curb the power of Spain through naval
attacks and colonization; the testimony of Fulke Greville shows how
persistently he warned Elizabeth of the danger from Philip and how
earnest he was in urging his plan of defense and counter attack. Greville
records his own dissatisfaction at being kept at court by the Queen and
tells how he ran away repeatedly, only to be denied the gracious presence for months at a time when he crept back. When, therefore, Spenser, alert, young, eager, realized that his stay in Ireland meant that he
was to be cut off from participation in these stirring projects, the revul-
sion of feeling, at first intense and terrible, found expression in his
splendid protest to Leicester in *Virgils Gnat:*

> Wrong'd yet not daring to express my paine,
>   To you (great Lord) the causer of my care,
> In clowdie teares my case I thus complaine
>   Unto yourselfe, that onely privie are.

But this mood, I am convinced, was temporary. Those biographers who represent Spenser as the poet of ideal beauty whose own life was disfigured by moroseness, who see in all his later work only the vain attempts of an imprisoned bird to regain its liberty, who regard him as a servile functionary ready to give literary sanction to barbarous and inhuman practices, snarling at the estate of poets, satirizing the vices and manifold corruption of court while doing everything in his power to gain a recall, are surely unjust. The warrant for such views apparently given by the *Teares of the Muses* is inapplicable, for this poem is incontestably early work and represents such conventional complaints as can be duplicated scores of times in the literature of the sixteenth century. The references, scattered through the *Faerie Queene,* to the wild and savage country in which he was compelled to do his work are more serious, but they too reflect mainly the conventional protestations of the poets for the meanness of their verses. The later books of the epic, particularly the fourth and the sixth, indicate peace and content, not moroseness or wild despair. The tract on Ireland cannot be defended as a work of pure literature, yet it has its merits notwithstanding, while the positive evidence of *Colin Clout* proves contentment with his lot rather than bitter disappointment, and the fifth book of the *Faerie Queene* shows the poet's art at its zenith. Spenser was not to be sent as ambassador on affairs of state, he was not to be associated with his friends in the great projects that made the air electric, but he was to be the laureate of the new England, defending that national policy which, however cruel and narrow in some of its applications, was to enable her to thwart the foes that threatened her destruction.

Like all sustained poems, the *Faerie Queene* suffers from its length. One reads the first book, notes the form of its stanza, the beauty of its descriptions, the liquid melody of its verse, perhaps the intricacy of its allegory. But the poem lacks the variety of the *Canterbury Tales* and the effect of unity given the separate stories in the *Idylls of the King.* Even *Paradise Lost* possesses the advantage of presenting its most interesting and thrilling narrative in the first two books, while Spenser's poem seems academic, and the triple allegory, even though one try to follow Lowell's advice, persistently intrudes. This is partly due to the fact that at least the first book represents early work, when the complicated allegory was the poet's chief object; it therefore suffers not only from the fact that allegory does not appeal to our naturalistic age but also because it has not the simplicity and directness of Bunyan or of Tennyson. It is in the last three books that we find a revelation of the mature thought of the poet that holds the attention. The fourth book is a complete exposition of his theory of love, supplementing admirably the *Foure Hymnes;* in the fifth is presented his theory of the state, and in this his mastery of allegory is complete; while the sixth develops from all points of view a theme that runs through all his works, the praise of the simplicity and sincerity of life away from the heated atmosphere of the court, and indicates at least an intellectual reconciliation with his environment.

In the fifth book we have no longer the personified virtues and vices of mediæval allegory, everything being subordinated to the treatment of problems of government. The book as a whole bears on the three crucial events in the reign of Elizabeth prior to the collision with Spain in 1588: the suppression of the rebellion in Ireland, fomented as it was by the policy of Philip; the trial and execution of Mary, also a necessary step in repelling Spanish aggression; and the direct attack on Spain through intervention in the Netherlands. The theme of the book is the necessity for the exercise of imperial power to the utmost in putting down rebellion active and incipient, the right of a strong nation to aid an oppressed and suffering people, and, in some minor passages, the right of England to establish an empire beyond the seas. The method of the book is to tell, by means of incidents suitable to a metrical romance, the story of Grey's experience in Ireland; to present from two points of view a defense of Elizabeth's execution of her rival; and to relate the experience of Leicester in the Low Countries. But deeper than this allegorical treatment of contemporary events lies the exposition of a theory of government that makes the book one of the most remarkable productions of its time.

The greatest space is given to the Irish problem. Irena (Ireland) must be delivered from Grantorto (Spain) by that queen whose glory it was to aid all suppliants and to be the patron of all weak princes (i, 4). Artegall, who represents Justice united with sovereign Power, on this occasion personified by Lord Grey, is deputed for the task. Then follows a series of incidents by which Spenser gives a vivid picture of the wretchedness of the country. The Squire mourning over the headless trunk of his love is a symbol of the woe wrought by murder and lawlessness (i, 13-30). The story of the Saracen and his daughter Munera (ii, 1-28) illustrates the evils of bribery and corruption in government. How directly this applied is revealed not only in Spenser's prose tract but in many of the letters and documents of the period. In the larger conception of the problem of government, it represents something more serious than lawlessness. Braggadocchio, who claims the victory really won by Artegall (iii, 14, 15; 20-22) represents those who by defamation of others and by self-seeking aim at securing credit not rightfully theirs. Here the historical reference seems to be to the quarrels among the English leaders in 1580; they plotted against each other, sought to thwart all plans for progress, and sent to England letters filled with petty jealousy and malice.[5] The larger significance of the story, including the account of the way in which all the people and even the knights themselves were unable to distinguish between the true Florimel and the false, is to show the danger to the government from men who are selfish and unscrupulous, a danger increased from the fact that the crowd does not accurately judge between merit and pretense. To enforce this distrust of the crowd (*vulgus*), Spenser introduces by way of parenthesis or interlude the story of the giant with scales (ii, 30 ff.), showing that socialistic theories of property and democracy are vain.[6]

Spenser now discusses the paramount right of the sovereign over all subjects (cantos iv ff.). The historical material is drawn from the events in the north from the uprising of the earls to the execution of Mary. The incident of the two brothers who quarrel over the treasure chest cast on the shore by the waves is somewhat obscure (iv, 4-20). At first sight, it is but another of the minor incidents scattered through the book to illustrate the simplicity of justice; other examples being the interesting modification of the judgment of Solomon, where Artegall discerns which of two knights truly loves a woman by proposing to cut her in half and give each a portion (i, 25, 26); the decision as to the true and the false Florimel (iii, 22-24); and the awarding of the horse to Guyon (iii, 35). But the incident is apparently founded on fact, since it refers, I believe, to the story of Northumberland's claim of treasure cast ashore in his jurisdiction in 1560, and possibly also to his claiming of the custody of Mary on the ground that she had landed in his territory.[7] In 1566 Parliament refused to sanction the Queen's claim to minerals wherever they might be found, thus recognizing Northumberland's objections to the attempt of the Queen to mine copper at Keswick.[8] Spenser probably means to assert the right of the Queen to lands, leavings of the sea, which had been discovered by her mariners, and the passage should be compared with his defense of Raleigh's projected expedition to Guiana (IV, xi, 22) and with the references, in *Colin Clout,* to Elizabeth as the Queen and to Raleigh as the Shepherd of the Ocean.

In the episode of Radigund, the great rebellion of the earls is again made use of, this time through the fact that Grey was concerned in it in some degree. Apparently Spenser attributes Grey's sympathy for Mary to the influence on him of her personal beauty (v, 12; vi. 1; viii, 1). By far the most interesting aspect of the case, however, is the application to Ireland. It will be remembered that Artegall, disarmed by the beauty of Radigund, is made to assume the dress of a woman and to perform the menial tasks of a woman (v, 23-25; vii, 37-41). With this should be compared the sad state of Turpine, found by Artegall in the power of women, his hands tied behind his back (iv. 22). Here we have an arraignment of womanish methods applied to the solution of the Irish problem; Artegall clad in woman's garments and with a distaff in his hand is a fit representative, says Spenser, of the course advised by some.

The story of Samient (viii) introduces more specifically the attempts of Philip to undermine the power of Elizabeth. She represents Ireland, and serves Mercilla, who represents Elizabeth's gentleness and mercy as Britomart represents her might.[9] Mercilla is in danger from the machinations of a mighty man

> That with most fell despight and deadly hate
> Seekes to subvert her crowne and dignity,
> And all his power doth thereunto apply.
>
> .　.　.　.　.　.　.　.　.　.　.
>
> Ne him sufficeth all the wrong and ill
> Which he unto her people does each day;
> But that he seekes by traytous traines to spill
> Her person, and her sacred selfe to slay;
> That, O ye Heavens, defend! and turne away
> From her unto the miscreant himselfe;
> That neither hath religion nor fay,
> But makes his God of his ungodly pelfe,
> And Idols serves: so let his Idols serve the Elfe!
>
> [Stanzas 19, 20]

Here is a pretty accurate picture of Philip: his secret plotting against England; his trust in his riches, an allusion to the vast stores of gold secured from the American voyages; his idolatry. The Saracens sent to destroy Samient represent the Spanish expeditions designed to wrest Ireland from England, one of which Grey destroyed at Smerwick. The triumph of Arthur over the Soldan prophesies the end of Philip.

The allegory is continued in the next canto in the account of the capture of Guile, described like one of the wretched outcasts that continually warred on the English in Ireland (ix, 8-11); his den, his flight, his many changes of form (ix, 12-19) give a vivid picture of the difficulties encountered by those who tried to stamp out the rebellion of the natives. It is noticeable that neither here nor in the story of Irena, nor, indeed, in any of the tracts dealing with the subject do we find Ireland identified with these outcast natives. To Spenser and his contemporaries Ireland is the fair realm to be made fit for habitation as a part of the English domain; the "wild Irish" do not enter into the calculation except as they may benefit by the peace that is to follow the subjugation of the rebellious chiefs and the casting-out of Spain. But in England itself would the lower classes have received a whit the more consideration in Spenser's time? And what of Fielding's and Goldsmith's accounts of the miseries of the poor and the injustice which they found in the courts and prisons of the eighteenth century? And Dickens? Why pour vials of wrath on Spenser's head for not being two or three centuries in advance of his time in respect to the doctrine of the equality of men?

The object of this lengthy analysis of the political allegory in the fifth book has been to show how admirable is Spenser's method and how complete his interpretation of contemporary history. The remaining cantos, dealing for the most part with the execution of Mary and the intervention in the Netherlands, require no special treatment; their excellence is apparent to any reader. There is, for example, the brilliant apology for the execution of Mary. In the seventh canto, Britomart, representing Elizabeth as the sovereign power of the nation, slays Radigund (Mary the seducer) without compunction; in the ninth, Mercilla, queenly but gentle and merciful, reluctantly passes judgment upon Duessa. Again, Prince Arthur, personifying the nation as distinct from the sovereign power, is at first inclined in Mary's favor, but is convinced by the evidence against her that no other course is possible. Artegall is no longer Lord Grey, but the Justice and Power that accompany sovereignty, unswayed by prejudice, and really sentences Duessa to death, because Mercilla

> Though plaine she saw, by all that she did heare,
> That she of death was guiltie found by right,
> Yet would not let just vengeance on her light:
> But rather let, instead thereof, to fall
> Few perling drops from her faire lampes of light;
> The which she covering with her purple pall
> Would have the passion hid, and up arose withall.

The Legend of Justice is a charming romance, and its moral allegory, less academic and symmetrical than that of the first book, answers to the fondness of the Renaissance for the epic of the perfect man. But it is much more. The most important events in the history of Elizabeth's development of a powerful government are treated, not baldly and incoherently as in the chronicles, but in an allegory that unifies and interprets. It is not of our modern type of philosophical history any more than it is modern chronicle, but it illustrates in a high degree that Renaissance tendency to interpret life by means of symbols so apparent in their sonnet, pastoral, novel, and epic. Finally, it possesses a higher interest even than these. The Renaissance created the State; it also produced many treatises on the theory of the State. In England this new interest was manifested not only in such books as *Utopia* or the *Boke of the Governour,* or in the translations of Machiavelli and collections of similar political axioms, but also in romances like *Arcadia* and the fifth book of the *Faerie Queene.* Fulke Greville says of Sidney's purpose in writing his novel: "In all these creatures of his making his intent and scope was to turn the barren Philosophy precepts into pregnant Images of life . . . lively to represent the growth, state, and declination of Princes." This comes very near anticipating Bolingbroke's famous saying, "History is Philosophy teaching by example," and both these aphorisms apply with surprising accuracy to this Legend of Justice. The whole book treats of the danger to England from Spanish aggression; of the need of centralization of power in the sovereign coupled with the inflexible manifestation of that power in dealing with plot and rebellion; and of the right of the Queen to rule the seas and to interfere in behalf of the oppressed people of the Netherlands. Each minor adventure leads toward the climax in the triumph of authority, showing how lawlessness, bribery, selfish quarreling and jealousy among the leaders, the danger from womanish theories of mildness, all contribute to thwart the purposes of the ministers of the sovereign. The story of Ireland's thraldom is twice told, in the accounts of Samient and of Irena; the might of the Queen and the awakened spirit of England combine to free her. Again, the story of Mary's fall is twice told, with consummate skill in its representation of Elizabeth as the personification of English sovereignty and in that other trial scene wherein Elizabeth the woman weeps that she must doom a sister to death. The story of the relief of the Netherlands is also presented in two aspects: as another illustration of the all-embracing tyranny of the Spanish monarch, and as a proof of the dawning sense in the English nation of the duty to aid a weaker people in distress. At the end of the book, in the story of the hags Detraction and Envy and in the hint of the ravages of the blatant beast of Scandal,[10] the theme descends from lofty philosophy to become intimate and tender in the story of how the faithful servant of the Queen returned unhonored, unthanked, and broken-hearted. Here in truth is a turning of the barren precepts of philosophy into pregnant images of life, a life not merely of men and measures, but also breathing the spirit of the new imperial England.

II

The *Veue of the Present State of Ireland* is the prose counterpart of the discussion of the Irish problem in the *Faerie Queene*.[11] I have shown elsewhere that in the main Spenser follows the theories of Machiavelli as to the subjugation of colonies foreign in language, customs, and religion.[12] The first part of the tract, which arraigns the life and customs of the Irish, is not materially different from other contemporary accounts; it seems to have been based as much on these chronicles as upon personal observation, or else all observers of the time are singularly agreed in their opinions and in their choice of topics. The curious poem by John Derricke, "The Image of Ireland," published in 1581, may have had some influence on Spenser's tract.[13] It is a fanciful description of the Irish girls as sirens and the kerns as satyrs; St. Patrick is blamed for killing the snakes instead of the kerns. There is detailed description of dress and manners, and one point in common with Spenser is the attack on the bards as aiming to incite rebellion by their songs praising the wild deeds of their forefathers. The course of action which Derricke thinks England should take is also as rigorous as that laid down in the *Veue:* "Rigour is meeteth where clemencie availeth not." The poem, which is in exceedingly crabbed verse, is dedicated to Sidney, and Harvey appar-

ently refers to it in a letter to Spenser in which he speaks of "an uncer-
tayne autor in certayn cantons agaynst the wylde Irishe" who used the
same peculiar verse as in *Gorboduc* and the *Steel Glas*.[14] Much of the
historical matter in the *Veue* comes from the earlier chronicles: Giraldus
Cambrensis, reprinted by Holinshed with continuations by Hooker,
Campion, and Stanihurst. Campion dwells on the manners and super-
stitions, on the Brehon laws, on the custom of redeeming crimes by
composition, on the glib, etc., as well as the usual matter about the origin
of the people.[15] This history, originally dating from 1571, was continued
in Holinshed by Stanihurst, who wrote an extremely euphuistic dedication to Sir Henry Sidney. There is a dialogue on the subject of snakes
which is thus described: "First therefore thou must understand, that his
booke is made in dialogue wise, a kind of writing as it is used, so commended of the learned. In these dialogs Irenaeus an Englishman and
Critobulus a Germane plaie the parts." [16] Stanihurst pays much attention to language, saying that "to this daie, the dregs of the old ancient
Chaucer English are kept," which he proceeds to illustrate by some not
very apposite examples. Spenser ridicules Stanihurst's philology, but he
himself makes comparisons between Irish words and some found in
Chaucer.[17] Hooker's account approaches Spenser's in that he proposes a
method of dealing with the Irish under the heads "How or by what
manner the land of Ireland is to be throughly conquered" and "How
the Irish people being vanquished are to be governed." He insists on
there being a sufficient force to punish severely all who rebel and advises
the English in time of peace to prepare for war; the people are treacherous and to be watched, they are "craftie and subtile"; they should be
deprived of arms.[18]

On the whole, a comparison of Spenser's tract with the contemporary accounts and the chronicles proves him to have been a careful
student of the subject, not merely a writer who gives impressions of his
personal observations. In none of these parallel documents is there anything approaching the thoroughness with which he worked out his plan,
subordinating the archaeological matter and the "ripping up of auncient
histories" to a clear analysis of the crisis presented by the ascendency of
the O'Neils and the presentation of a theory of procedure based on an
accurate understanding of *Il principe*. This plan has been harshly criticized for its cruelty, but a brief statement of the situation in 1595 will
show the seriousness of the crisis. Since the recall of Grey in 1582,

Burghley had temporized, chiefly in order to save expense. Tyrone, while professing great loyalty, was secretly preparing for revolt. In the early nineties Fitzwilliam, the lord deputy, became alarmed at the developments; he was charged with corruption, but appears to have been a brave man, though no military strategist. He was succeeded in 1594 by Sir William Russell and almost at once the great revolt was on. Tyrone leagued with Spain; Jesuits and seminary priests swarmed into the country. The resident English army was made up of men said to be of the type impressed by Falstaff. Russell's hands were tied by the presence of a special commission. A fiery letter from the Queen complains that the more inclined to mercy she showed herself the more insolent the rebels became; the commission addressed Tyrone as "loving friend" and "our very good lord"; the Queen seemed inclined to trust his professions, though Russell said the only course was to capture him and put him to death.[19] Without going any more fully into the subject it is easy to see that in the conflict of authority and in the difficulties imposed by distance, to say nothing of the rabble soldiery intent only on plunder, things had got to such a pass that it is small wonder that Spenser, a student of affairs for many years, a man thoroughly conversant with the situation and alive to the fatal weakness of the English course for fifteen years of his residence in Ireland, should advise "strong medicine." Frequent changes of administration, each of them rightly interpreted by the Irish chiefs as signs of the incompetence of the government to deal with the situation; equally frequent changes of plan, blowing now hot, now cold, had brought matters to a desperate state. In the mean time the miseries of the poor were increased, the country was not developed though a source of enormous expense to the crown, life for the English "undertakers" was not safe, Spain was more anxious than ever before to profit by English incompetence: surely these considerations ought to prove the wisdom of Spenser's advice. . . .

The truth of the matter is that the vituperation and abuse that have been poured forth upon the *Veue* are based on two misconceptions: it is regarded as an example of religious intolerance, being due to Spenser's hatred of the Irish because they were Catholics, and it is read without proper regard to its historical setting. How far the first is from being just may be seen by anyone who will take the trouble to read what the author has to say about religion. His quarrel, he distinctly says, is not that they are Papists, but that they are such bad Papists, being "soe blindly and brutishly enformed (for the most part) as that you woulde rather thinke them Atheistes or Infidells." "I doe not blame the christening of them, for to be sealed with the marke of the Lambe, by what hand soever it be done rightlye, I hold it a good and gracious work." [20] He blames those priests who dwell beyond seas with the Queen's professed enemies and "converse and are confederate with other traytors and fugitives which are there abiding." [21] He protests against the plotting of the emissaries from Douay and elsewhere, which he says is more openly carried on in Ireland than in England, where stern measures of repression have been taken.[22] As to the second point, I have tried to show by reference to other tracts and documents the reality of the danger to the crown that Spenser repeatedly refers to. He praises Ireland as being goodly and commodious, but fears lest God has reserved it for some secret scourge which shall by her come into England.[23] His defense of Grey is based on the altogether incontestable ground that the prisoners at Smerwick were not "lawefull eneymes," being sent by enemies of England "into another Princes dominions to war." [24] The common people are not to blame for their course, for they are the tools of the rebel chiefs; Tyrone owes his power to the encouragement received from "the greatest King of Christendome," as well as from the "great fayntness in her Majesties withstanding him." [25] The advice he gives is to send tried soldiers, well paid and well commanded, to capture the rebel chiefs; then to send colonies of Englishmen to settle the country, after scattering the Irish so that they may no longer be subject to the ambitious chiefs or the comfort of Spain; this done, to give the laws and settled policy that will bring peace and prosperity to English and Irish alike. He has no hatred for the country; it is no wild and forbidding place, but rather "a most beautifull and sweet countrey as any is under heaven, seamed throughout with many goodly rivers, replenished with all sortes of fish, most aboundantly sprinckled with many sweet Ilands and goodly lakes, like little Inland Seas, that will carry even ships upon theyr waters, adorned with goodly woodes fitt for building of houses and shippes, soe commodiously, as that yf some princes in the world had them, they would soone hope to be lordes of all the seas, and ere long of all the world." [26] Here speaks the imperialist, longing to see so fair a land reclaimed to ancient glory,

> When Ireland florished in fame
> Of wealth and goodnesse, far above the rest
> Of all that bear the British Islands name.[27]

III

From her accession to the year 1588 Elizabeth's policy had of necessity been defensive. With the execution of Mary, however, and the humbling of Philip's pride, the party represented by Walsingham, Raleigh, and Drake became insistent that a bolder national course should be followed. With the great increase of interest in travel and the knowledge that rich territories might easily be brought within British dominion, to say nothing of the success Philip had attained in making his colonies pay the expenses of his wars, they found public opinion gradually coming to their views. But Elizabeth and Burghley still hesitated. The "forward school" urged that the victory over the Armada be followed up by increasing the navy and planting colonies in opposition to those of Spain. Had this course been followed, England would not have been so handicapped in her later attempts at colonization, and the terrible expense of the Irish campaigns of the nineties, due once more to Philip's plotting, would have been saved. The most that the Queen would allow, however, was piracy under government protection; one finds nearly all the projects presented to the Queen during this period stressing the possibilities of securing rich booty. Men like Walsingham and Raleigh saw the larger possibilities in founding a new empire beyond seas, but Burghley was not a statesman of that type. After the death of Burghley, his son Robert inherited his power and his policies; madly jealous of Raleigh and Essex, he blocked all plans for progress.[28]

Throughout the most critical years of this period, from 1579, when the Alençon marriage was imminent and the active campaign of Rome and Spain in England, Scotland, and Ireland was beginning, to 1595, when Elizabeth, confronted by the results of Spain's plotting in Ireland and by the fact that her great rival was stronger than ever on the sea and in the possession of colonies that were rich sources of supplies, became convinced of the need of a more vigorous policy, the course of Spenser was absolutely consistent. In the earlier period he stood with Leicester and Sidney; later he gave the support of his literary genius to Walsingham and defended the memory of Grey; in the nineties he agreed with the colonial policy of Raleigh and Essex. I am well aware of the danger in thus comparing the visions of the bard of fairy-land with the deeds of men who, like him, saw visions of England's destiny but who risked their lives and fortunes to make these dreams realities.

In the flush of youth, when he was received into the brilliant circle at Leicester House, I am convinced that Spenser meant to be a man of action as well as a writer of verse; no doubt in the later years when far distant from the court he wrote the epic that his friends were living he often felt the ineffectiveness of his life. Like Sordello, prevented from being a man of action, he sought through the imaginative interpretation of heroic deeds to realize, in some sort, his ideal. Drake, it has been finely said, was an ocean knight-errant, smiting and spoiling in knightly fashion and for a great cause; a scourge of the enemies of his country and of his faith.[29] And Spenser, looking in his mirror of Shalott, saw, in reflection it is true, the deeds of these knights-errant and interpreted them. He who reads the records in the calendars of state papers, the letters dealing with the crises and the projects of these eventful years, the journals of returned travelers, can hardly fail of the impression that most of these men had little conception of the vast significance of their work; intrigue and chicane in dealing with foreign powers, penurious-ness and vacillation in dealing with Ireland, greed for gold in every charter granted Gilbert and Raleigh and Drake, marked the policy of Burghley. A few men conceived, perhaps prematurely, an England greater than any continental power, and to these men Spenser gave his genius and his pen.

Fulke Greville's account of Sidney is less a biography than a record of conversations. From these we may get an idea of the topics that were discussed when Spenser was on intimate terms with his first idol. We are repeatedly told of his sense of the danger from Spain and the folly of temporizing;[30] he saw that Philip's power rested largely upon the rich-ness of his mines in America;[31] he advised open attack on Philip himself and indirect attack by fetching away his golden fleece;[32] to him Eliza-beth was the Queen of the Seas, and should keep a strong fleet upon her ocean;[33] as a natural consequence, England should herself establish col-onies abroad:[34] The revelation which these pages give of a man whose range of thought and knowledge and whose grasp of great problems of government were so remarkable helps to make clear how extraordinary must have been the contagion of his character. Every one of these lead-ing ideas was reflected by Spenser. Every one of them was contrary to the settled policy of Burghley.

Next to Sidney, Raleigh had the greatest influence on Spenser's political opinions. When the company of shepherds asked Colin to tell the subjects of the songs exchanged between him and the Shepherd of the Ocean, he told a modest story of the loves of the Bregog and the Mulla, and then told of his friend's joy at being again in the good graces of that Cynthia who was Queen of the Seas:

> For land and sea my Cynthia doth deserve
> To have in her commandement at hand.

There is no need to outline Raleigh's great achievement, in action and in his writings, toward the making of an imperial Britain; Spenser's name for him, the Shepherd of the Ocean, is at once a stroke of genius and a proof of understanding and sympathy that outweighs any tract on colonial expansion that the poet could have written. All these men were students of government. Gilbert early gave himself to "studies perteining to the state of government and to navigations." [35] In the *Arcadia* and in the conversations reported by Greville, Sidney gave proof of his interest in large problems. In the "Maxims of State" in which Raleigh summed up his conception of these same problems we have a work drawn, like Spenser's *Veue*, from *Il principe* and laying down exactly the same principles which Spenser maintained should govern the course of England with respect to Ireland.[36]

Besides the references in *Colin Clout,* Spenser gives other evidences of interest in the English vikings and in the development of colonies. The eloquent passage in the *Veue* has already been cited.[37] The allegory of the two brothers and the dispute about the treasure chest, with the conclusion that lands set apart from other lands by the power of the sea belong to him who seizes them, seems to be a justification for the right of discovery.[38] That Spenser read with interest the accounts of the journeys to lands formerly unknown is proved by the stanza about the "hardy enterprize" through which daily "many great regions are discovered." [39] Moreover, he saw in his own epic the reflection of the journeys of these travelers through uncharted seas:

> Like as a ship, that through the Ocean wyde
> Directs her course unto one certaine cost,
> Is met of many a counter winde and tyde,
> With which her winged speed is let and crost,
> And she herselfe in stormie surges tost;
> Yet, making many a borde and many a bay,
> Still winneth way, ne hath her compasse lost:

> Right so it fares with me in this long way.
> Whose course is often stayd, yet never is astray.[40]

In all this mass of literature, written through the fifteen most eventful and critical years of Elizabeth's reign, is revealed a course unswerving as it is lofty. I have elsewhere alluded to the folly of supposing that *Mother Hubberds Tale* was called in because of Burghley's jealousy of a brilliant young poet who dared resent his failure to secure a good appointment.[41] The present study, I think, throws further light on the reasons for Spenser's hatred of the great chancellor. To Spenser, Burghley represented Machiavellism according to Gentillet; the craft and temporizing and deceit of politicians of this school was abhorrent to his high-souled idealism as it was to Sidney's. This hatred was expressed not only in the *Tale* but throughout the *Faerie Queene* and in *Colin Clout*. In a time when references to political subjects were exceedingly dangerous, when certain passages in Holinshed alluding to Ireland were canceled and when even such a work as Drayton's metrical version of the Psalms was recalled,[42] it required courage of a high order to write as Spenser wrote. Moreover, he did not hesitate to rebuke Burghley in a way impossible of misunderstanding, as the splendid defense of love in the proem to the fourth book of the *Faerie Queene* proves. Artegall's censure of Burbon refers directly, of course, to Henry of Navarre, but it is noticeable that the policy that he censures,

> To temporize is not from truth to swerve,
> Ne for advantage terme to entertaine,

represents also the very element in Burghley's political philosophy that Spenser detested.[43] Even the sonnet addressed to the Lord Treasurer on the publication of the *Faerie Queene* contains no compliment, and is subtly defiant. Spenser's course was consistent and manly; he was not, like Dryden, ready to change his politics and his religion wherever there was hope of personal gain; his attack on Burghley was due to ideals of government and conduct which he held throughout his life, not to wounded self-love.

Taken as a whole, these writings of Spenser's present an interpretation of Elizabethan political idealism without parallel elsewhere. To regard him as a "functionary" of Leicester, of Essex, or of any other man, or to regard him as a morose and disappointed applicant for the favors of the great, is wholly unjust. Those who find in him the master of a sweetly flowing verse that has made him the "Warwick of poets" shall have their reward. But he was more than this. Dreamer of dreams, Galahad of the quest for Beauty, he was also of good right a member of that little group of men who saw beyond the welter of court intrigue and petty politics the glorious vision of an imperial England. He had his limitations, it is true; at first sight he seems to fail to realize the idea of the nation in the larger sense; one does not find in him the passionate love of native land that quivers through the lines attributed by Shakspere to the dying John of Gaunt. His loyalty is personal; he conceives the State as Machiavelli conceived it; to him the Prince is the State. Yet on the whole, the two great poets who were the glory of Elizabethan England are of one accord. The splendid lines of Faulconbridge defying a conqueror to set foot on British soil breathe the spirit that animates all Spenser's work, and the England of Gaunt's adoration was to the poet of allegory his sovereign lady queen.

NOTES

1. "The Influence of Machiavelli on Spenser," *Modern Philology*, October, 1909; "Spenser and the Earl of Leicester," *Publications Mod. Lang. Assn.*, September, 1910; "The Shepheards Calender," *ibid.*, September, 1911.

2. *Letter Book*, p. 66.

3. Tucker Brook, *Mod. Lang. Notes*, XXVI, 13.

4. In the masque it is shown that Diana lost Zabeta (Elizabeth) years before and now finds her still a virgin though a queen; she begs her not to marry, but Iris, coming from Juno, entreats her not to listen to Diana, since it is possible for her in this place where she has passed a pleasant day to enjoy "a world of wealth in wedded state" and there withal to "uphold the staff of her estate." Thus plainly did the earl plan to tell the Queen that by marriage with him she would make her position secure; moreover, a son was promised her. But apparently Elizabeth left somewhat abruptly and the masque was not presented, though Gascoigne tells us everything was ready, every actor in his garment, two or three days before she left. Therefore, Gascoigne was in the service of Leicester in 1575, as Spenser was four years later; it was the habit of the great earl to make use of poets to further his personal ambitions.

5. *Carew Papers*, February, 1581.

6. Spenser is not complimentary to the intelligence of the common people (stanzas 33, 48, 51, 52), who are of the type of the rabble in Ibsen's *Brand*. The giant is a demagogue who has ideas about communism and proposes to set right the world. But to his questions about the mysteries of the universe Artegall makes the reply that God gave Job.

7. Pollard, *Polit. Hist. of Eng.*, 1547-1603, 278 ff.

8. *Ibid.*, 282.

9. Cf. viii. 17:

> And strongly beateth downe
> The malice of her foes, which her envy
> And at her happiness do fret and frowne;
> Yet she herselfe the more doth magnify,
> And even to her foes her mercies multiply.

10. That the blatant beast is Scandal is indicated by a passage in the *Return from Pernassus* (Arber ed., p. 69): "We are fully bent to be Lords of misrule in the world's wide heath: our voyage is to the Ile of Dogges, there where the blatant beast doth rule and reigne, Renting the credit of whom it please."

11. Spenser indorsed it "finyss 1596" and it must have been written very near that time. There is a sarcastic reference to Stanihurst (Globe ed., pp. 632, 633), whose *Plaine and Perfect Description of Ireland* was published 1586. The reference to the founding of the "new college" indicates a date later than 1591, perhaps later than 1593 (Morley, *Ireland under Elizabeth and James,* 128). Probably Spenser wrote about 1595-96, when the fickleness of the governmental policy had driven men who had to live in the country nearly to distraction. There is a MS dialogue in the Irish State Papers, 1598, which purports to be the work of one Thomas Wilson and is dedicated to Essex. The interlocutors are Peregryn and Silvyn, suggesting Spenser's two sons, and the style is similar to that of the *Veue* (Bagwell, *Ireland under the Tudors,* III, 302).

12. *Modern Philology,* October, 1909.

13. Reprinted, Edinburgh, 1883, pp. 56 ff., 65 ff.

14. Smith, *Eliz., Crit. Essays,* I, 126.

15. Pp. 25, 28 ff.

16. Holinshed (ed. 1808), VI, 10 ff.

17. Globe ed., pp. 639*b*, 676*b*.

18. Holinshed, *loc. cit.,* 229-232.

19. Bagwell, *Ireland Under the Tudors,* III, 261-274.

20. *Veue,* Globe ed., 646*a*.

21. *Ibid.,* 621*a*.

22. *Ibid.,* 680*a*.

23. *Ibid.,* 609*a*.

24. *Ibid.,* 656*a*.

25. *Ibid.,* 658*a*.

26. *Veue,* Globe ed., 616*b*.

27. *Faerie Queene,* VII, vi, 36. As is well known, these cantos on mutability perhaps refer to the constant changes in the English policy, which prolonged the struggle. That Spenser here and in the *Veue* was in exact accord with so capable and farsighted a man as Raleigh is seen in the account of Raleigh by Edwards (I, 104): "He was often called into council in relation to these affairs of State and government in Ireland, and was always of one mind about them. His face was set, as flint, against piddling interferences and temporizing expedients in dealing with great evils. To cut the tap root, rather than to spend precious time in pruning the branches, was his maxim." It is also worth noting that in this respect of strong medicine both Raleigh and Spenser differed from Burghley, as they differed from him in other points. See Burghley's letter to the Queen. *Hatfield House,* II, 308-10, in which he advised extreme mildness.

28. For the facts on which this summary is based, see Innes, pp. 375-83; Pollard, pp. 414 ff.

29. Innes, p. 347.

30. Reprint of the first edition by the Caradoc Press, pp. 32, 33, 62, 83, 85 ff.

31. P. 65.

32. Pp. 67, 76.

33. P. 70.

34. Pp. 78, 81-85, 88, 89, etc. It will be remembered that Sidney was sent to Holland to prevent him from accompanying Drake.

35. Hooker, in Holinshed (ed. 1808), VI, 368.

36. Oxford ed. of the *Complete Works,* VIII, 1 ff. Cf. also his *The Cabinet Council, Containing the Chief Arts of Empire and Mysteries of State,* published by Milton.

37. At p. 19.

38. *Faerie Queene,* V, iv, 19.

39. *Ibid.,* II, proem, stanza 2.

40. *Faerie Queene,* VI, xii, 1. Cf. also I, xii, 1 and 42, and compare the references to his course through Faerie Land in VI, proem, 1 and elsewhere. The simile of the ship is also applied to Guyon, II, vii, 1.

41. *Pub. Mod. Lang. Assn.,* XXV, 560.

42. Sheavyn, *Literary Profession in the Elizabethan Age,* 45.

43. *Faerie Queene,* V. xi, 56.

TEN

W. L. RENWICK

Philosophy (1925)*

The basic fact of the Renaissance, so difficult to isolate, has been held to be the escape of human reason from the bonds of authority. It would be true also to say that it was the escape of human temperament from the bonds of reason, from the habit of categorical division which is the mark of the legalistic mind of the Middle Ages. The mediæval man kept things separate, and attended to one at a time. The Griselda of the Clerk's Tale, for instance, offends a modern reader by her lack of proper pride; the Clerk's Tale, however, is not about proper pride, but about patience. So also the passivity of Emily in the Knight's Tale is sometimes cited as a social document, evidence for the position of women in the Middle Ages, but the Knight's Tale is not about the relations of a young lady with two young men who are fighting over her, nor about her ideas or emotions, but about the relations of two friends who find themselves in enmity, and about the proper conduct of their quarrel. On the larger scale, the simple emotion of the *Acta-Sanctorum* is divided from the austere logic of the *Summa Theologiæ;* Guillaume de Lorris expounds a law that is neither Canon nor Civil, but chivalric; the religious emotion of the story of the Saint Graal does not affect the ethics of the story of Tristram and Iseult in the same book. This separation of human functions and interests could not last for ever, and when it weakened there began the Renaissance, the discovery of man as a whole, indivisible, mind and body and soul together—the discovery of the central inclusive fact of Life. On one hand the evasion of tempera-

*Reprinted from *Edmund Spenser: An Essay on Renaissance Poetry,* pp. 151-176.

ment broke down the dominion of mediæval intellectualism, leading philosophy away from metaphysics, which exercised only logic, to ethics, which implies the co-operation with intellect of intuition and feeling; and on the other hand it removed ethics from the sole jurisdiction of dogmatic and inexpugnable ecclesiasticism, to be examined in the light of thought and experience. Men discovered that their own actions and emotions were really the most interesting subject in the world, and felt they were not receiving the serious attention they deserved. Scholastic philosophy ignored them, the Church pronounced judgment upon them, sometimes in accordance with an ascetic ideal too high for the ordinary mortal and sometimes in accordance with clerical aims which the world's honesty condemned, and the secular literature of chivalry dealt with them only in the limited sphere of social convention.

Love between man and woman, for example, could not be discussed by scholastic philosophers with any profit to lovers. The Church regarded sex as an evil—even if it were a necessary evil—and recognized its existence only by imposing restrictions on it. The chivalric poets treated of it without regard to ethics at all: Sir Gawaine's reason for refusing to commit adultery, for instance, is purely social—it would be discourteous to the husband, who is his host.[1] But this was one of the great human facts whose interest the Renaissance felt pressing, and it had to be considered in all its bearings. So also with Justice and Temperance and Glory, and all the other vital factors in man's existence; they escaped the categories of truth and falsehood, of holiness and sinfulness, of good form and bad form, not because these categories did not apply, but because they all applied. Taken separately in the mediæval manner, they were too narrow and too rigid, and so men turned to the classics, where the conditions of man's life and the factors of his destiny are treated under wider and more elastic terms of good and evil. In the classics, again, a less dogmatic theory of the state, the ideas of civic duty and of expediency, the political virtues and vices, were included among those conditions and factors, and the sense of beauty and its cultivation in art, disregarded by the Schoolmen and denounced by the Church, but very living in the eager temperament, permeated all the thought and expression of the ancients. Few of the humanists, perhaps, and few of their disciples, could have formulated what it was that satisfied them in Plato and Cicero and Virgil, but the instinct, however obscure, was powerful, and when the new poets set themselves to school to the classics it was to acquire not only the finer art, but this wider scope, this adequacy to life as a whole, which even the best of the vernacular poets had missed. The humanists led them to Lucretius, the poet who was a philosopher, and to Plato, the philosopher who was a poet, and they, proposing to themselves the creation of a philosophic poetry, a poetry which should treat of human life in all its aspects and under all the categories of judgment, sought wisdom from the philosophers just as they sought guidance in their art from the critics.

One of the purposes of the new poetry was to bring into circulation among the modern peoples the treasures of the world's thought, for the sake of whatever use the peoples might make of them. The ideas of the philosophers formed part of Spenser's academic training, and part of the *materies* which it was his duty to treat in his dissimilar English manner. He incorporates into his own poems, accordingly, fragments from philosophic as well as from other writers, and for the same variety of reasons. When, for instance, he insets into his somewhat mediæval description of the Court of Venus the first thirty-odd lines of the *de Rerum Natura* of Lucretius,[2] the passage has no special Epicurean significance; the procedure is purely literary. In this Book Spenser was treating largely of Love. For the complete presentation of his theme he had been studying Lucretius, and when his poetic precedents called for a hymn to Venus, he imitated this excellent one. Here the literary motive is clear enough, but less purely artistic imitations cause endless doubt and difficulty, which can be overcome only by tactful consideration by the reader of each example as it occurs. A fragment of Aristotle or Seneca or Plato may be borrowed, not only for its beauty, but because it expressed more or less clearly some feeling which Spenser was trying to make explicit, and it may be borrowed just as a phrase or a story might be borrowed from Virgil or Ariosto. The use of quotations may be proof of study, but is not necessarily proof of intellectual discipleship, still less of complete acceptance of a system of thought. Nor did quotations necessarily come direct from their originals, for many phrases and arguments had done duty many times, and not always the same duty or in the same connexion.

By an ordinary process, again—and we have seen Spenser bear his part in it—technical expressions, divorced from their original bearing, pass into the common stock of allusion, and thence, losing precision of reference and meaning by the way, into the common stock of current speech. It is one of the difficulties that confront the student of the Renaissance that the process was then both rapid and voluminous. Many common words and phrases, now almost empty of content, may at any occurrence in Renaissance work be understood as having their original connotation, or their modern, or anything between, and this is particularly noticeable in the work of Spenser, who kept a loose grip on language, and is apt, moreover, to use the technical terms of philosophy just as he uses those of law or of falconry, but with scarcely the same precision. In such a passage as the following, for instance, the term "Idea" is explicitly the technical term of Platonism:

> Faire is the heaven . . .
> More faire is that, where those Idees on hie
> Enraunged be, which Plato so admired.[3]

When in the *Hymne of Heavenly Love* the poet speaks of "th' Idee" of God's "pure glorie," [4] the difficulty of the conception may be caused by loose thinking—he means, presumably, the divine glory as seen in itself, not in an earthly reflection. In two of the *Amoretti*, however, the term appears to mean an image or representation in the mind:

> Within my hart, though hardly it can shew
> thing so divine to vew of earthly eye,
> the fayre Idea of your celestial hew
> and every part remaines immortally.[5]

> Ne ought I see, though in the clearest day,
> when others gaze upon theyr shadows vayne:
> but th' onely image of that heavenly ray
> whereof some glance doth in mine eie remayne,
> of which beholding the Idaea playne
> through contemplation of my purest part
> with light thereof I feed my love-affamisht hart.[6]

These have been taken as a confession of Platonic faith, the record of progress from desire of beauty seen in the flesh to desire of beauty conceived in the intellect. The first, however, is a well-known commonplace, used by Marot[7] and derived from Serafino da Aquila. The second is closely related not only to Sonnet xxxv, but to Petrarch's Sonnet lxxi and Canzone xii, and still more to one of Bembo's *Rime:*

> Mentre 'l fero destin me toglie, et vieta
> Veder Madonna, e tiemmi in altra parte

La bella immagin sua veduta in parte
Il digiun pasce, e i miei sospiri acqueta.[8]

The Platonic source of Spenser's phrasing is obvious—he might not, perhaps, have disclaimed a Platonic sub-intention—but the use of the term "idea" to mean "image" can be paralleled in Ronsard [9] and Montaigne,[10] and the employment of philosophical tags in many of Ronsard's sonnets, as here:

O lumière enrichie
D'un feu divin qui m'ard si vivement
Pour me donner et force et mouvement
Estes-vous pas ma seule Entelechie? [11]

which is not an Aristotelian psalm, but a compliment to his lady's eyes. If, finally, Spenser intended the full Platonic significance to be attached to these sonnets, then he was a bad or at least a reluctant Platonist, for surely the philosopher should rejoice at his achievement of a step nearer the One, and here Spenser mourns.

It is not safe to argue Spenser's adherence to a system of philosophy upon such uncertain evidence, and as for more extensive borrowings, let the warning of three quotations suffice. "It is easie to verifie," says Montaigne, "that excellent authors, writing of causes, do not only make use of those which they imagine true, but eftsoones of such as themselves believe not: always provided they have some invention and beautie. They speake sufficiently, truly and profitably, if they speake ingeniously. We cannot assure ourselves of the chiefe cause: we hudle up a many together, to see whether by chance it shall be found in that number." [12] According to Ronsard, as we have seen, the aim of the poet is "to imitate, invent, and represent the things which are, or can be, or which the Ancients believed to be true." [13] And after discussing the variety of knowledge required by Ariosto for his heroic poem, Pigna continues: "And since in such variety of different professions there may be opinions of many philosophers, with which he comes in contact, he is here a Stoic, there a Platonist, and on one hand one opinion is followed, on another, another." [14] Literary imitation and the careful exhibition of wide scholarship might almost be supposed to account for the appearance in Spenser's work of philosophic matter, were it not that deep thought was required of the new school of poetry, and that one of his purposes in *The Faerie Queene*, and that not the least important, was "to fashion a gentleman or noble person in vertuous and gentle discipline." Holding such a purpose, he did not attempt to construct an original independent theory of morality. He lived in days before it was necessary to gain a reputation as moralist by showing that unchastity is chastity or that purity of soul is best manifested in a Russian debauch. True to his classical training and to the profound common sense of his English character, trying to arrive at the central truth, the essential common factor which all men must recognize, he attempted rather an exposition of the general consensus of the best ethical doctrine. Such a purpose required all the course of philosophic reading on which his Cambridge studies entered him, as well as his native and inherited instincts.

The method of *The Faerie Queene* is, to display each virtue completely in all its forms and phases, not as a simple characteristic, but as defined by the various trials and experiences operating to its perfection, by the various actions proper to its possession, and, negatively, by the diverse vices and defects opposed to it. A single exemplar is not enough. Guyon and the Palmer present Temperance arising from two different moral bases, highmindedness and restraint; Britomart and Belphœbe and Amoret, different conceptions of chastity—that which depends on strength and faithfulness, that which is a noble fastidiousness removed from common frailty, and that which is a natural attribute of womanly character. Spenser drives home his lesson by repeated variations, adding additional illustrations by additional characters and episodes. Sir Calidore, to take the simplest instance, represents Courtesy: his principal task is to restrain malice and evil speaking—the "Male-Bouche" of the chivalric allegorists—he also teaches mercy and mildness, championship of woman, tenderness to the sick, politeness to honest inferiors.[15] Cruelty, haughtiness, inhospitality, treachery, insincerity, are his opposites, though not necessarily his personal opponents in the story.[16] Tristram and the Hermit show that Courtesy, though rightly "named of court," belongs to "the gentle blood" and not to worldly position; the Savage Man, that goodwill and right instinct are its primary conditions. Incidental illustrations are given in the old knight Aldus, who tempered his grief for his son's wounds

> and turned it to cheare
> To cheare his guests, whom he had stayed that night
> And make their welcome to them well appeare,[17]

and in the quaint worldly-wise diplomacy of Calidore's explanation of the lady Priscilla's absence from home.[18] Courtesy, again, is allied to Justice in Prince Arthur's punishment of Turpine,[19] its place in the sphere of Love illustrated by the episode of Mirabella,[20] its interpretation extended by the vision of the Graces and Colin Clout's explanation.[21] Nor does this very rapid analysis by any means exhaust the complexity of Spenser's conception, which appears often in a phrase or even a pregnant word.

To frame and exhibit this complex conception of the virtues, then, required more than the current body of conventional social habit, and so Spenser draws upon the philosophers. The Sixth Book, as might be expected, contains least matter from classical sources: there are evident reminiscences of Seneca in many places,[22] but Chaucer and the romancers,[23] and the example of the best contemporaries, were authorities enough for Courtesy. Books which deal with more difficult questions, and questions which have been treated of by many minds, display a greater variety of sources, and Spenser evidently made a special study of the main authorities for each Book. It is only in the Sixth Book that Senecan borrowings appear in any quantity; the Stoic doctrine of the right of suicide, for instance, is mentioned only to be condemned by the Red Cross Knight.

The Bible contributes much matter and phrase to the First Book, as well as the methods already noticed, because it is the authority for Holiness, as Aristotle is for Temperance and for Justice; but "in the multitude of professions" other authorities are quoted, and the complete ethical conception—for be it noted that even Holiness is an ethical conception, with only the slightest mystical infusion in the last canto—the complete conception is built up of many fragments drawn from many sources. The Books of Chastity and Friendship, which really deal with Love, are drawn from Lucretius as well as from the Nicomachean Ethics: that Spenser follows Aristotle generally in the Book of Justice by no means precludes his following Boethius or Plato, the Hebrew prophets, the institutes of chivalry, or the police system of contemporary Ireland, in any one passage. Some of Spenser's debts to the philosophers have been studied, and there is matter enough for more, but unfortunately none of these separate studies, though valuable in themselves, can give a proper idea of Spenser's philosophy, for the character of his thought, here as elsewhere, can be appreciated better through a rough grasp of his peculiar mixture of sources than by a complete study of one.

The difficulty—and the interest—arises from his equal acceptance of all available authorities: it should not be increased by over-simplification, by trying to confine Spenser to a school. He could accept all the ancient schools, all "that the Ancients believed to be true," just because they were all equally superseded by revealed religion. The fundamental fact about his ethics is that they were those of a Christian, a Protestant Christian with a tendency—not an indulged tendency—towards Calvinism. Like all the modern world, he inherited much ancient philosophy in the tradition of the Church and of society, which made easier the interfusion of one with another, but where he deliberately seeks the aid of the Schools it is as supplementary to the teaching of the Church of England, and borrowings should be read only for their value at the moment and not as committing Spenser to an alien, still less to a pagan system. He draws upon Seneca, and at the same time upon the Epistle of St. James, upon Aristotle, and upon the Apocrypha, the Prophets, the Book of Job, the Revelation of St. John. All are intimately mingled together, but the Bible of all books was his principal source, as it was the foundation of his faith.

This attempt to combine the best of all the philosophies within a predominant Christianity, the intimacy with which the various borrowings are mingled, and the occasional confusion which results, are typical of the time, not only of the poets, but also of professed philosophers. The men of the Renaissance, unlike those of the French Revolution, were not seeking for a simplification; they had, as we have seen, just escaped from one, and they rejoiced in the variety and complexity of life, of human activities and possibilities, of human thought. They were somewhat bewildered and confused by that variety, those possibilities, but they faced them. There was no one dominant or leading philosophy as there was in the thirteenth century or even in the nineteenth, and no system could be evolved until the intellectual excitement had calmed: only Calvin succeeded in working out a complete system, and his system, confined to the sphere of theology, excludes many considerations very important to the average thinker of the time. Calvin succeeded because he worked by pure logic, but in this he was alone in his time: his contemporaries could not keep their temperament out of their thinking, and their doctrines, and the choice of authority to support them, are not the result of severe process. Thinking to them was an art and an indulgence, and it is by strength of temperament rather than by novelty of thought, that that passionate thinker Giordano Bruno is the typical Renaissance philosopher. Bruno has been held to have influenced Spenser, but they worked towards different ends, Bruno in ardent speculation, Spenser in solid ethics. The phrases of Bruno may appear in Spenser, but the ideas they hold in common are not those peculiar to Bruno, but those which they could both find in Lucretius and Plato, and even the phrases are uncertain, for both phrase and idea were of the common stock of the time. The curious mixture of schools, and the loose handling and uncertain application of terms and formulas taken from various and often from conflicting sources, resulted from the attempt to gather and reconcile all the philosophies and to relate the mass to Christianity. It is the same process, though in the wider sphere and with much less security in outcome, as we have seen in the critical thought of the new poets, and it is to be found in such popular philosophical works as that of Leone Hebreo, and in commentaries like that of Loys le Roy on the Symposium, work which may be only of historical interest, but must not therefore be neglected.

All these men were strongly affected by Platonism, for the reconciliation of ancient philosophies with Christian doctrine began with the Platonic Academy of Florence. Why Platonism was so attractive to the Renaissance mind is sufficiently clear from what has gone before—in Plato's works temperament and intellect move in harmony, humane feeling and exalted speculation, ethics and the spiritual universals, somehow interpenetrate and are fused into one. There was some common ground in the unrecognized Platonic element in the tradition of the Church, and still more community in the temper of thought, for Plato was not only the philosopher who taught, like the Church, that earth is but the shadow of heaven, but the philosopher of Love and Beauty and Desire, the poet-philosopher of the beautiful, spiritual tales. Platonism, then, was cultivated, compressed, and spread abroad. The treatises of Ficino, Politian, Pico della Mirandola—especially his commentary on the Platonic *canzone* of Benevieni—passed the tenets of the Florentine school into the mind of all Europe. To put it bluntly, Platonism was the fashion. It marched well with Petrarchism, it certainly was inspiring, and it had not caught this fashion along with all the others of his time: where he found the material for the *Hymnes in Honor of Love and Beauty* is more difficult. He certainly knew some of Plato's works at first hand, and used them, but the systematic method of the *Hymnes* is of the Renaissance. Ficino, the master of all Renaissance Platonists, would be his master also, but the phrase of Lucretius,

Mother of love and of all worlds delight [24]

was already brought into Platonic exposition by Loys le Roy[25]; Bruno's *degli Heroici Furori* may have supplied some of the matter, and so may Bembo's *Asolani*, and Castiglione's *Corteggiano* (newly translated by Sir Thomas Hoby), and Leone Hebreo, and Pico, and Benevieni. It is more likely that Spenser knew all these than that he did not: in any one of them he would find all or nearly all he required for the *Hymnes,* and his slight uncertainties of thought are probably due to this, that he was versifying the common floating conception—though not far from his books—rather than one hammered out in his mind.

In Italy the Church had to restrain the growing cult of systematized Neo-Platonism, for though the intention was to reconcile it with Christian dogma, the Platonism tended to swallow up the Christianity. In France and England Neo-Platonism did not antagonize the Churches, for the Reformation had preceded its introduction, and the fact of open conflict upon well-defined grounds forced men to take a side for one Church or another and attached them the more passionately to the central tenets of their creed. The infusion of Platonism into the thought of Christian men could do no harm, for there was no possibility of competition and no possible place for paganism. In the dedicatory epistles prefixed to the *Fowre Hymnes* Spenser apologizes for those in honour of Love and Beauty as having been written "in the greener times of my youth," and in the *Hymnes* of Heavenly Love and Heavenly Beauty he attempts to sanctify his old Neo-Platonism by treating the Neo-Platonic scheme as a myth, to symbolize the progress of the Christian soul. The attempt, though productive of some beautiful phrases, is neither very lucid philosophy nor very downright theology; it required more logic than Spenser cared to spend in a poem; but it shows that the Platonic fashion ceased to prevail with a man isolated from fashion and deeply engaged in the war of the Churches. Platonism attracted him, always, could be romanced about. There would be room for surprise if Spenser as it attracted many of his contemporaries, more as an emotion than as a creed—in which he was perhaps the nearer Plato.

For the purposes of *The Faerie Queene* the Neo-Platonists were less useful than the practical teachers of ethics like Aristotle and Seneca: which means, of course, that Spenser was less interested in the Neo-Platonists. When Castiglione wrote his treatise *Il Corteggiano*, he, like Spenser, intended it "to fashion a gentleman or noble person in vertuous and gentle discipline," and when he broached the inevitable problem of the relation of the sexes he put into the mouth of Bembo, as the author of the *Asolani*, a brief resumé of Platonic doctrine, telling how the lover progresses from desire of beauty in one human embodiment to desire of that beauty divorced from flesh, so to desire of universal beauty, and so to God, Who is Beauty Itself. Now this is just what Spenser did not do in the poem into which he poured all he knew and felt and learned about the good life. In view of a common tendency among writers on this subject it is necessary to premise that to derive from Plato any and every conception of love higher than the brute instinct is a libel on mankind. There have been honourable souls in other states than Athens, and one element in the Platonic temperament, the yearning mood, the vague desire for far-away or half-imagined beauty, is common to all youth and to many peoples—to Kormak the Icelander, and Jaufré Rudel, and many an old poet of Germany and Ireland. "Platonic Love" as a deliberately accepted and conclusive ethic flourished in Italy, and, with Maurice Scève, in the Italianate city of Lyons: it may be doubted whether it suited the solid mind of the North, except as a scholarly elegance. The exaltation of beauty into something divine flattered the Renaissance temperament—almost gave an excuse for indulgence—and the spiritualization of love was easily grafted on the tradition of *amour courtois* to make a courtly refinement. But that very tradition carried a principle hostile to the Neo-Platonic scheme. Under Renaissance Neo-Platonism the only duty of woman is to be beautiful, to awaken desire, and then to disappear, leaving the desire to be nursed into an ecstasy in which she has no place: this cannot be reconciled with the principle of personal loyalty, the first clause of the law of *amour courtois* as it was the basis of the whole mediæval system. And behind the principle of personal loyalty lies the secular instinct of the North, obvious enough for a stranger like Tacitus to have observed it, giving the woman her equal share in a love which exists for both man and woman together, and exists by virtue of their being man and woman.

Plato contributed largely to Spenser's thought, but he was not the only source of principle, nor was he the final authority. He enforced the truth that love is a spiritual activity, but the complementary truth that love is a primary function of the animate universe, essential to its continuance, was set forth with equal force by Lucretius, and these two principles were reconciled for Spenser in the final authority, the teaching of the Church of England, defined in the Marriage Service of the Prayer Book. Heavenly Love and Earthly are not eternal antagonists, but complements one of the other, and so the story of Chastity is a love-story. All Spenser's virtues are positive fighting virtues, and Chastity among them: its representative is neither nun nor sage, but a redoubtable knight who is also a woman in love, destined to the honourable estate of matrimony and the procreation of a noble line; for chastity is nothing other than truth and honour in the question of sex, sanctified by the spirit of God, Who is Love, and serving the world as His agent. Chastity is attended by Prudence, but depends on its own strength and courage. It is as free from the asceticism of the Middle Ages and the asceticism of the Neo-Platonists as it is from the frauds and counterfeits, the weaknesses and the perversions it combats, for its end is not in the solitary individual soul, but in the universe, through love, of which it is the necessary condition.

This is the mark of Spenser's Puritanism. His removal from Cambridge took him out of the ecclesiastical controversies about vestments and altar-tables into a wider sphere of thought, but the essential of Puritanism remained with him, the sense of personal responsibility which cannot be transferred to priest or king. In his preaching of this doctrine he was, perhaps, as well in the example of his art, the master of Milton, who in a famous passage of *Areopagitica* dared think him "a better teacher than Scotus or Aquinas." False Puritanism is distinguished by its negations, but the true Puritan is not an ascetic, undergoing privations as a sacrifice or in self-distrust, but an athlete and a soldier, disciplining himself against indulgences which would unfit him here and now for his duty, and for the reward to be earned, not by the privations, but by the duty accomplished. The individual is responsible for himself, for his own destiny, and for more than his own: he is a combatant in the eternal strife between good and evil for the dominion of a universe in which spiritual and material are one. His victories and his defeats affect the universe as a whole, and he is never fighting alone. Ethics, then, takes a large place in Puritan thought, as the rule of a daily life which is an activity of the universe.

Individual human conduct, though perhaps concerned in any one instance with small material conditions, extends into the great movement which is ultimately spiritual, just as the individual human life is part of the universal. In his study of love as the law of life Spenser extends ethics into speculation, for in it there is some hint of a solution to the problem which recurs through all his work, the problem of change. The mutability of things, the brevity of life, the inevitable end of human beauty and greatness, haunted the Renaissance as it haunted the Middle Ages; but unlike the mediæval poets Spenser was not content to accept it only as tragedy or as a subject for moralizing, for the problem was enlarged, made more poetic in being made more philosophical, by Lucretius. On this note *The Faerie Queene,* as we have it, closes, and we do not know how Spenser proposed to treat the Legend of Constancy, but it is in all his thought. His astronomical knowledge, however incomplete, destroyed for him even the poetic fiction of the changeless stars:[26] all earth was involved in change. That he learned to accept as a universal law: substance is constant, form changes according to universal law; and Universal Law is God.

> What wrong then is it, if that when they die,
> They turne to that, whereof they first were made?
> All in the powre of their great Maker lie:
> All creatures must obey the voice of the most hie.[27]

That is the theological statement, in a passage based on the second chapter of the first Book of Samuel and on Lucretius: it is stated again in the sixth canto of the Third Book, in the famous myth of the Garden of Adonis, compiled from the *Phaedrus,* the *Tabula* ascribed to Cebes, Aristotle *de Anima,* Lucretius, and the Book of Genesis. Here the principle of continuance in change is the Venus of Lucretius, presiding over procreation, and representing "nothing other than the power of God." Thus Love is doubly sanctified, matter and spirit are reconciled, and the tragedy of mutability is resolved, not by blind submission or by abstention, but by comprehension.

That is one solution of the problem of change: form begets form in perpetuity according to the will of the Creator; but man cannot forget that which was, and in a universe of unceasing change his desire is for stability. In the last resort the only permanence is with God:

> When I bethinke me on that speech whyleare
> Of Mutabilitie, and well it way,
> Me seemes that though she all unworthy were
> Of the Heav'ns Rule, yet very sooth to say,
> In all things else she beares the greatest sway:
> Which makes me loath this state of life so tickle,
> And love of things so vaine to cast away
> Whose flowring pride, so fading and so fickle,
> Short Time shall soon cut down with his consuming sickle.
>
> Then gin I thinke on that which Nature sayd,
> Of that same time when no more change shall be,
> But stedfast rest of all things, firmely stayd
> Upon the pillours of Eternity,
> That is contrayr to Mutabilitie;
> For all that moveth doth in Change delight:
> But thence-forth all shall rest eternally
> With Him that is the God of Sabaoth hight:
> O! that great Sabaoth God, grant me that Sabaoths sight.[28]

But the positive spirit of England, of the time and the man, would not allow Spenser to wait in mystical contemplation for the coming of the Kingdom of Heaven. In this world of change men must strive for such stability as may be won by the strength of their virtues, and so the ethical ideal returns with renewed importance and validity. Yet Puritanism did not make Spenser a rebel. Just as the individual must be a well-disposed member of the universal life, so he must be a well-disposed citizen, for the state and the universe are maintained by order and control. The lesson of *The Faerie Queene* is the same throughout: society must be held together by concord or Friendship, the individual must be controlled by Temperance, the state by Justice. The recurrent victory of the trained and disciplined knights over "the rascal many" was more than an inheritance from the aristocratic Middle Ages, or an echo of Tudor statesmanship, or a memory of Irish insurrections. All these were in Spenser's mind, but they were contained within the greater idea, the necessity of stability. The rabble is crushed because it is a rabble, incapable of constant policy of united action.

Spenser's political attitude is thus similar to that of Shakespeare, and for good cause. As *Paradise Lost* proclaims the individualism of the seventeenth century, so *The Faerie Queene* sums up the lesson of English history for a century and a half. There was reason in the adulation of Queen Elizabeth: she stood for the sixteenth-century virtues as Queen Victoria for those of the late nineteenth, and she had given England something approaching civil and religious stability for over thirty years when the first part of *The Faerie Queene* was published. In English history Shakespeare saw the clash of personality and the permanence of England: Spenser, less interested in the dramatic personality than in the idea of movement, saw the eternal vicissitude of things exemplified, and the need for stability enforced. Partly this may be the reflection of the official mind, largely it is the conclusion of the philosophical temper. The great vision of Spenser is the vision of Mutability, the alteration of the stars in their courses, the succession of the months and seasons and centuries, the cycle of birth and death, the sequence of kings and dynasties, all subject to the universal law.

> For all that lives, is subject to that law:
> All things decay in time, and to their end do draw.[29]

Yet there is the permanent factor:

> That substance is eterne, and bideth so,
> Ne when life the decayes, and forme does fade,
> Doth it consume, and into nothing go,
> But chaunged is, and often altred to and fro.

> The substance is not chaunged, nor altered,
> But th' only forme and outward fashion.[30]

So in every particle of existence, in man, in society, in the state, the temporary form is important as a phase of the permanent, and must therefore be brought to its best mode and noblest function.

Here, then, is justified the cultivation of all the activities of human life which was the contribution of the Renaissance to the progress of the world. Spenser could not set aside the material for the sake of the spiritual, nor could he live in the material in despite of God. All knowledge, art, beauty, emotion, government, manners, were important as promoting the fine fashioning of the universal substance, and as fashioning it towards permanence, for permanence is possible only in perfection.

We do not know what were the twelve virtues which together made up Magnificence, but they were not merely theological virtues. The six we have are Holiness, a spiritual virtue; Temperance and Chastity, personal virtues; Justice, a political virtue; Friendship and Courtesy, social virtues; and all these are shown to be intimately interrelated and equally required of the inclusive virtue of Magnificence. This complete and balanced cultivation of all the powers of man was the ideal of the Renaissance: Sidney displayed it in his life, Shakespeare dramatically, Spenser philosophically. The great man must be competent in each function, must possess the capacity for thought, the capacity for feeling, and the capacity for action, all trained and cultivated, and all in equilibrium. Hamlet, Lear, Othello are subjects of tragedy because one of their capacities is overbalanced, though it may be only for the time, by the others: Spenser's ideal knights are victorious, because they are in possession and in control of all three. The only permanence is in perfection—that is, in God—but something may be done on earth by the careful maintenance of equilibrium. Thus Temperance is the personal ideal which gives its due place to all the faculties of mind and body by refusing dominion to any one, Justice the political ideal which gives' its due rights to each unit of the state, prescribes to each its duties and keeps each within its rights and its duties, Courtesy the social ideal which gives each man his due of proper regard in his degree and restrains the overbearing and the ungracious.

How much of this Spenser learned from Aristotle is very obvious, as his debt to Plato is obvious, but as we have seen, he was thirled to neither of them. The attempts that have been made to discover the source of the Twelve Virtues in Aristotle or in his commentators have all been unsuccessful, and it would be more surprising to find than to miss it. Some credit must be given to Spenser: just as the new poets combated the notion that all the world's store of poetic power has been expended on the earlier races, so they would have claimed for the modern age some power of thought, if only because Christianity had reoriented many of the ancient problems. There were to be twelve Books in *The Faerie Queene* because that was the correct number for an epic poem, not because there were any twelve virtues; and the phrase of Spenser "the twelve private morall vertues, as Aristotle hath devised," is best and most simply understood to mean "the twelve moral virtues which are such as Aristotle would call *private* virtues." Artistic motives must be kept in mind as well as philosophic, and temperament as well as reason. Thus Plato appealed to the spiritual and artistic nature of the poet, and Lucretius to his feeling for this world that is caught in the whirl of change—and, since temperament must judge of temperament, one reader at least feels that the deeper communion of spirit was between Spenser and Lucretius, that there is a depth of tone in the Lucretian passages of *The Faerie Queene* more moving and more heartfelt than the somewhat shrill straining of the *Hymnes* of Love and Beauty. But if one name be asked for, as of him who most formed the thought, and the habit of thought, of Spenser, then it were best, here also, to turn back to his early training, and there, of all thinkers that he would be made to study, we find the prose idol of the humanists, Cicero. *The Faerie Queene*, with much in it *de Natura Deorum*, is the *de Officiis* and the *de Finibus* of the Renaissance, deriving the elements of a complex civic and personal ideal from the opinions of many philosophers, aiming at stability and the proper distribution of rights and duties in an uncertain world, with a backward glance at the pristine virtues of the past and yet a wide outlook on the universe, preaching the search for "what order may be, what it may be that is seemly and fitting, a measure in speech and action," observing man's relations with God, with his fellows, and with the state.

Spenser was not a mere critic of life, but a constructive idealist, and intent on a possible ideal. All his virtues, as has been said, are positive fighting virtues, and go to build up the positive ideal of Magnificence, magnanimity. Magnificence seems vague and uncertain. The place of Prince Arthur in the epic-romance was never quite clearly worked out; his appearances are fitful and unrelated, and this naturally obscures the expression of the virtue he represents, but we know that Magnificence includes all the others, and its difficulty is due to its complexity. The Renaissance would forgo nothing and would shirk nothing, but endeavoured to combine in one comprehensive plan of life all personal and political good, religion, learning, and all arts and elegances. It is the most complex ideal that any poet ever attempted to express, inclusive of all that Virgil ceded to Greece and all he claimed for Rome, all the gifts and graces of Chaucer's knight and squire and clerk and parson, and all the art of Virgil and Chaucer with them. Intellect and feeling had to combine in it, and to combine equally. Spenser's philosophy lacked the lucidity and system of severe intellectual process, but at least it did not attain lucidity and system by a severe process of exclusion of all that might interfere with its security. And among all our philosophic poets that may be said of Spenser alone.

NOTES

1. *Gawaine and the Green Knight,* lines 1773-5.
2. Book IV, x, 44-7.
3. *Hymne of Heavenly Beautie,* 78-83.
4. *Hymne of Heavenly Love,* 284.
5. *Amoretti,* xlv.
6. *Amoretti,* lxxxviii.
7. Elegie xvi, 72-99.
8. Ed. of 1548, fol. 31 *vo.* "While cruel fate seizes me and forbids me to see my Lady, and keeps me in another place, her fair image seen in part feeds my hunger and quiets my sighs."
9. See quotation on p. 139 [of Professor Renwick's book].
10. II, vi: *Of Exercise.*
11. *Amours,* I, lxviii.
12. III, vi: *Of Coaches:* tr. Florio.
13. *Art Poétique,* p. 321.
14. *I Romanzi,* p. 81.
15. Book VI, i, 40 ff.; ii, 14; ii, 47-8; ix, 6-7, 18.
16. Crudor, Briana, Maleffort, Turpine, Blandina.
17. Canto iii, 6.
18. Canto iii, 12-19.
19. Canto vi, 18-vii, 27.
20. Canto vii, 27-viii, 30.
21. Canto x, 21-24.
22. Cf. i, 12, 5-6 and Seneca, Ep. xxxv; vi, 6 ff., and Ep. viii, l, lxviii; vi, 14, and Ep. ix, xxv, lxiii; ix, 20 ff., and Ep. ii, iv; etc.
23. Alluded to, iii, 1. Cf. Wife of Bath's Tale, 257-60; *Rose,* 2196-7 *et passim.*
24. *Hymne in Honor of Beautie,* 16.
25. 1559. Du Bellay translated the verse quotations for him.
26. Introduction to Book V; VII, vii, 49-55.
27. V, ii, 40.
28. VII, viii—the last fragment of *The Faerie Queene.*
29. III, vi, 40.
30. III, vi, 37-38.

ELEVEN

CHARLES G. OSGOOD

*Spenser and the Enchanted Glass (1930)**

Said the Duchess: "I can't tell you just now what the moral of that is, but I shall remember it in a bit."

"Perhaps it hasn't one," Alice ventured to remark. "Tut, tut, child!" said the Duchess. "Everything's got a moral, if only you can find it. . . . O 'tis love, 'tis love, that makes the world go round!"

Thus lightly doth the satirist touch a modern fashion in criticism. For the disparagement of moral values in art and in literature has for a generation or two been the cant of critics. As moral values have sunk into such abatement and low price, so too have sunk such poetical stars of first magnitude as Milton and Pope and Spenser, and their diminished following have latterly fallen back from stout defence to feeble denial.

For example, a recent reviewer: "Much is sometimes made of Spenser's moral intention in composing the *Faerie Queene* and, indeed, Spenser rather paraded it himself. But in reality this moral intention amounts to little."

That notable Spenserian, Mr. Courthope, remarks "the absence of depth in Spenser's moral allegory," and another, both teacher and editor of Spenser, avers that "we should learn to dwell more upon the imaginative and picturesque qualities and less upon the purely ethical elements of the *Faery Queen* in order to prevent this poetic treasure from being consigned to oblivion."

Good Spenserians, I take it, will not worry about the oblivion of the poet. Moral or no moral, his great poem will take care of itself. And

*Professor Osgood delivered this lecture to the Tudor and Stuart Club of the Johns Hopkins University on February 27, 1930. It was printed in *The Johns Hopkins Alumni Magazine,* XIX (November, 1930), 8-31.

in passing, we may recall that over against the notion which I have cited are arrayed—emphatically, sincerely, formidably—men no less than Raleigh, Milton, Pope, Gray, Wordsworth, Shelley, Tennyson—poets all—and poets, be it remembered, by their peculiar rights in Spenser, have the first and the last word.

Rather, next to the last. For the last and the first are properly those of Spenser himself, whose opinion is, after all, of greatest weight in this matter which concerns him most. It is easy but unfair and dangerous to assume, as writers do at times for their own ends, that even as great a man as Spenser did not know his own mind. If not he, how much less they? But what has Spenser to say?

Of the obvious and oft noted glories of his work Spenser seems to have been quite aware.

> The waies through which my weary steps I guyde,
> In this delightfull land of Faery,
> Are so exceeding spacious and wyde,
> And sprinckled with such sweet variety,
> Of all that pleasant is to eare or eye,
> That I, nigh ravisht with rare thoughts delight,
> My tedious travell doe forget thereby.

Here he notes in effect the splendors of pageantry, of spectacle and music, that delight all readers of the great poem, its scope and range, its variety, its wealth of antiquities, its other-world enchantment; he is aware, too, of the dazzling coruscation of grand ideas inwoven with the poem's fabric and subtly suggested throughout.

He would, then, approve our pleasure in the poem's pageantry, the fair processions of men old and young, of frolicking children and of dancing maidens and graces

> with girlands dight,
> As fresh as flowres in medow greene doe grow,
> When morning deaw upon their leaves doth light:
> And in their handes sweet timbrels all upheld on hight.

Grotesque ballets, of satyrs and Sins and sea-monsters; strange mysterious rites; sun-flooded gardens; dark and deep reaches of forest-shade or sea depths, inland rivers, rich old myth and symbolism, grim castles and gorgeous palaces—I cannot help wondering that some designer of murals for a great library has not discovered the infinite store of subject, all sketched and colored, in effect ready to his hand, in the vast spaces of the *Faery Queen*.*

Spenser surely approves our pleasure in all this; but it is not his whole, nor even his chief concern. He abridges the pageantry of Marinell's wedding because

> The pride of ladies, and the worth of knights,
> The royall banquets, and the rare delights
> Were worke fit for an herauld, not for me:
> But for so much as to my lot here lights,
> That with this present treatise doth agree,
> True vertue to advance, shall here recounted bee.

But, one may ask, was Spenser's declared and avowed purpose his real one? When, at the outset, he announced,

> Fierce warres and faithfull loves shall moralize my song,

did he mean it? When he wrote to Sir Walter Raleigh that "the generall end therefore of all the booke is to fashion a gentleman or noble person in vertuous and gentle discipline," was he sincere? When he cites the great heroic poets as his precedents for moral intention, is he honest? When he claims the authority of Aristotle for his ethical doctrine, is he only making a fashionable humanistic gesture? In his October eclogue of the *Shepherd's Calendar* wherein Piers and Cuddie debate whether poetry really pays, Piers, who speaks for Spenser, exclaims:

> Cuddie, the prayse is better then the price,
> The glory eke much greater then the gayne:
> O what an honor is it, to restraine
> The lust of lawlesse youth with good advice,
> Or pricke them forth with pleasaunce of thy vaine,
> Whereto thou list their trayned willes entice!

Do these numbers ring hollow? At any rate, they woke an echo in a corner of the realms of gold as far and high as Milton's *Lycidas*.

Thus Spenser again and again both declares and implies that his moral purpose as an artist transcends and draws up into itself all other purposes of the poem.

---

*In April, 1945, Mr. Lee Woodward Zeigler completed his series of seventeen mural paintings of scenes from the *Faery Queen* for the Enoch Pratt Free Library in Baltimore, Maryland.—ed.

We can, I think, on sober reflection, conclude only that the poet meant what he said, and that he would have regarded as partial, and in so far fallacious, all criticism and scholarship concerned which not only failed to take into account his moral intention, but failed to see it as the very soul and informing agent of his achievement.

But, apart from fashions in criticism and scholarship—for even the Learned Ladies have a weakness for styles—one very good reason offers itself for the neglect of Spenser's moral teaching. On closer consideration it proves not vague, but somehow inarticulate, unmeasurable. Ruskin talks of Spenser's moral system. But I fear it is Ruskin's system, not Spenser's which he unfolds. The veil of Spenser's allegory clothes no moral system, as Dante's allegory clothes a system. Dante inherited a definite frame and coherent structure of doctrine and symbols necessary to purposes of sustained allegory, and favorable, therefore, to the concrete, detached, scientific modes of modern scholarship. But Spenser lived in an age too late. For him and his world, the old system has passed, and he finds himself clinging only to its glittering fragments.

To be sure, there was Calvinism, systematic enough, but Calvinism was new. And for the uses of great poetic allegory more than consistency is necessary. Centuries of thought, and use, and symbol must accumulate. Hence the efforts of certain excellent scholars to trace the system of Calvin beneath the veil of the *Faery Queen* tend to reveal in effect only a misfit.

It was inevitable, therefore, that an allegory on so grand a scale as the *Faery Queen*, erected in a time so confused and paradoxical, must prove in the execution fortuitous, casual, in a sense fragmentary, for lack of a system.

"Oh but," some will say, "has he not claimed for himself the system of Aristotle as laid down in the *Nicomachean Ethics?*" And they cite the familiar words in Spenser's letter to Raleigh: "I labour to pourtraict in Arthure, before he was King, the image of a brave knight, perfected in the twelve private morall vertues, as Aristotle hath devised, the which is the purpose of these first twelve books: which if I finde to be well accepted, I may be perhaps encoraged to frame the other part of poiliticke vertues in his person, after that he came to be king." Arthur then is to represent Magnanimity or Highmindedness, the epitome of all the virtues. Spenser continues: "But of the xii. other vertues I make xii. other knights the patrones . . . of which these [the first] three bookes contayn three. The first of the Knight of the Redcrosse, in whome I expresse holynes" etc. Here at all events seems to be system enough—indeed the very scheme for an epic—a complete duodecimal framework—on which six, twelve, or twenty-four books may be set up according to the time-honored epic example.

But difficulties are in the way. Not to mention others, Aristotle himself disclaims any intention of rearing a system of virtues. He nowhere makes a sharp distinction such as Spenser implies between private and public virtues. To Aristotle they are all essentially public. Furthermore Spenser's list doesn't correspond with Aristotle's. For his First Book wears the label Holiness; the Second, Temperance; the Third, Chastity; the Fourth, Friendship; the Fifth, Justice; the Sixth, Courtesy; and a fragment of another, Constancy. Now scholars are put to it in this matter—some, indeed, beyond the point of dispassionate observation. At one extreme M. Jusserand finds the discrepancy between Spenser and Aristotle so wide as to suggest that Spenser never read the *Ethics* at all. But there comes another who is at great pains to prove—by brute force if necessary—that Spenser's scheme is just what he promised, Aristotle's and *only* Aristotle's, and as Dr. Johnson would say, "there's an end on't." Alas, this is not the end on't.

For illustration, let us consider Spenser's Second Book, the Book which tells the story of Sir Guyon, the Knight of Temperance. Now Mr. Padelford has had no trouble in showing that, for all his label, "Temperance," Spenser exhibits in Sir Guyon not Temperance, but Continence, which is indeed quite a different matter. It is a distinction the artistic possibilities of which may have been suggested to Spenser by Castiglione in the Fourth Book of his *Book of the Courtier,* and which, for Spenser's moral purpose, is highly important.

Virtue, in Aristotle's famous definition, is a "state of deliberate moral purpose consisting in a mean . . . determined by reason." And as Temperance is a virtue, it is a state of character. Furthermore, Aristotle implies that Temperance, like any other moral state or virtue, is a result and an achievement of moral discipline under the dictates of reason, and that a man is not temperate until by practice and discipline he has at last achieved the state of temperate habit, both in action and in the desire that prompts to action. In short he has struggled up the steep, and now travels the exalted, though unvaried and less interesting, plateau of Temperance. Henceforth his reasonable moderation in both pleasures and desires is assured. And of course we are glad of his final success and wish him well. But the thing in which we are interested is not this state of virtue, but his struggle to attain to it. Witness Bunyan, Dante, Everyman, and the thousand and one other versions of the Psychomachia in all times. Witness also Spenser's free use of Aristotle. Now Aristotle's Ἐρκράτεια, Continence, or Self-Control, for which Spenser exchanges Temperance, if it is ever a state of virtue at all, is at any rate more nearly a state of unstable equilibrium. Continence implies that in the struggle between right and wrong, the natural desires, as allies of wrong, are more evenly matched against reason and intelligence, the allies of right, than in the case of Temperance; that a man is continent so long as reason wins, but incontinent when the natural desires get the best of it. The struggle is always recurring. Of course reason may win every time. Or it may lose every time.

And where the struggle is less apparent, and the hero is more securely virtuous, Spenser provides an external struggle between the perfected virtue of the hero and conditions of the world about him with which the virtuous knight-errant or reformer finds himself at variance. Was this not after all very much the situation of Spenser himself—as of one who experienced the inner moral struggle, while he contended with the conditions of his own time?

But another, among the great ancients, was closer to Spenser than was Aristotle. The poet—idealist that he was—had a natural instinct and affinity for Platonic and neo-Platonic ways of thinking or intuitions. You remember Plato's figure of the loved one as a glass in which the lover really beholds himself, though he knows it not. Spenser seems to have recognized himself in Plato—not in the whole of Plato—but at least in Plato's idealism, especially his idealization of the romantic passion. Spenser's cast of mind is in great measure Platonic, and whatever he derives from Aristotle is ancillary and subject to his prevailing Platonic enthusiasm. From the *Shepherd's Calendar* to the *Prothalamion* this quality of the poet's mind reveals itself again and again. Furthermore when the Platonic phrase or thought is not in evidence, a deep Platonic undertone is easily distinguishable, that mingles with the whole, fills it with import, and renders both music and meaning of the poem more rich and strange. Thus it is not a system of thought which Spenser derives from Plato, any more than from Aristotle, or the Middle Ages, or Calvin, but rather certain congenial ideas, and a pervading quality.

Somewhat wilfully and arbitrarily he ranges among the thoughts of others, particularly Aristotle and Plato. He is "ravisht with rare thoughts delight." Like Milton, he feeds

                                    on thoughts that voluntary move
Harmonious numbers.

He appropriates here and there such conceptions and ideas as fit exactly his own intense experience and aspirations. These great fragments, newly vitalized with the energy of his own spiritual life, and projected in concrete form, constitute his poetry.

But what, one may ask, was there about Spenser to generate the energy and heat of his moral convictions? What indeed, but the conflict that awaits every idealist born into the world? No idealist was ever more keenly aware than Spenser of the sharp clash between the ideal world as he conceived it, and all that is finite, mundane, actual. As early as the *Shepherd's Calendar* he sets a worthless clergy over against an ideal cure of souls, a worldly, faint-hearted poet over against one of pure devotion to his art, and puts the question, "the price or the praise?" In *Mother Hubbard's Tale* and in *Colin Clout's Come Home Again* he contrasts a corrupt and immoral court of the Renaissance with ideal service to Prince and Commonwealth. This contrast extends by implication throughout the *Faery Queen*. Such the antinomy between actual and ideal which ranges through all his varied transcriptions of life even to his last poem. But in the *Faery Queen* the warfare is most fierce and acute. The struggle between false and true is ever renewed, never finally settled. I find no compromise, no truce between these extremes. And this struggle but bodies forth the war in the poet's soul, and the clash between his vision of an ideal world and the moral flaws of the world into which he was born. Fierce wars and faithful loves do indeed moralize his song—the wars and loves, the struggles and adorations of the man himself. Subtle gradations and fine shadings of mingled good and evil abound, to be sure, especially in the later Books. The Fourth, for example, is a symphonic treatment of many widely varied themes of amatory love in relation to friendship. But the main issue everywhere none the less prevails—the issue between good and evil, between right and wrong, between life as it is and life as it ought to be.

The *Faery Queen* as Spenser left it consists of six Books. What so natural as to regard the six Books, one virtue to a Book, as six separate and systematic poetical essays on six several virtues—Holiness, Temperance, Chastity, and such? It is easy to imagine each of these Books as a compartment of esoteric, abstract truth, first accessible only to him who can discover the right manipulation of wards, tumblers, and combinations. At any rate some Spenserian scholars have exhibited feats of highly elaborate and subtle lock-picking. Now I cannot but suspect that there is no need of such subtlety; that the doors are unfastened, nay, ajar; that, once inside, nothing especially strange, or subtle, or esoteric will be found, unless it be some fanciful and ingenious construction which the student himself, in his zeal, has unwittingly "planted" there. In short, the secret of the moral allegory, if secret there be, is but the character and quality of Spenser himself, the wars and the loves and aspirations of his own spiritual problem, and of the world in which he moved.

Thus the structural cleavage or division of the *Faery Queen* is not up and down, between Book and Book, virtue and virtue; but latitudinal, between these personal moral issues of the poet, which horizontally traverse and pervade the entire work.

First and most prevalent is the moral issue between carnal lust and pure affection or chastity. It is not the issue of the Third Book especially, but is ubiquitous, because Spenser was more interested in the experience and spiritual potentialities of romantic love than in anything else.

No one can read Spenser's poetry without seeing that he was peculiarly susceptible to the charms of women. The trait is almost as conspicuous in him as in Byron and Burns. He did not marry till he was forty-two, and it is probable, nay certain, both from his verse, and the nature of the man, that he had experienced at least one unhappy love affair, to the memories of which he clung with strange fondness. Whether the lady was Rosalind or who else matters little. Such experience, not to mention the erotic fashions in high life of the time described in *Colin Clout's Come Home* and familiar to every reader, precipitated and prolonged the conflict in his own nature between sensuality and an idealistic or Platonic influence of the grand passion upon his own spiritual life. Had he married early the two elements might early have become reconciled. And indeed in what may be his post-marital poetry the issue seems to grow less acute. Spenser, like most men, had not attained to the stable equilibrium of Aristotle's virtuous man. As in most men inclined to behave themselves, the struggle between continence and incontinence was in him continuous or recurrent. In so highly sensitive and idealistic a man it must have been singularly acute, but with a difference. As a substitute for Aristotle's "reason," his chief reinforcement to continence is an idealism partly Platonic, partly Christian, "another law, warring against the law of his mind." Such seems to me the first moral issue in Spenser's poetry.

Aristotle says that continence pertains not to carnal desires alone, but also to the passion of anger, love of honor, and the love of gain. Whether Spenser had a troublesome temper, I cannot say. Angry violence was surely a besetting sin of his times. But his desire for honor and gain, for prominent position and wealth, admits no denial. Ashamed as he was of it, he could never rise wholly superior to his ambition in politics and at court. With Spenser the infirmity was chronic and incurable. In even his latest lines it mingles with more tranquil notes to effect some of his sweetest and most moving melody.

> Calme was the day, and through the trembling ayre
> Sweete breathing Zephyrus did softly play,
> A gentle spirit, that lightly did delay
> Hot Titans beames, which then did glyster fayre:
> When I, whom sullein care,
> Through discontent of my long fruitlesse stay
> In princes court, and expectation vayne
> Of idle hopes, which still doe fly away,
> Like empty shaddowes, did aflict my brayne,
> Walkt forth to ease my payne
> Along the shoare of silver streaming Themmes;
> Whose rutty bancke, the which his river hemmes,
> Was paynted all with variable flowers,
> And all the meades adornd with daintie gemmes,
> Fit to decke maydens bowres,
> And crowne their paramours,
> Against the brydale day, which is not long:
> Sweete Themmes, runne softly, till I end my song.

Nor did he ever recover from the humiliation of his early failure in public life—a failure which seems to have been predetermined in his youth by imprudent public utterance at the time when his hopes were highest. The very imprudence of *Mother Hubbard's Tale* has something characteristic of the idealist in it, such an idealist as has often been the helpless fool of mean and selfish politicians. Later attempts to redeem his failure with the help of his incomparable performances in literature came to naught; and I see in him a man whose worldly ambitions were continually at war with his sense of their unworthiness and his appreciation of higher values. He longed for conspicuous position, while he knew its real worth in spiritual terms. This, I believe, is the second of the moral issues that dominate the *Faery Queen*.

This issue is interwoven with the whole fabric, appearing and reappearing in such places as the Palace of Lucifera, in the ghastly laystall of the world's greatest at the posterngate in the Cave of Mammon, and the golden chain of Philotime (a temptation, be it noted, that prostrated the good Sir Guyon as did no other), in the episode of Pollente and Munera, of Philterra and Amidas, of old Malbecco.

I read it also in the suggestions of true and solid fame—more with Spenser than a Renaissance convention—in his Gloriana, his Cleopolis, his choice of Clio as his Muse instead of Calliope, the legitimate mother of epic; for had he not read that Clio is the Muse named for κλέος, i.e., fame? Spenser never could resist an etymology. But in this instance more is involved—his ambitions, worthy and unworthy, ever at war.

A greater artistic effect, however, seems to have sprung from this issue. It appears, as I see it, in the detachment—sometimes pathetic, sometimes wistful, sometimes grim—of his great heroes. They are singularly alone, unassociated, unacclaimed, toiling along the unfrequented road to Cleopolis. Had Milton, I wonder, caught a poetic impulse from this moral value in his sage and serious Spenser, which drew forth his cadences on "the last infirmity of noble minds?"

As Spenser saw other men easily gaining the prizes that in the worldly part of himself he so passionately desired, and saw them to that end closely involved in intrigue, duplicity, and false dealing, these methods must, to one of Spenser's moral sort, have been either a matter of daily temptation, or of intense hatred. On every hand at Court and in Ireland he encountered them, and honest and confiding as he was, he suffered disillusionment after disillusionment until he distrusted all appearance. Hence everywhere in the Faery world he asserts and reasserts the moral issue between false and true. The bluff of the monsters Error and Orgoglio, of Braggadocchio, the shifting and baffling disguises of Archimago and Duessa, the undoing speciousness of Lucifera, and Phaedria, and Acrasia, and Despair, the host of "such malengine and fine forgerie" as Dolon, and Guizor, and Guile, Malice, and Despite, the archenemies of Mercilla—and many more. Everywhere this motive runs, but is most sustained in the story and counter-story of the true and the false Florimel—false Florimel who proved everyone a victim to mere appearances but the great Britomart.

No wonder Spenser exclaims:

> What man so wise, what earthly witt so ware
> As to discry the crafty cunning traine,
> By which Deceipt doth maske in visour faire,
> And cast her coulours, died deepe in graine,
> To seeme like Truth, whose shape she well can faine,
> And fitting gestures to her purpose frame,
> The guiltlesse man with guile to entertaine?

Then as the years dragged on, soul-weary with disappointment, with disillusionment, with the heart-sickening situation in Ireland, Spenser comes to grips with the depression that weighs down his soul; and as the brave pageant moves by, one catches the recurring undersong of despondency:

> Blisse may not abide in state of mortall men.
>
> Nothing is sure that growes on earthly grownd.
>
> So feeble is mans state, and life unsound.
>
> Nothing on earth mote alwaies happy beene.
>
> For who will bide the burden of distresse
> Must not here thinke to live: for life is wretchednesse.
>
> Here on earth is no sure happinesse.
>
> Litle sweet
> Oft tempred is . . . with muchell smart.
>
> What on earth can always happie stand?
> The greater prowesse greater perils find.
>
> O why doe wretched men so much desire
> To draw their dayes unto the utmost date,
> And doe not rather wish them soone expire,
> Knowing the miserie of their estate,
> And thousand perills which them still awate,

> Tossing them like a boate amid the mayne,
> That every houre they knocke at Deathes gate?

Pageant after pageant is disrupted by brute force, or fate, and dissolves into naught, like the exquisite idylls in the Sixth Book. One embodiment of depression succeeds another like Despair, Amavia, the weeping nymph, the Garden of Proserpina; and the malady invades even the exalted souls of Britomart and Arthur.

The reason why the Seven Deadly Sins are no more than seven is doubtless a pretty reason. Yet, like the seven stars, they once were eight, and the missing sin, Tristitia, chronic despondency, points another of the moral issues in the poet's soul and in his poem.

Small wonder if such a man should lean more and more to Heraclitus, should see about him a mutable and unstable world, wherein all is in flux, and naught shall abide; that he should, in his spiritual warfare, join this issue repeatedly throughout his poem and eventually design a whole Book on the theme.

It was and had been a common theme of mediæval and Renaissance art, but Spenser resumes it with a frequency, especially towards the end, that implies deep and warm conviction. It reaches its culmination in the superb fragment of Mutability, who in all earthly things

> Beares the greatest sway:
> Which makes me loath this state of life so tickle,
> And love of things so vaine to cast away;
> Whose flowring pride, so fading and so fickle,
> Short Time shall soon cut down with his consuming sickle.

Not only his shattered ambitions but his long years amid the insecure conditions of a half-civilized frontier, and his foreboding of the terrible storm of rebellion that eventually swept him away to poverty and death, bore in upon him the conviction that all earthly things are fleeting.

These, then, would appear to be the moral issues within the soul of the idealist Spenser—sensuality over against idealized love or Chastity; worldly ambition over against high, honorable, and chivalrous dealing; despondency and despair in a fluctuating world over against cheerful security in a sense of Absolute Goodness and Beauty.

In two explicit arraignments of public life in his time Spenser indicts the age and the Court for lust, greed, ambition, envy and malice,

violent and sudden anger, and specious pretence. Of certain of these we
have already observed the counterpart in his own moral problem. Two
others of them at least preoccupied him as vices of his time—Violence
and Slander.

This habit of sudden, violent, disruptive temper which he saw on
every side of him—in the daily quarrels of such men as Essex, and Oxford, and even his own friend Raleigh, in the bloodstained violence of
Shan Oneall and his kind, he must have viewed as a barbaric obstacle
to civility and the realization of a great imperial England.

> Firebrand of hell, first tynd in Phlegeton
> By thousand furies, and from thence out throwen
> Into this world, to worke confusion
> And set it all on fire by force unknowen.

The motive is ubiquitous in the *Faery Queen* from the first sudden,
dangerous indignations of the Red Cross Knight to the rage of the
Blatant Beast at the close.

Envy, too, and Slander he clearly suffered both on his own behalf
and on behalf of his friends, since these were inescapable in political life
then—if one may say that they have ceased to be since. That he hated
them with a white-hot hatred none can doubt. You will recall that the
arch-enemy of Calidore, the Knight of Courtesy, is not an obvious opponent—Boorishness, or Violence, or Savagery—but the Blatant Beast,
which imports envious Slander, who after Calidore had subdued and
bound him, broke his bonds, and escaped.

> So now he raungeth through the world againe.

Invidious Slander is also the last foe of Justice. In the moment of
his supreme triumph Artegall is beleaguered by two Irish hags, Envy
and Detraction, and the Blatant Beast. And his death is foretold "by
practise criminal of secret foes."

The poet's hatred of this monster never sleeps. Consider the terrible
sonnet against one who had slandered him to his lady-love:

> Venemous toung, tipt with vile adders sting,
> Of that selfe kynd with which the Furies fell
> Theyr snaky heads doe combe, from which a spring
> Of poysoned words and spitefull speeches well,
> Let all the plagues and horrid paines of hell

> Upon thee fall for thine accursed hyre,
> That with false forged lyes, which thou didst tel,
> In my true love did stirre up coles of yre.

These simple, and perhaps obvious, antinomies—critical and dangerous in the poet's spiritual life, and, as he thought, in England, mingle with the whole fabric of the *Faery Queen.*

The First Book is a fair illustration. No theoretical or abstract Aristotelian virtue is the Red Cross Knight. He is almost autobiographical. His whole story is the story of a struggle towards virtue very much like that of Spenser himself.

Spenser was already engaged on his First Book during his twenties, in the heyday of his youthful hopes, and doubtless finished it while still a young man. Meanwhile he learned about women from Rosalind, or whomever; his aspirations as a man of the world burgeoned, broke into luxuriant bloom, under the favor of Sidney, Leicester, and the Queen, and then suddenly faded and fell. He found himself in Ireland—as it were, in the Philippines, Balkans, Anatolia—for an indefinite stay, and with leisure to make what moral character and poetry he could out of his disillusionments.

The gentle knight who comes pricking o'er the plain into the first stanza of the First Book is a wholly inexperienced young man. He is an Englishman, with the blood of Saxon kings in his breeding, but wholesomely combined with a boyhood and youth spent close to the soil in a farmer's household. Spenser, in so presenting him, could hardly, I suppose, have been thinking of his own aristocratic origin and bourgeois youth. The hero of the story, with all the winsome enthusiasm of a high-spirited and well-bred lad, throws himself into his career. There is a girl—a lovely creature, one among all women for her purity and sweetness and fidelity, but not of the sort that makes a furore among men. The young man does not at once fall deeply in love with her, and indeed takes her almost casually, though her partly maternal, partly romantic interest in him no one but the lad himself can fail to see.

His first adventure is a fight with the monster Error, a gruesome and filthy she-dragon in the direct literary line that stretches from Grendel's dam to the Jabberwock. But what kind of Error is this? For all the commentators say, it might be just plain Error in general, if such there be. But how, one might ask, if the Red Cross Knight first overcomes Error in general, does he fall into so much error later on? Ruskin seems to be right, however, when he finds a clue in the not very tidy line, "Her vomit full of bookes and papers was." Clearly this is Error of doctrine, of books, multiclamorous cant, and evil counsel, which din in the ears of every young person during the period of his education. The fight is vigorous, but not doubtful. The young man is proof by very breeding against silly and specious ideas from whatever authority. He refutes them by a sort of habit and instinct. They fall naturally from his mind. Such Error is easily vanquished. But the harder task remains to validate and prove the truth of his experience.

And he has not long to wait, for here comes a gentle inoffensive old man, whom the Red Cross Knight addresses with just a trace of assurance caught partly from his first easy triumph and partly from the girl's admiring congratulation on his success. But the old man is a Deceiver, to wit the notorious Archimage, and he imposes upon the ingenuous but self-assured young person with pathetic ease. A series of cleverly managed misrepresentations deceive the young man, and he falls out with the woman who is the mainstay of his life, yet whom he does not really know. He then picks up with a more intriguing female—to all appearances more desirable, as the world desires. What is more, he wins her by his personal prowess from another man.

I notice two very natural touches in Spenser's narrative at this point. First, in a fit of righteous indignation, and with something of the absolute downrightness of youth,

> His eie of reason was with rage yblent.

Then he deserts Una without any attempt to explore the matter. Thus he wanders aimlessly far away.

> Still flying from his thoughts and gealous feare:
> Will was his guide, and griefe led him astray.

Clearly he misses not Una so much as he resents—with a touch of youthful selfishness perhaps—the reflection which her apparent infidelity casts upon his dignity.

Such grief is easily dispelled the moment a popular woman shows interest in him, especially if, as in this case, she drops another man to take him up. She is too artful to try to capture him with gaiety. She appeals to his warm but unseasoned heart as one in sad plight, "friendlesse, unfortunate."

Soon they are engrossed in a flirtation, which for him is innocent and most consoling. Forgotten are his troubles, forgotten is Una, forgotten his career, forgotten all but the present delicious moment, when they are interrupted by a fantastic episode that would have put him on his guard against this dangerous but delightful girl, had she not quickly played her highest trump-card and fainted in his arms.

Clearly, she sees, he needs something to take his attention—something engrossing. She introduces him into Society, that is, to the Palace of Pride, a Renaissance Court, the beau-monde—by whatever name it is the same perennial thing, gorgeous, ostentatious, unsubstantial, thronged, fickle, yet fascinating. Everybody is there—at least everybody that counts —all agog for the favor of her who is arbitress of their social success. Of course there is a deal of iniquity beneath this gorgeous spectacle, but the callow young knight cannot yet discern it. He finds himself at once a social favorite. Why not? He is young, able, handsome, has already scored at least two conspicuous successes, and his natural charm suffers nothing by a certain ingenuousness, the basic ingredient in many a social triumph. All this is pleasant enough for a time. At length he happens to fall foul of a quarrelsome gentleman named Sans Joy, who will take it out of him, willy nilly. But the Lady Lucifera, the social leader, with an eye single to successful social events, stops the impromptu fight, and turns it into a society affair. She stages a magnificent duel for her guests. Though his opponent escapes defeat by a trick, the Red Cross Knight gains the credit of a victory, and enormous vogue for the moment.

But something is queer about this place. Even he sees that, though he is not discerning enough to explain the rather inscrutable behavior of his lady Duessa, who is really playing a double game. Meanwhile with a lurking instinct quite natural in a well-bred youth, that this is no place or company for him, he stumbles upon the reverse view of the whole situation—the broken hearts and bitter thrall that have overtaken all who devoted themselves to this kind of success. Such are Croesus, Nimrod, Sulla, Tarquin, Cleopatra, nay heroes like Alexander, Scipio, Hannibal, and the great Julius himself.

I confess I can never read these passages without reflections upon Spenser's own ever-recurring illusion and disillusion of like kind. But after his quiet escape what? Nothing. He has no aim apparently beyond sitting in a pleasant spot luxuriating in the loveliness about him. The lady, whom he has deserted in somewhat the same inconsiderate fashion of his parting from Una, will not let him off so easily. She overtakes him, and with pretty reproaches reduces him again to helpless subjection. Idly he stoops to refresh himself with a draft from a shady spring.

> Eftsoones his manly forces gan to fayle,
> And mightie strong was turned to feeble frayle
> His chaunged powres at first them selves not felt,
> Till crudled cold his corage gan assayle,
> And chearefull blood in fayntnes chill did melt,
> Which, like a fever fit, through all his body swelt.

> Yet goodly court he made still to his dame,
> Pourd out in loosnesse on the grassy grownd,
> Both carelesse of his health, and of his fame.

The situation is clear. He has had nothing thus far but success and popularity and attention. True he lost his first lady Una, but that was her fault, he thought, and he has suffered little wrong but injured pride. Now he is without a purpose, without vision or inspiration. He is unaware of what he has lost in Una, grows self-gratulatory and impotent, and easily falls prey to the least formidable of his adversaries, the braggart Orgoglio. Captive in the dungeon of this giant he has leisure to review his course and realize his plight. But if he has to all appearances failed by trusting too much his own powers, ever vigilant and devoted Una has not relaxed her efforts to save him. Arthur comes to her aid, overcomes Orgoglio, forces the dungeon, and she rescues the hero in the last stages of depression over his failure.

Now he sees the real devotion of Una and beholds, stripped of all her blandishments, Duessa and all her kind. May I call attention here to a rather exquisite touch in Spenser's narrative? When Una, overjoyed, reclaims her hero, not a thought of blame enters her mind. With almost maternal partiality she excuses all that has happened:

> Ah, dearest lord! what evill starre
> On you hath frownd, and pourd his influence bad,
> That of your selfe ye thus berobbed arre,
> And this misseeming hew your manly looks doth marre?

> But welcome now, my lord, in wele or woe,
> Whose presence I have lackt too long a day;

> And fye on Fortune, mine avowed foe,
> Whose wrathful wreakes them selves doe now alay,
> And for these wronges shall treble penaunce pay
> Of treble good: good growes of evils priefe.

The Red Cross Knight in shamed realization of her true worth has no word to utter. But his full sense of his own defection is yet to come. As it grows upon him, he is face to face with Despair. And though he enters upon this deepest and most subtle of his trials with a trace of his old swagger, he falls quickly by the specious reasoning of guilty depression into such deep and agonizing remorse that he madly rushes upon suicide. In the very act Una again saves him.

> Out of his hand she snatcht the cursed knife,
> And threw it to the ground, enraged rife,
> And to him said: "Fie, fie, faint hearted knight!
> What meanest thou by this reprochfull strife?
> Is this the battaile, which thou vauntst to fight?"

With faultless sense of his predicament she forces him from contemplation of a miserable and hopeless past to consider the redeemable future in service to her. And he is saved forever.

Rightly enough expositors have interpreted this episode and the whole Book as an illustration of Spenser's Platonic faith in the power of pure and noble love to redeem the soul of man. But to me it is something more than Platonic; it is Spenserian. Spenser has authenticated the exalted teaching of Diotima in the *Symposium,* nay of the Gospels themselves, through his own struggle in the clash of noble and ignoble in his own soul. The last cantos, especially the tenth and twelfth, ring with the sound conviction of one who knows these things because he has lived them.

Only one episode remains. Out of his recovery he rises with Una or superhuman Truth at his side to a vision of supreme values, to a point whence he beholds all things human in their true light and relationship. Henceforth he is established, mature, reliable, and betrothed forever to her who is above all lovely, faithful, and good. In her service his real career begins just as the Book closes.

The Age of Elizabeth presents certain strong analogies with our own time and land. Like ours it was parvenu.

Within a century England had become a new country—as new as

ours. The old order had perished in complete revolution. Old feudal society had crumbled under the strong hand of the Tudors. The old faith had been superseded. The old monastic and ecclesiastical order had been abolished. Everyone in England was affected, profoundly affected, by the change. A parvenu family was on the throne, and a new theory of absolutism prevailed. Even the aristocracy was new, and with the strong reassertion of individualism careers were open to all talents that could command them. But as in Italy, so in Tudor England such careers lay open primarily through the Court and the Prince's favor. Plungers and adventurers abounded. The game, with sudden and incredible wealth or power as its prize, flattered men into venturing all. The world flocked to London. The sensational or brilliant rise and fall at Court was an almost everyday occurrence. All things were possible. Our young men seek success in the west or south; the young Elizabethan dreamed of it at all four receding points of the compass. Luxury and dissipation increased with wealth. So did ostentation. So did extravagance. The reins fell slack upon the mad passions of men. High as Elizabethan achievement often rose, yet with it went intrigue, trickery, scandal, envy, and all questionable practice. Graft was almost universal, and easily condoned. Men boasted, quarrelled, and broke into lawless violence. Of such times the *Faery Queen* is the faithful mirror.

Elizabethan England was not only parvenu, but it was conscious through increasing intercourse with Italy and the rest of the world of its provincialism. Hence perhaps the lively discussion of theories of education and manners during the century, and the number of works bearing thereupon of which Elyot's, Lyly's, Ascham's, Hoby's, and Mulcaster's are most conspicuous. The *Faery Queen* too was clearly regarded by Spenser as such a work—a work to help civilize Englishmen, to make of the imperfect England about him the great imperial England which he and his associates envisioned. Such transformation must be moral. It must work with the individual. Of this he was sure. Sir Philip Sidney in his *Defence* so maintains, and so doubtless did Spenser in his lost treatise on poetry. So he clearly states in his *View of the Present State of Ireland*, where the talk falls upon the Irish Bards:

I have reade that in all ages Poets have beene had in speciall reputation, and that (me thinkes) not without great cause; for besides their sweete inventions, and most wittie layes, they have alwayes used to set foorth the praises of the good and vertuous, and to beate downe and disgrace the bad and vitious. So that many brave young mindes, have oftentimes thorough hearing the praises and famous eulogies of worthie men sung and reported unto them, beene stirred up to affect the like commendations, and so to strive to the like deserts. [And Irenaeus (Spenser) rejoins] It is most true, that such Poets as in their writings doe labour to better the manners of men, and thorough the sweete baite of their numbers, to steale into the young spirits a desire of honour and vertue, are worthy to bee had in great respect.

"To steale into the young spirits a desire of honour and vertue." "To entice," as he said years before—"To entice with pleasance of his vein." Not by bald precept nor by neat admonition, but by enchantment through ear, eye, fancy, mind, to capture the imaginations of men, and release in their souls, thus made susceptible, moral forces effectual for their regeneration, and for the regeneration through them of their times.

The young Britomart, destined to mother great England, began her high career "by a vision." As she gazed into the enchanted glass of Merlin, she beheld, as she supposed, the image of her lover-to-be, the heroic knight of Justice, Artegall. In reality she beheld herself, for this enchanted glass is but the Platonic mirror of the *Phaedrus,* in which the lover "beholds himself, but he is not aware of this." Nay it hath power

> to shew in perfect sight
> What ever thing was in the world contaynd
> Betwixt the lowest earth and hevens hight . . . .
> Forthy it round and hollow shaped was,
> Like to the world it selfe, and seemed a world of glas.

Such is the enchanted glass of the *Faery Queen.* As we gaze and meditate upon its shifting pageant, its lights and shadows, its images of passion and heroic magnitude of mind, we gain truer intimations of moral values than we can seize groping amid the noise, dust, and confusion of the actual world. In this enchanted glass of the poet we discern the image of Spenser himself, of his world, of *the* world, nay, of ourselves, of much perhaps that he did not there see himself. He would have been the first to approve. For such heightened and corrected vision —heightened and corrected by long contemplation—is one of this poet's peculiar gifts, and one which has made him a begetter of poets.

Unsubstantial and ineffectual all this pageant, were it not informed with the moral energies generated in the poet's warfare with evil in himself and his time.

As subtle, as powerful, as pervasive as this, seems to me the moral element in the *Faery Queen*. And who—critic or scholar—can ever measure its fulfilment of the poet's intention during these last three centuries and more, or for all time to come?

TWELVE

B. E. C. DAVIS

Romance (1933)*

Humanism and Romanticism imply two distinct modes of consciousness and expression. The humanist imparts significant form to objects perceived with detachment; the romantic, identifying self with object, represents concepts of the associative imagination. To the humanists of the Renaissance classical antiquity stood for a composite civilisation, an intelligible whole; but the Middle Ages were barbarous, intangible, meaningless, an opinion that appeared to be fully confirmed by the most typical of mediæval literary monuments. For chivalric romance, from its origin, reflected the artificiality of the society which had created it and to which it was addressed. The replacement of primitive *comitatus* by Douzeperes and Round Table, of the *Volsungasaga* and the *Chanson de Roland* by the *Nibelungenlied* and *The Four Sons of Amon* meant the dilution of ancient epos to suit the taste of a feudal community; and the universal popularity of romantic tales among all classes quickly opened the way to every sort of commonplace absurdity and extravagance. The minstrel scored his success not by apt presentation of the age and body of the time but by skill in the invention and refurbishing of monsters and marvels utterly remote from human experience. The incredible fictions, the unnatural setting and disorderly conduct of romance in its dotage contravened every principle of classic decorum.

With good reason, therefore, Thomas Nashe could follow the lead of Montaigne in fulminating against "worne out impressions of the feyned no where acts of Arthur of the rounde table, Arthur of litle

---

* Reprinted from *Edmund Spenser: A Critical Study*, pp. 78-99.

Brittaine, Sir Tristram, Hewon of Burdeaux, the Squire of low degree, the foure sons of Amon." [1] Others, like Vives, Roger Ascham and Francis Meres, based their objection chiefly upon moral grounds. But none the less these "worn out absurdities" continued to divert a large public and to supply material for heroic poetry throughout the Renaissance era. A typical specimen is *Amadis of Gaul,* originally a Portuguese product of the fourteenth century, which enjoyed an immense vogue up to the time of Sir Philip Sidney and, together with two other works, survived the conflagration of Don Quixote's library. With *Amadis* as chief exemplar of its kind, it is not surprising that Italian poets of the new school, with the logical and critical instinct of their race, showed scant reverence for their romance originals. Luigi Pulci (1432-84) amused the wits of Medicean Florence with the burlesque fable and low comedy of his *Morgante Maggiore.* At Ferrara romance fared better, as a thing of beauty which, though faded, was worthy of retention. Count Matteo Maria Boiardo (1434-94) founded the plot of his *Orlando Innamorato* upon the rival suits of Orlando and Rinaldo for Angelica, a typically romantic situation of conflict between love and honour. Lodovico Ariosto (1474-1533), whose *Orlando Furioso* nominally completed the unfinished *Orlando Innamorato,* shifted the interest to the fortunes of Ruggiero and Bradamante, traditional ancestors of his patron, Cardinal Ippolito d'Este. Both Boiardo and Ariosto fully appreciate the bravery and fine sentiment of their theme; but the romantic illusion serves them only as fair game for the exercise of poetic fantasy. They refuse to believe in it, to quit solid earth in pursuit of shadows. Boiardo's hero is in love, and this is sufficient to make him slightly ridiculous. To Ariosto, for all his moralising and mock gravity, the main argument is irresistibly comic, a wild-goose chase after an impossibly elusive heroine, admitting endless wonders and wizardry by way of diversion. Romance, so sceptically treated, is three parts on the way towards mock heroic. The alternative, in Italy, was romantic epic, first attempted by Trissino in his tedious *Italia Liberata* (1547-8) and finally brought to perfection by Tasso, whose *Gerusalemme Liberata* (1581) provided a pattern for all subsequent work of the same kind.

But in England the *chanson de geste* was a native heritage, transmitted by direct line from the Anglo-Norman writers of the twelfth century. Arthur, Lancelot, Bevis, Guy, and a score of others still held their own, and had even gained ground since the invention of printing.

The first Christian worthy was a British prince, still venerated as the national hero and therefore ranking in a class apart from foreign rivals like Orlando or Godfrey, whose chief claim to recognition lay in their legendary repute as champions of the true religion. Elizabeth and her court could draw the analogy between their princely pleasures and the tourneys of the Round Table; but the real strength of Arthurian romance lay in the familiarity which for generations had endeared it to the masses.

Among all Spenser's originals the place of honour must be assigned to Malory's *Morte Darthur*, that "booke of Chevalrie" which, despite the objections of pedant and Puritan, preserved the most complete record not merely of the hero himself but, as Caxton reminds his readers, of all the finer elements of antique usage:

And I accordyng to my copye have doon sette it in enprynte, to the entente that noble men may see and lerne the noble actes of chyvalrye, the ientyl and vertuous dedes that somme knyghtes used in tho dayes, by whyche they came to honour, and how they that were vycious were punysshed and ofte put to shame and rebuke; humbly bysechyng al noble lordes and ladyes wyth al other estates of what estate or degree they been of, that shal see and rede in this sayd book and werke, that they take the good and honest actes in their remembraunce, and to folowe the same. Wherin they shalle fynde many Ioyous and playsaunt hystoryes, and noble and renomed actes of humanyte, gentylnesse and chyvalryes. For herein may be seen noble chyvalrye, Curtosye, Humanyte, frendlynesse, hardynesse, love, frendshyp, Cowardyse, Murdre, hate, vertue and synne. Doo after the good and leve the evyl, and it shal brynge you to good fame and renommee.

The proximity between these reflections and the ethic of *The Faerie Queene* is so close as to suggest that Spenser planned his allegory with Caxton's preface in mind, admitting within his scheme the virtue of Courtesy, which he could not have found in Plato or Aristotle. True, in the unmoral world of old romance, of lawless love self-justified in scorn of consequence, the issue between right and wrong with due assignment of reward or punishment is hardly so plain and direct as Caxton would infer. But his defence of "noble chyvalrye" carries more weight than Ascham's attack upon its "bold Bawdry," and won a better following. In the history of Arthur, Spenser, like Sidney, could find nothing to displease a soldier, but rather the very mirror of nobility, the pure heroic mettle without fear or reproach, unsullied by custom and unshattered by abuse. The sinewy strength of authentic romance, rarely recaptured by the Italian poets, springs spontaneously from the naïve, pregnant English of Malory:

> And soo the knyght arose up hastely and putte his helme upon his hede, and gat a grete spere in his hand, and without ony moo wordes he hurled unto sir Tristram, and smote hym clene from his sadel to the erthe, and hurte hym on the lyfte syde that sir Tristram lay in grete perylle. Thenne he wallopped ferther, and fette his cours, and came hurlynge upon sir Palomydes.
>
> And thenne he tooke hym a scarlet cote so that shold be in stede of his sherte, tyll he had fulfylled the quest of the Sancgreal; and the good man fond hym in soo merveillous a lyfe, and soo stable, that he merveilled and felte that he was never corrupte in flesshely lustes.[2]

Spenser, in comparison, is diffuse and artificial; but at points of dramatic climax he is often nearer to Malory than to Ariosto:

> So stoutly he withstood their strong assay;
> Till that at last, when he advantage spyde,
> His poynant speare he thrust with puissant sway
> At proud Cymochles, whiles his shield was wyde,
> That through his thigh the mortall steele did gryde:
> He, swarving with the force, within his flesh
> Did breake the launce, and let the head abyde.
> Out of the wound the red blood flowed fresh,
> That underneath his feet soone made a purple plesh.[3]

The similarity extends from diction to tone, suggesting kinship of mind, a common attitude towards a common theme.

This community of spirit is more significant than any specific borrowings; for so freely does Spenser adapt his material that it is impossible to determine precisely the extent of his debt to any one original. As the invincible knight-errant, Prince Arthur resembles his namesake in *Arthur of Little Britain;* and the conception of a "faery knight" was authorised through his traditional association with the ladies of the lake, his departure to Avalon and the popular report, preserved by Malory, that he was yet alive and would one day return. But his career prior to his accession is briefly dismissed by most of the earlier romancers. Spenser follows Malory in stating that the hero, after being taken from his parents in infancy, was entrusted to the care of a guardian ("Ector" in Malory, "Timon" in Spenser), and to the tutelage of Merlin, who endows him with supernatural power; but the suitor of Gloriana is substantially a new invention. Merlin is the child of a nun, seduced by a spirit, as stated by Geoffrey of Monmouth. He meets his end, as in Malory, through the guile of a false lady of the lake, but is "buried under beare" and inhabits the underground cave of enchantment before and not after he has met his doom. Spenser again follows Malory in his account of Tristram's ancestry and early career, but makes nothing of the more important part of the story. The familiar motive of knight and dame bound upon the same quest, parted through misunderstanding or treachery and finally reunited, occurs in the tales of Gareth and of Geraint, though it might equally well have been suggested by the episode of Olympia and Bireno in Ariosto. The "wylde man" who beneath a churlish exterior hides a noble heart is a commonplace of Renaissance fiction, anticipated, however, by Malory's Balen in his retort to the disdainful damsel:

Worthynes and good tatches and good dedes are not only in arrayment, but manhood and worship is hyd within mans persone and many a worshipful knyghte is not knowen unto all people, and therfore worship and hardynesse is not in arayment.[4]

The castle of Radigund resembles the castle of maidens assailed by Galahad and both maintain a similar "wicked custom." The episode of Crudor and Briana probably derives from Malory's story of King Ryence, who, after working himself a mantle from the beards of Arthur's knights, demanded that of the King himself for its completion. The Blatant Beast is Malory's "Questing Beast," "that hadde in shap a hede lyke a serpentes hede, and a body lyke a lybard, buttocks lyke a lyon, and foted lyke an herte, and in his body there was such a noyse as hit had ben the noyse of thyrtty coupel of houndes questyng, and such a noyse that beest made where somever he wente."[5] Finally, Malory supplies such names as Placidas, Pelleas, Pellenore, Percivall, Joyous Gard, all redolent of romantic suggestion.

Besides *Le Morte Darthur* the common stock of romance, with which Spenser was well acquainted, provided him with abundant material. Most of the chronicle canto (II, x) and of Merlin's prophecy concerning Britomart's offspring (III, ii) comes from Geoffrey of Monmouth and the sixteenth-century historians, including Holinshed who "muche furthered and advantaged" Spenser in his "Epithalamion Thamesis." The scheme of knights-errant owing allegiance to one sovereign and setting out upon successive quests of deliverance is common to many of the cycles and may have been partly suggested by *The Seven Champions of Christendom,* which undoubtedly supplied hints for Book i. The situation of the Red Cross Knight resembles that of Libeaus Desconus, the original of Gareth, while the adaptation of this motive to an allegory of the Christian's pilgrimage to salvation had already been attempted by Stephen Hawes in his *Pastime of Pleasure.* Cambell and Canacee come from *The Squire's Tale,* completed through the invention of a lover for Canacee and the introduction of a favourite romantic *motif,* the sealing of eternal friendship between two mortal foes meeting in combat. *The Parliament of Fowls,* possibly also its original, the *De Planctu Naturæ* of Alain de l'Isle, gave suggestions for the trial of Mutability and the pageant of seasons in Book vii. Huon of Bordeaux is mentioned once in connection with Guyon, though nothing is made of his relations with Oberon and the fairy train. The belt of Chastity which serves to distinguish the true from the false Florimell has several analogues. In *The Boy and the Mantle* a mantle fulfils the same function at Arthur's court; in the fable of *The Wright's Chaste Wife* the lady's fidelity is vindicated by means of a magic girdle; and at the conclusion of *Gawain and the Green Knight* the hero's peers agree to wear green belts in token of his victory over temptation.

But for particular details Spenser stands far more deeply indebted to Ariosto and Tasso than to any single mediæval author. The episodes, images and phrases which he has adapted from the former are so numerous as to suggest that *Orlando Furioso* was open at his side while he was penning his work; and though his debt to *Gerusalemme Liberata* is mainly confined within certain episodes, particularly that of Armida, the influence of Tasso's glowing and coloured descriptions was sufficient to enable Fairfax, when translating Tasso, often to do little more than reproduce Spenser. But though Spenser derived from Tasso the idea of an allegorical romance his ethic differs fundamentally from Tasso's militant Catholicism, while from Ariosto, in spirit, he is worlds apart. Purporting to be a serious poem of love and chivalry presented through a succession of diverting scenes, the *Orlando Furioso* is dominated by the imp of mischief and mockery. Throughout one-third of it the nominal hero, driven desperate at the news of his lady's infidelity, cuts the ludicrous figure of a maniac rending his clothes, uprooting trees, stealing horses, slaying their owners and performing such impossible feats as swimming the Straits of Gibraltar. Ruggiero, the principal character, in the fourth book is abruptly separated from the heroine by a flying hippogryph and transported to Alcina's enchanted island. Astolfo, having neither razor nor scissors to cut the lock of hair that confers immortality upon Orrilo, holding the severed head of the magician by the nose, shears the lock with his sword. And through all this comedy sparkles the irony of the poet's grave reflections and assurance. How fortunate were the old-time cavaliers who could find in deserts, caves and forests ladies of such beauty as cannot now be seen in palaces! The wonderful tales which Turpin related of Ruggiero he knew to be true, but you must believe as you list. Achilles, Æneas and the rest owe their renown not to their own merits but to the generosity of their descendants, to the villas and palaces presented to poets who, as everyone knows, are the greatest of liars.

Such levity, the very life and soul of the *Orlando Furioso,* is incompatible with the aim and temperament of Spenser, who will often adapt Ariosto's mocking sallies to his own serious purpose. The reconciliation between Guyon and Britomart at the opening of Book III calls forth a eulogy of ancient chivalry freely translated from a stanza in the first canto of *Orlando Furioso.* But the difference in situation is characteristic. Whereas Guyon abandons the fight solely at the instigation of Prince Arthur and Palmer, Rinaldo and Ferrau compose their differences for the very good reason that the lady for whom they are fighting has vanished. The praise of woman and of her heroic achievements, which serves to introduce the legend of Britomart, derives from the bantering preamble to the account of Orontea and her domain, in which ten men are allowed to every hundred women. Ariosto's admonition to the squeamish reader of the Host's very merry tale (*Orlando Furioso,* xxviii), which is on a par with Chaucer's similar apology for his churls, inspires the introduction to the tragic history of Malbecco and Hellenore.

But despite fundamental difference in temper Spenser's debt to the *Orlando Furioso* is profound and far-reaching. Artegall and Britomart are modelled on Ruggiero and Bradamante, and both pairs of lovers are encouraged to pursue their adventures by prophecies of their ultimate union and glorious progeny, in the one case the D'Este family, in the other the Tudor dynasty. Guyon's temporary submission to the charms of Phædria recalls Ruggiero's sojourn at the island of Alcina, the original of the Bower of Bliss. Alcina, like Acrasia, treats her victims with Circean hospitality and, when unmasked, proves hideous and deformed as Duessa. Astolfo, like Fradubio, transformed into a tree discovers himself at the wounding of the bark, though here Spenser adds a dramatic touch by allowing the enchantress Duessa to be present and to overhear the recounting of her victim's wrongs. Radigund and her realm are suggested by Orontea and her Amazons. Braggadochio, the one purely comic figure in *The Faerie Queene,* is much nearer the norm of Ariosto than of Spenser, and all the main details respecting him—the horse-stealing that leads to his advancement, his boastfulness, cowardice and final "uncasing"—are paralleled in *Orlando Furioso.* The adventures of the Squire of Dames in the performance of his vow form a milder version of the host's tale of Giocondo. Trompart is another Pinabello. Most of Spenser's supernatural machinery comes from the same source. Arthur's shield and horn, Artegall's sword, Chrysaor, and Britomart's magic lance have the same virtues as the shield of Atlante, the horn presented by Logistilla to Astolfo and the lance of Bradamante. "Briga-dore" is an anglicised version of "Briglia d' oro," the name of Orlando's horse.[6]

The parallel extends to language and imagery. Guyon attacks two knights simultaneously, like a ship rolled by two contrary waves. Satyrane restrains the monster pursuing Florimell as a husbandman dams a sudden flood. Talus defends Artegall against an unruly mob like hawk descending upon a "flush of Ducks." Irena, learning of her deliverance, revives like a withered rose at the first drops of rain. Malbecco, watching the satyrs around Hellenore and finding himself cuckolded in his own demesne,

> out of the bush
> Upon his handes and feete he crept full light,
> And like a Gote emongst the Gotes did rush;
> That, through the helpe of his faire hornes on hight,
> And misty dampe of misconceyving night,
> And eke through likenesse of his gotish beard,
> He did the better counterfeite aright.[7]

For all these and many like figures Ariosto gave the suggestion; and though comparison affords good evidence of his brevity beside Spenser's diffuseness the adaptation is often little more than free translation. If any one work may be described as the original of *The Faerie Queene* it is the *Orlando Furioso,* Spenser's first model, as we learn from his correspondence with Harvey, duly honoured along with the ancient epics in his prefatory letter and transparently imitated in each of the six legends.

While Ariosto had fully exploited the possibilities of chivalric romance as theme for narrative poetry Tasso refined upon the work of his uninspired predecessor, Trissino, in imparting to his romantic material the solidity of an heroic poem fashioned after conventional design. The *Gerusalemme Liberata* is a regularly constructed epic, consisting of one continuous action to which all digressions are directly related; and the religious object which inspired it impels a high seriousness of tone more akin to that of *The Faerie Queene* than of *Orlando Furioso.* But Tasso's fidelity to classic authority forbade the intrusion of much romantic commonplace freely admitted by Ariosto and Spenser. There is a world of difference between the apparition of angels or devils as ministers of grace or disaster to a crusader and, on the other hand, the astonishing array of dragons, orcs, monsters and phantoms which people Ariosto's kingdom of nonsense; between an epic strictly observing the traditional laws of design and a romance of Faerie in which time and space count for nothing. Reverencing the heroic spirit and fine sentiment of romance, Tasso had no use for its irresponsibility, for the pursuit of the quaint or fantastic on its account. His burden is not

> Le donne, i cavalier, l' arme, gli amori,
> Le cortesie, l' audici imprese,

"of Knights and Ladies gentle deeds," "of Faerie Knights, and fayrest Tanaquill," but

> l' armi pietose, e 'l Capitano,
> Che 'l gran Sepolcro liberò di Cristo.

The first concern of his heroes is neither amorous adventure nor the pursuit of virtue, but a crusade on behalf of true religion.

Temperamentally Spenser had not a little in common with Tasso, whose epic is specifically cited in the legend of Friendship.[8] Both were idealists with a profound sense of spiritual values, thwarted outwardly by circumstance and inwardly by a restlessness of disposition which, in

the case of Tasso, bordered on insanity. Whilst Ariosto could supply
Spenser with copious fine material his poem is totally lacking in the
gravity essential to an allegory of virtue, and this defect Tasso made
good. His heroes are no carpet cavaliers seizing the present moment to
gratify their passing fancies but, like Spenser's, stout champions united
in their devotion to a common object. His women likewise—Erminia,
Clorinda, the warrior maid, won to the truth through love, even the
enchantress Armida—are more closely related to Una, Britomart or Belphœbe than to any of Ariosto's volatile damsels. Without slavishly following either of his Italian masters Spenser could learn from them both.
The Faerie Queene combines the exuberance and irresponsibility of
Ariosto's romantic medley with the austere solemnity of Tasso's sacred
epic. In Spenser we miss the intimacy of Ariosto, who is continually
obtruding himself, nudging his readers and chuckling at his characters.
On the other hand his Muse works with less effort than that of Tasso,
who sacrifices something of his freedom as a poet to his admiration for
his models, particularly for the elegance and dignity of Virgil.

The first impression created by such diversity of motive and matter
is one of Gothic inconsequence rather than of classic coherence. Pigna's
note on *Orlando Furioso*—"'D' errante persone è tutta la poema"—is
still more applicable to *The Faerie Queene,* in which every character
possesses the ubiquity of Artegall,

> ne wonneth in one certeine stead,
> But restlesse walketh all the world arownd.[9]

Whereas Ariosto relates every digression and side-show to the main
design, leaving nothing unexplained, Spenser has considered neither
beginning, middle nor end of his fable, apart from the allegory to which
it is related. Guyon, or the Red Cross Knight—there is some ambiguity
as to which—turns up unexpectedly with Britomart. Calidore drops out
of the picture throughout half the legend that bears his name. Most surprising of all, Arthur offers no response to Scudamour's tale of woe
concerning the loss of Amoret when he himself, at that very moment,
has the unfortunate lady under his protection and almost within ear-
shot. Spenser has, in fact, clean forgotten Amoret, who forthwith dis-
appears from the field, unrestored to her lover.[10] The stock apparatus of
romantic fiction and drama adds further complexity and improbability.
The appearance of a phantom Florimell occasions much of the adven-

ture and intrigue in Book IV. Mistaken identity and disguising play a prominent part in the legends of Britomart and Artegall, especially in the stories of Dolon and of Samient. The pastoral interlude in Book VI, clearly influenced by *Arcadia*, perhaps also by Sidney's originals, Montemayor, Longus and Heliodorus, embodies all the traditional *motifs* of its kind—the foundling heroine, the birthmark disclosing her identity, the warrior turned shepherd, his clownish rival, the rescue of the heroine from the wild beast. In moments of crisis everyone behaves in orthodox romantic fashion. Hearing that Artegall has been worsted by a "tyrannesse," without waiting for explanations Britomart rushes to her chamber, nursing her delusion till restored balance of mind impels her to return to Talus and learn the truth. Timias, scorned by Belphœbe for infidelity, betrays his remorse by carving her name on every tree and ultimately recovers grace through the good offices of a dove which bears his jewel to its donor, the disaffected lady.

Even the principal figures of *The Faerie Queene*, though ostensibly distinguished as allegorical types, are for the most part conditioned by their romantic setting. The hero does not make the legend but evolves within it. St George is neither holier than Guyon nor less courteous than Calidore. The difference lies in presentation rather than in character, arising from the division of the fable into six distinct types of romance.

The Red Cross Knight pays the common penalty of "blameless fool" in having no mind of his own. His crudity and inexperience are stressed from the outset, when he appears as "a tall clownish younge man," seated upon the floor, "unfitte through his rusticity for a better place." With Truth herself as guide and despite her warnings, at the first provocation he accepts the advances of a suspicious-looking stranger and deserts her. Duped by Duessa, whom he continues to accompany after she has lured him into the disreputable House of Pride, he falls an easy victim to Orgoglio and would have succumbed to Despair, but for the timely aid of his mistress. Finally, after a special course of discipline at the House of Holiness, he succeeds in quelling the dragon only after three days' conflict and with the aid of magic balm. In so pale and ethereal a "Saint George of mery England, the signe of victoree" the sturdy dragon slayer of *The Golden Legend* and *The Seven Champions* is scarcely recognisable; for the interest aroused by his story depends upon neither personality nor adventure but upon the adaptation of both to an allegory of the Christian pilgrimage.

The Odyssey of Guyon, Spenser's nearest approach to travel romance after the order of the *Argonautica,* allows for much firmer character delineation. The adventurer pursuing the quest for Acrasia's bower is of pure heroic mould, no neophyte but thoroughly versed in the ways of chivalry and the pitfalls of knight-errantry. Playing the active and unselfish part, as rescuer of the distressed, he appears to better advantage than the Red Cross Knight, who is fully occupied in extricating himself from difficulties occasioned through ignorance and indiscretion. Guyon's impulsiveness, evinced throughout his earlier adventures before he has fully acquired the virtue of Temperance, appears as the natural outcome of heroic virtue; and his temporary submission to the charms of Phædria is more in keeping with the part than his subsequent treatment of Acrasia. That the trial at the cave of churlish Mammon, unlike the counsels of Despair, should prove utterly unavailing is only to be expected. For Guyon possesses strength of will together with instinctive gentleness and nobility, a gracious combination befitting the type of chivalric virtue in active life.

The character of Artegall, on the other hand, suffers through the entire subordination of romance to allegory. His supernatural origin, his relations with Britomart and the prophecies respecting their royal descendants endow him with heroic attributes second only to those of Prince Arthur himself. But the nature of his exploits and the unseemly ministrations of his henchman Talus tend to convert him into an inhuman symbol of justice, unseasoned by mercy. His story is one long record of terrorism. The drowning of Pollente and Munera may have been a public necessity; but we might have been spared the barbarous mutilation of the victims and the exposure of their remains. Arguments with demagogues and interference in property disputes better become the legislator than the knight at arms, especially as Artegall's methods of executing justice have more in common with the Elizabethan criminal code than with the goodly usage of chivalry. The fable cannot be classed under any traditional type, but falls into a series of mechanical episodes manufactured to point the moral and culminating in the artless reduplication of the last two cantos. In Book v the politician completely overrides the romancer; Arthur, Lord Grey, has eclipsed the memory of Arthur and the Table Round.

At the opposite pole to Artegall is Calidore, the "very perfit, gentle knight" of Courtesy, a purely chivalric virtue, standing second on the list prefixed by Caxton to *Le Morte Darthur*. The opening to Book VI spells an entire change of *motif* and atmosphere, transporting us from grim reality to the idyllic fantasy of *Arcadia* and the Greek romances. Calidore, Tristram and the wild man belong to the Saturnine age of natural living and primitive refinement. The knight of Courtesy is a man of peace, subduing violence by arbitration and reform. His easy settlement of differences in the episodes of Crudor and Briana, of Aladine and Priscilla offer a welcome contrast to the rough justice of Artegall; and having early abandoned the heroic life for the bucolic he leaves the field with the minimum of bloodshed, claiming only Maleffort and Pastorella's abductors as victims of his sword.

The legend of Courtesy evolves from that of Justice. But the way for Calidore has already been prepared by the scenes and actors of Books III and IV, in the course of which faery society has undergone considerable transformation. The knight of Holiness wooing his mistress Truth, Prince Arthur serving a phantom Gloriana, Guyon the celibate captor of Acrasia are far removed from the traditional romantic lover. But the story of Britomart, with its attendant episodes, allows for the tempering of heroic virtue by heroic sentiment. The pure flame of passion that held Lancelot and Guenevere, Tristram and Iseult—elemental, self-sufficient, subversive—is inadmissible within the ideal commonwealth of *The Faerie Queene*. But passion spiritualised urges its possessor towards the highest good. Britomart is no unsexed Radigund but the ornament of "true feminitee," hiding beneath the armour of a valkyrie the "amiable grace" of woman, a rose secured from the spoiler by thorns and briars. She enters as the child princess of romance, sleepless for love of a knight unknown, confiding in her nurse, saying her prayers "with great devotion and with little zele." Everything about her betrays the natural touch—her confusion on being taxed by Guyon as to the reason for her disguise, her perversity when slandering Artegall in order to learn the truth about him, the womanly arts whereby she would stay his departure:

> And by the way she sundry purpose found
> Of this or that, the time for to delay,
> And of the perils whereto he was bound,
> The feare whereof seem'd much her to affray;
> But all she did was but to weare out day.
> Full oftentimes she leave of him did take;

> And eft againe deviz'd some what to say,
> Which she forgot, whereby excuse to make;
> So loth she was his companie for to forsake; [11]

finally the pitiful scene of her desolation:

> One day when as she long had sought for ease
> In every place, and every place thought best,
> Yet found no place that could her liking please,
> She to a window came that opened West,
> Towards which coast her love his way addrest:
> There looking forth, shee in her heart did find
> Many vaine fancies working her unrest;
> And sent her winged thoughts, more swift than wind,
> To beare unto her love the message of her mind. [12]

The entry of Britomart brings the love *motif* into the foreground, where it is represented under every aspect—as physical and spiritual desire, at once a disease and a remedy, as friendship, domestic affection, idyllic sentiment. The Christian champion has yielded priority to the romantic lover, whose trials and adventures tend to obscure the basic moral issue. The "loose life" and "ungentle trade" at Malecasta's castle prefigures a new and welcome secularity. As the noise of war diminishes to the milder note of joust and tourney interest becomes more evenly distributed among minor actors and episodes included "rather as accidents than intendments" and less remote from common experience. Abstract figures of good and evil give place to familiar types of chivalric legend—to "Cupid's man" Scudamour, to Braggadochio the comic mountebank, to Paridell, Blandamour and the Squire of Dames, whose worldly wisdom and urbanity make ample amends for their easy virtue. A train of fair ladies follows the warrior heroine—Belphœbe, vital and majestic as Diana, Florimell, forlorn type of fugitive beauty, Amoret, chosen of Venus, the very embodiment of afflicted innocence and fidelity, Pastorella, another "Flora, peering in April's front." Two-dimension figures, confined within their romantic setting, they are timeless.

The faery world which Spenser has fashioned from the raw material of myth and folk tale, legend and chronicle is no less peculiar to himself than is his diction. The unseen Gloriana has little in common with the mistress of Launfal, still less with a fairy Mab no longer than an agate stone, commanding an airy palace with walls of spiders' legs,

windows of cats' eyes and roofing of bats' skin. Hers is no golden age
when

> All was this land fulfild of fairye:
> The elf queene with her joly compaignye
> Daunced ful ofte in many a grene mede.[13]

Guyon was knighted by Huon of Bordeaux "when with King Oberon
he came to Faeryland." But Oberon has left none of his faery crew, none
of the pucks and hobgoblins exorcised in *Epithalamion;* nor is this surprising since Oberon is actually no faery monarch but King Henry VIII.
For the defenders of Gloriana life is a grim business and any approach to
the wonder and delight of traditional faerie stands suspect. Guyon may
not submit to the charms of Acrasia nor Scudamour tarry within the
Temple of Venus. Spenser's faery lore is a lore within itself.

The diversity of his material covers a single poetic concept. *The
Faerie Queene,* for all its inconsequence, preserves unity of place, un-
broken from the entry of the Red Cross Knight to the capture of the
Blatant Beast. "The reader never knows where he is, but still he knows,
from the consciousness within him, that all is as natural and proper, as
if the country where the action is laid were distinctly pointed out, and
marked down in a map." [14] The romantic device is not artificially contrived by the compounding of this and that original but evolves as a
whole, "out of space," from creative imagination. The fable, apart from
the allegory, has neither beginning, middle, nor end. Scenes change,
figures enter and vanish without prologue, epilogue or relevance to their
context. But the complete spectacle conveys the kaleidoscopic effect of a
dream, where disconnected objects and incidents merge easily without
abrupt transition. "All is marvellous and extraordinary; yet not *unnatural* in one sense, as it agrees to the conceptions that are readily
entertained of these magical and wonder-working Natures." [15] Nothing is
unexpected. Sansloy, Braggadochio, Scudamour and the rest, entering
suddenly out of the void, seem to have been there all the time. Against
the charges of incoherence and discursiveness the poet—a Pygmalion, be-
guiled by his own handiwork—proffers an unanswerable defence:

> The waies, through which my weary steps I guyde
> In this delightfull land of Faery,
> Are so exceeding spacious and wyde,
> And sprinckled with such sweet variety

> Of all that pleasant is to eare or eye,
> That I, nigh ravisht with rare thoughts delight,
> My tedious travell doe forget thereby;
> And, when I gin to feele decay of might,
> It strength to me supplies, and chears my dulled spright.[16]

For this land of Faerie is but a concrete symbol of the poet's dream, the ideal realm of fantasy expressed under different attributes through epic, pastoral and allegory but common to them all. Without conscious effort the faerie way of writing, with its quaint diction, haunting music and phantom imagery, effects spontaneously "that willing suspension of disbelief, which constitutes poetic faith":

> A shepeheards boye, (no better doe him call,)
> When Winters wastful spight was almost spent,
> All in a sunneshine day, as did befall,
> Led forth his flock, that had bene long ypent:
>   So faynt they woxe, and feeble in the folde,
>   That now unnethes their feete could them uphold.

> A gentle Knight was pricking on the plaine,
> Ycladd in mightie armes and silver shielde,
> Wherein old dints of deepe woundes did remaine,
> The cruell markes of many a bloody fielde.[17]

Here is no palpable artifice for the gradual inducing of atmosphere. The spell works at a stroke, plunging us into the middle of things.

Though we may not always follow our bearings the objects that we encounter are sharply outlined and easily recognisable. The one exception is the House of Busirane, deliberately set in the conventional romantic atmosphere of wonder and terror; for here the nature of the tale, embodying the Child Roland-Comus *motif* of rescue from an enchanter, calls for the full paraphernalia of horror—prolonged suspense, mysterious inscriptions, midnight thunder, ritual drama—half masque, half Black Mass—the sealing of the spell with the blood of the victim. But as a rule Spenser prefers open daylight and quick-changing spectacle to gloomy interiors and lengthy concentration upon the eeriness of the unseen. His giants, witches and monsters, though of incredible strength and dimension, are supernormal rather than supernatural, creatures of the same universe as their opponents. Though treacherous and malicious they lie within reach of attack and fight in the open. Their few supernatural allies are too familiar to cause any cold shudders; "snowy Florimell" too closely resembles a common harlot, Archimago a "Vice," or Lord of Misrule, often more comic than sinister. Magic armour, healing waters, love wizardry are freely adopted as narrative machinery; but the mumbo-jumbo of sorcery is only fair game for laughter:

> But th'aged Nourse, her calling to her bowre,
> Had gathered Rew, and Savine, and the flowre
> Of Camphora, and Calamint, and Dill;
> All which she in an earthen Pot did poure,
> And to the brim with Coltwood did it fill,
> And many drops of milk and blood through it did spill.
>
> Then, taking thrise three heares from off her head,
> Them trebly breaded in a threefold lace,
> And round about the Pots mouth bound the thread;
> And, after having whispered a space
> Certein sad words with hollow voice and bace,
> She to the virgin sayd, thrise sayd she itt;
> "Come, daughter, come; come, spit upon my face;
> Spitt thrise upon me, thrise upon me spitt;
> Th'uneven nomber for this business is most fitt".[18]

Heroic argument calls for the semblance of actuality, for vigour and energy in presentation. Far more typical than the Busirane episode at the close of Book III is Book v, canto ii, in which fifty-four stanzas suffice to describe the combat with the Pagan, the drowning of Munera and the overthrow of the giant with his adherents. Time and again dramatic touches vivid as those of Chaucer or Ariosto serve to connect the land of Faerie with common experience. The woeful history of Florimell, despite her fugitive appearances, is a most effective study in pathos developed through complex intrigue to a highly theatrical dénouement. Another striking instance of such contact between fantasy and fact is the scene after the slaying of the dragon:

> Some feard, and fledd; some feard, and well it faynd;
> One, that would wiser seeme then all the rest,
> Warnd him not touch, for yet perhaps remaynd
> Some lingring life within his hollow brest,
> Or in his wombe might lurke some hidden nest
> Of many Dragonettes, his fruitfull seede:

Another saide, that in his eyes did rest
Yet sparckling fyre, and badd thereof take heed;
Another said, he saw him move his eyes indeed.

One mother, whenas her foolehardy chyld
Did come too neare, and with his talants play,
Halfe dead through feare, her litle babe revyld,
And to her gossibs gan in counsell say;
"How can I tell, but that his talants may
Yet scratch my sonne, or rend his tender hand?"
So diversly them selves in vaine they fray;
Whiles some more bold to measure him nigh stand,
To prove how many acres he did spred of land.[19]

In Spenser romantic sentimentality is tempered and controlled by the objective alertness of the humanist who would repair the ruins and rekindle the dying embers, not content to stand entranced before their half-spent radiance. The fairyland of his poetic consciousness is no ruin peopled by misty wraiths and shadows, like the erections of his early "Gothic" admirers, but a well-defined structure, peopled by the figures of living originals or lively conventions, vividly imaged and portrayed. Its history, as he naïvely reminds his reader, is hardly more astounding than the logs of voyagers to "Indian Peru," "Amazon huge river," "fruitfullest Virginia" or other unknown lands—authorities in which the incredulous could have found authentic record of Fancy's painted plumes,

Like as the sunburnt Indians do aray
Their tawney bodies in their proudest plight,

of Maleger turning at bay,

As wonts the Tartar by the Caspian lake,
Whenas the Russian him in flight does chace,

or of the features, dress and gestures of "salvage men." [20] The defence, offered but half seriously, bears upon his poetry as a whole. His ideal concept is an image of the actual, he extols the past as a pattern for the present, breathing new life into a dying tradition. The numerical correspondence between the twelve knights of the Round Table, the twelve virtues of Aristotle and the twelve books of the heroic poem is the outward symbol of an inward union between the old world and the new.

The last of those "lofty fables and romances which recount in solemn cantos the deeds of knighthood" becomes the epic of Humanism.

NOTES

1. Gregory Smith, *Elizabethan Critical Essays,* Oxford, 1904, I, 323.
2. *Le Morte Darthur,* X, ii; XVI, vi.
3. *F.Q.* II, viii, 36.
4. *Le Morte Darthur,* II, ii.
5. *Ib.* IX, xii.
6. T. Warton, *Observations on The Fairy Queen.* London, 1807, I, 272 ff.
7. *F.Q.* III, x, 47.
8. *Ib.* IV, iii, 45.
9. *Ib.* III, ii, 14.
10. The 1590 version of Book III closes with the reunion of Scudamour and Amoret; but in subsequent issues the five stanzas recording this were dropped and three others substituted, doubtless with the object of sustaining interest in the fortunes of the two lovers throughout the later books.
11. *F.Q.* IV, vi, 45.
12. *Ib.* V, vi, 7.
13. Chaucer, *Wife of Bath's Tale,* 3 ff.
14. Coleridge, *Lectures on Shakespeare.* London (Bohn's Standard Library), 1900, 67.
15. *The Works of Edmund Spenser,* ed. H. J. Todd, 1805, II, clxxi.
16. *F.Q.* VI, Pr. I.
17. *S.C.* "January," I ff.; *F.Q.* I, i, I.
18. *F.Q.* III, ii, 49, 50. The episode is adapted from the pseudo-Virgilian *Ceiris.*
19. *Ib.* I, xii, 10, 11.
20. *Ib.* III, xii, 8; II, xi, 26; L. Whitney in *Mod. Phil.* XIX (1921), 143 ff.

THIRTEEN

C. S. LEWIS

The "Faerie Queene" (1936)*

. . . Let us return to the Knight and the Lady in the opening stanzas. The knight has a red cross on a silver shield; the lady is leading a lamb. The lamb has puzzled many readers; but we now know[1] that it had a real function in earlier versions of the legend of St. George, and (what is much more important) we know that the lady was commonly represented leading her lamb in the pageants of St. George and the dragon. In other words, the two figures which meet us at the beginning of *The Faerie Queene* were instantly recognized by Spenser's first readers, and were clothed for them not in literary or courtly associations, but in popular, homely, patriotic associations. They spoke immediately to what was most universal and childlike in gentle and simple alike. This at once suggests an aspect of Spenser's poetry which it will be fatal for us to neglect, and which is abundantly illustrated in the First Book. The angels who sing at Una's wedding probably come from the same pageant source as the lamb.[2] The well in which St. George is refreshed during his fight with the dragon comes from *Bevis of Southampton*.[3] The whole similarity between his allegory and that of Bunyan, which has exercised many scholars, is best explained by the fact that they have a common source—the old-fashioned sermon in the village church still continuing the allegorical tradition of the medieval pulpit.[4] Innumerable details come from the Bible, and specially from those books of the Bible which have meant much to Protestantism—the Pauline epistles and the Revelation. His antipapal allegories strike the very note of popular, even of

*Reprinted from Parts II and III of the last chapter of *The Allegory of Love*, pp. 297-360.

rustic, Protestant aversion; they can be understood, and enjoyed by the modern reader (whatever his religion) only if he remembers that Roman Catholicism was in Spenser's day simply the most potent contemporary symbol for something much more primitive—the sheer Bogey, who often changes his name but never wholly retires from the popular mind. Foxe's *Book of Martyrs* was in every one's hands; horrible stories of the Inquisition and the galleys came from overseas; and every nervous child must have heard tales of a panel slid back at twilight in a seeming innocent manor house to reveal the pale face and thin, black body of a Jesuit. The ghosts crying from beneath the altar in Orgoglio's chapel, and the mystery of iniquity beneath that other altar of Gerioneo are accurate embodiments of popular contemporary horror at these things.[5] Gerioneo himself, who

> Laught so loud that all his teeth wide bare
> One might have seene enraungd disorderly
> Like to a rancke of piles that pitched are awry[6]

is the genuine raw-head and bloody-bones of our remembered night nurseries. A dragon's mouth is the "griesly mouth of hell" as in medieval drama.[7] Mammon is the gold-hoarding earthman of immemorial tradition, the gnome. The witcheries of Duessa, when she rides in Night's chariot and "hungry wolves continually did howle," [8] or of the hag with whom Florimel guested, are almost incomparably closer to the world of real superstition than any of the Italian enchantments. We have long looked for the origins of *The Faerie Queene* in Renaissance palaces and Platonic academies, and forgotten that it has humbler origins of at least equal importance in the Lord Mayor's show, the chap-book, the bedtime story, the family Bible, and the village church. What lies next beneath the surface in Spenser's poem is the world of popular imagination: almost, a popular mythology.

And this world is not called up, as Ariosto may call up a fragment of folk lore, in order to amuse us. On the contrary, it is used for the sake of something yet deeper which it brings up with it and which is Spenser's real concern; the primitive or instinctive mind, with all its terrors and ecstasies—that part in the mind of each of us which we should never dream of showing to a man of the world like Ariosto. Archimago and Una, in their opposite ways, are true creations of that mind. When we first meet them we seem to have known them long before; and so in a sense we have, but only the poet could have clothed them for us in form and colour. The same may be said of Despair and Malengin, of Busirane's appalling house, and of the garden of Adonis. For all of these are translations into the visible of feelings else blind and inarticulate; and they are translations made with singular accuracy, with singularly little loss. The secret of this accuracy in which, to my mind, Spenser excels nearly all poets, is partly to be sought in his humble fidelity to the popular symbols which he found ready made to his hand; but much more in his profound sympathy with that which makes the symbols, with the fundamental tendencies of human imagination as such. Like the writers of the New Testament (to whom, in the character of his symbolism, he is the closest of all English poets) he is endlessly preoccupied with such ultimate antitheses as Light and Darkness or Life and Death. It has not often been noticed—and, indeed, save for a special purpose it ought not to be noticed—that Night is hardly even mentioned by Spenser without aversion. His story leads him to describe innumerable nightfalls, and his feeling about them is always the same:

> So soone as Night had with her pallid hew
> Defaste the beautie of the shyning skye,
> And refte from men the worldes desired vew[9]

or,

> whenas chearelesse Night ycovered had
> Fayre heaven with an universall cloud,
> That every wight dismayed with darkenes sad[10]

or, again,

> when as daies faire shinie-beame, yclowded
> With fearefull shadowes of deformed night,
> Warnd man and beast in quiet rest be shrowded[11]

And, answering to this, in his descriptions of morning we have a never failing rapture: mere light is as sweet to Spenser as if it were a new creation. Such passages are too numerous and too widely scattered (often at unimportant places in the story) to be the result of any conscious plan: they are spontaneous and the better proof of the flawless health, the paradisal naïveté, of his imagination. They form a background, hardly noticed at a first reading, to those great passages where the conflict of light and dark becomes explicit. Such is the sleepless night of Prince Arthur in the third book, where the old description of lover's insomnia is heightened and spiritualized into a "statement" (as the musicians say) of one of Spenser's main themes;

> Dayes dearest children be the blessed seed
> Which darknesse shall subdue and heaven win:
> Truth is his daughter; he her first did breed
> Most sacred virgin without spot of sinne.[12]

It is no accident that Truth, or Una, should be mentioned here, for she is indeed the daughter of Light, and through the whole First Book runs the antithesis between her father as emperor of the East and Duessa as queen of the West [13]—a conception possibly borrowed from *Reason and Sensuality*—and in the Fifth canto of that book we meet Night face to face. The contrast between her "visage deadly sad" as she comes forth from her "darksome mew" and Duessa

> sunny bright
> Adornd with gold and jewels shining cleare,[14]

(though Duessa is but pretended, reflected light!) is, of course, a familiar example of that pictorial quality which critics have often praised in Spenser—but praised without a full understanding of those very unpictorial, unpicturable, depths from which it rises. Spenser is no dilettante, and has a low opinion of the painter's art as compared with his own.[15] He is not playing mere tricks with light and shade; and few speeches in our poetry are more serious than Night's sad sentence (the very accent of a creature *dréame bedéled*)

> The sonnes of Day he favoureth, I see[16]

And yet it is characteristic of him that the constant pressure of this day and night antithesis on his imagination never tempts him into dualism. He is impressed, more perhaps than any other poet, with the conflict of two mighty opposites—aware that our world is dualistic for all practical purposes, dualistic in all but the very last resort: but from the final heresy he abstains, drawing back from the verge of dualism to remind us by delicate allegories that though the conflict seems ultimate yet one of the opposites really contains, and is not contained by, the other. Truth and falsehood are opposed; but truth is the norm not of truth only but of falsehood also. That is why we find that Una's father, King of the East and enemy of the West, is yet *de jure* King of the West as well as of the East.[17] That is why Love and Hatred, whom the poet borrows no doubt from Empedocles, are opposites but not, as in Empedocles, mere opposites: they are both the sons of Concord.[18] And that, again, in the passage we were discussing, is why Aesculapius, a creature of Night's party, asks Night the formidable question,

> Can Night defray
> The wrath of thundring Jove that rules both night and day? [19]

The other antithesis—that of Life and Death, or, in its inferior degrees, of Health and Sickness—enables Spenser to avoid the insipidity of representing good as arbitrary law and evil as spontaneity. His evils are all dead or dying things. Each of his deadly sins has a mortal disease.[20] Aesculapius sits in the bowels of the earth endlessly seeking remedies for an incurable fever.[21] Archimago makes Guyon "the object of his spight, and *deadly food.*" [22] Despair is an immortal suicide,[23] Malbecco lives transfixed with "deathes eternall dart." [24] The porter of the garden of intemperance, the evil genius, is the *foe of life,*[25] and so are the violent passions, red-headed and adjust, who attack Guyon in the earlier stages of his pilgrimage.[26] Over against these mortal shapes are set forces of life and health and fecundity. St. George, in combat with the beast who

> was deadly made
> And al that life preserved did detest[27]

is refreshed with water from the well of life and saved by the shadow of the tree of life. Babies cluster at Charissa's breasts:[28] Belphoebe's *lilly handës twaine* crush virtuous herbs for the healing of wounds:[29] in the garden of Adonis,

> Ne needs there Gardiner to sett or sow,
> To plant or prune: for of their owne accord
> All things, as they created were, doe grow,
> And yet remember well the mighty word
> Which first was spoken by th' Almighty Lord,
> That bad them to increase and multiply[30]

and throughout the whole garden "franckly each paramor his leman knowes." [31] The love of Britomart is enobled by prophecies of famous offspring. The poem is full of marriages. Una's face unveiled shines "as the great eye of heaven," [32] and Cambina carries a cup of Nepenthe.[33]

The whole shining company of Spenser's vital shapes make up such a picture of "life's golden tree" that it is difficult not to fancy that our bodily, no less than our mental, health is refreshed by reading him. . . .

III

In considering *The Faerie Queene* as a consciously allegorical poem I shall neglect entirely its political allegory. My qualifications as an historian are not such as would enable me to unravel it; and my critical principles hardly encourage me even to make the attempt. By his political allegory Spenser doubtless intended to give to his poem a certain topical attraction. Time never forgives such concessions to "the glistering of this present," and what acted as a bait to unpoetic readers for some decades has become a stumbling-block to poetic readers ever since. The contemporary allusions in *The Faerie Queene* are now of interest to the critic chiefly in so far as they explain how some bad passages came to be bad; but since this does not make them good—since to explain by causes is not to justify by reasons—we shall not lose very much by ignoring the matter. My concern is with the moral or philosophical allegory.

In approaching this latter, the modern reader needs a little encouragement. He has been told that the *significacio* of *The Faery Queene* is not worth looking for. Critics have talked as if there were a fatal discrepancy between Spenser's spiritual pretensions and the actual content of his poetry. He has been represented as a man who preached Protestantism while his imagination remained on the side of Rome; or again, as a poet entirely dominated by the senses who believed himself to be an austere moralist. These are profound misunderstandings.

The first—that of unconscious or involuntary Roman Catholicism —may be answered pretty shortly. It is quite true that Una is dressed (in her exile) like a nun, that the House of Holinesse is like a conventual house, that Penaunce dwells there with a whip, and that Contemplation, like the hermit of Book Six,[34] resembles a Catholic recluse. It is equally true that we can find similarly Catholic imagery in Bunyan; and I know a man in our own time who wrote what he intended to be a general apologetic allegory for "all who profess and call themselves Christians," and was surprised to find it both praised and blamed as a defence of Rome. It would appear that all allegories whatever are likely to seem Catholic to the general reader, and this phenomenon is worth investigation. In part, no doubt, it is to be explained by the fact that the visible and tangible aspects of Catholicism are medieval, and therefore steeped in literary suggestion. But is this all? Do Protestant allegorists continue as in a dream to use imagery so likely to mislead their readers without noticing the danger or without better motive than laziness for incurring it? By no means. The truth is not that allegory is Catholic, but that Catholicism is allegorical. Allegory consists in giving an imagined body to the immaterial; but if, in each case, Catholicism claims already to have given it a material body, then the allegorist's symbol will naturally resemble that material body. The whip of Penaunce is an excellent example. No Christian ever doubted that repentance involved "penaunce" and "whips" on the spiritual plane: it is when you come to material whips—to Tartuffe's *discipline* in his closet—that the controversy begins. It is the same with the "House" of Holinessse. No Christian doubts that those who have offered themselves to God are cut off *as if* by a wall from the World, are placed under a *regula vitae*, and "laid in easy bed" by "meek Obedience"; but when the wall becomes one of real bricks and mortar, and the Rule one in real ink, superintended by disciplinary officials and reinforced (at times) by the power of the State, then we have reached that sort of actuality which Catholics aim at and Protestants deliberately avoid. Indeed, this difference is the root out of which all other differences between the two religions grow. The one suspects that all spiritual gifts are falsely claimed if they cannot be embodied in bricks and mortar, or official positions, or institutions: the other, that nothing retains its spirituality if incarnation is pushed to that degree and in that way. The difference about Papal infallibility is simply a form of this. The proper corruptions of each Church tell the same tale. When Catholicism goes bad it becomes the world-old, world-wide *religio* of amulets and holy places and priestcraft: Protestantism, in its corresponding decay, becomes a vague mist of ethical platitudes. Catholicism is accused of being much too like all the other religions; Protestantism of being insufficiently like a religion at all. Hence Plato, with his transcendent Forms, is the doctor of Protestants; Aristotle, with his immanent Forms, the doctor of Catholics. Now allegory exists, so to speak, in that region of the mind where the bifurcation has not yet occurred; for it occurs only when we reach the material world. In the world of matter, Catholics and Protestants disagree as to the kind and degree of incarnation or embodiment which we can safely try to give to the spiritual; but in the world of imagination, where allegory exists, unlimited embodiment is equally approved by both. Imagined buildings and institutions which have a strong resemblance to the actual buildings and institutions of the Church of Rome, will therefore appear, and ought to appear, in any Protestant allegory. If the allegorist knows his business their prevalence will rather mean that the allegory is not Catholic than that it is. For allegory is *idem in alio*. Only a bungler, like Deguileville, would introduce a monastery into his poem if he were really writing about monasticism. When Spenser writes about Protestant sanctity he gives us something like a convent: when he is really talking about the conventual life he gives us Abessa and Corceca. If I might, without irreverence, twist the words of an important (and very relevant) Protestant article, I would say that a Catholic interpretation of *The Faerie Queene,* "overthoweth the nature of an allegory." Certainly, a Catholic reader anxious to do justice to this great Protestant poem, would be very ill advised to read it in that way. Here, as in more important matters, frontier courtesies do not help; it is at their fiery cores that the two faiths are most nearly in sympathy.

The charge of actual sensuality and theoretical austerity cannot be answered so briefly. The spear-head of this attack is usually directed against the Bower of Bliss, and it is sometimes strengthened by the statement that the Garden of Adonis is not sufficiently distinguished from it; and an analysis of these two places is as good a method as any other of beginning a study of Spenser's allegory. The home of Acrasia is first shown to us in the fifth canto of Book Two, when Atin finds Cymochles there asleep. The very first words of the description are

> And over him art, striving to compare
> With nature, did an Arber greene dispred.[35]

This explicit statement that Acrasia's garden is art not nature can be paralleled in Tasso, and would be unimportant if it stood alone. But the interesting thing is that when the Bower of Bliss reappears seven cantos later, there again the very first stanza of description tells us that it was

> goodly beautifide
> With all the ornaments of Floraes pride,
> Wherewith her mother Art, as halfe in scorne
> Of niggard Nature, like a pompous bride
> Did decke her, and too lavishly adorne.[36]

In order to be perfectly fair to Spenser's hostile critics, I am prepared to assume that this repetition of the antithesis between art and nature is accidental. But I think the hardest sceptic will hesitate when he reads, eight stanzas further,

> And that which all faire workes doth most aggrace,
> The art which all that wrought appeared in no place.[37]

And if this does not satisfy him let him read on to the sixty-first stanza where we find the imitation ivy in metal which adorns Acrasia's bathing-pool. Whether those who think that Spenser is secretly on Acrasia's side, themselves approve of metal vegetation as a garden ornament, or whether they regard this passage as a proof of Spenser's abominable bad taste, I do not know; but this is how the poet describes it,

> And over all of purest gold was spred
> A trayle of yvie in his native hew;
> For the rich metall was so coloured
> That wight who did not well avis'd it vew
> Would surely deeme it to bee yvie trew.[38]

Is it possible now to resist the conviction that Spenser's hostile critics are precisely such wights who have viewed the Bower "not well avis'd" and therefore erroneously deemed it to be true? Let us suppose, however, that the reader is still unconvinced: let us even help him by pointing out stanza fifty-nine where the antithesis is blurred. But we have still to deal with the garden of Adonis; and surely all suspicion that the insistence on Acrasia's artificiality is accidental must disappear if we find throughout the description of the garden of Adonis an equal insistence on its natural spontaneity. And this is just what we do find. Here, as in the description of the Bower, the very first stanza gives us the key-note: the garden of Adonis is

> So faire a place as Nature can devize.[39]

A few stanzas later, in lines which I have already quoted, we are told that it needs no Gardiner because all its plants grow "of their owne accord" in virtue of the divine word that works within them. It even needs no water, because these plants have eternal moisture "in themselves." [40] Like the Bower, the Garden has an arbour, but it is an arbour

> not by art
> But of the trees owne inclination made.[41]

and the ivy in this arbour is living ivy not painted metal. Finally, the Bower has the story of a false love depicted by art on its gate,[42] and the Garden has faithful lovers growing as live flowers out of its soil.[43] When these facts have once been pointed out, only prejudice can continue to deny the deliberate differentiation between the Bower and the Garden. The one is artifice, sterility, death: the other, nature, fecundity, life. The similarity between them is just that similarity which exists between the two gardens in Jean de Meun;[44] the similarity of the real to the pretended and of the archetype to the imitation. *Diabolus simius Dei.* . . .

The reader may well be excused if he has, by this, forgotten that the whole subject of nature and art arose out of our analysis of the Bower of Bliss and the Garden of Adonis. But the Bower and the Garden (the very names, I trust, have now become significant) are so important that we have still not exhausted them. We have dealt only with their contrast of nature and art. It still remains to consider the equally careful, and even more important, contrast between the explicitly erotic imagery of the one and the other. We here approach a subject on which Spenser has been much misunderstood. He is full of pictures of virtuous and vicious love, and they are, in fact, exquisitely contrasted. Most readers seem to approach him with the vulgar expectation that his distinction between them is going to be a quantitative one; that the vicious loves are going to be warmly painted and the virtuous tepidly—the sacred draped and the profane nude. It must be stated at once that in so far as Spenser's distinction is quantitative at all, the quantities are the other way round. He is at the opposite pole from the scholastic philosophers. For him, intensity of passion purifies: cold pleasure, such as the scholastics seems to approve, is corruption. But in reality the distinction has very little to do with degree or quantity.

The reader who wishes to understand Spenser in this matter may begin with one of his most elementary contrasts—that between the naked damsels in Acrasia's fountain and the equally naked (in fact rather more naked) damsels who dance round Colin Clout.[45] Here, I presume, no one can be confused. Acrasia's two young women (their names are obviously Cissie and Flossie) are ducking and giggling in a bathing-pool for the benefit of a passer-by: a man does not need to go to fairie land to meet them. The Graces are engaged in doing something worth doing—namely, dancing in a ring "in order excellent." They are, at first, much too busy to notice Calidore's arrival, and when they do notice him they vanish. The contrast here is almost too simple to be worth mentioning; and it is only marginal to our immediate subject, for the Graces symbolize no sexual experience at all. Let us proceed to something a little less obvious and more relevant: let us compare the pictures Venus and Adonis in the house of Malecasta with the real Venus and Adonis in the Garden. We find at once that the latter (the good and real) are a picture of actual fruition. Venus, in defiance of the forces of death, the Stygian gods,

> Possesseth him and of his sweetnesse takes her fill.[46]

Nothing could be franker; a dainty reader might even object that the phrase "takes her fill" brings us too close to other and more prosaic appetites. But daintiness will be rebuked (as Spenser is always ready to rebuke it) if any one tries to prefer the pictured Venus on Malecasta's wall. For she is not in the arms of Adonis: she is merely looking at him,

> And whilst he bath'd, with her two crafty spyes
> She secretly would search each daintie lim.[47]

The words "crafty," "spies," and "secretly" warn us sufficiently well where we have arrived. The good Venus is a picture of fruition: the bad Venus is a picture not of "lust in action" but of lust suspended—lust turning into what would now be called *skeptophilia*. The contrast is just as clear as that in the previous example, and incalculably more important. Thus armed, we may now return to the Bower. The very first person we meet there is Cymochles. He has come there for pleasure and he is surrounded by a flock of wanton nymphs. But the wretched creature does not approach one of them: instead, he lies in the grass ("like an Adder lurking in the weedes") and

> Sometimes he falsely faines himselfe to sleepe
> Whiles through their lids his wanton eies do peepe.[48]

The word "peepe" is the danger signal, and once again we know where we are. If we turn to the Garden of Adonis we shall find a very different state of affairs. There "all plenty and all pleasure flowes": the garden is full of lovers and "Franckly each Paramor his leman knowes." [49] And when we have noticed this it ought to dawn upon us that the Bower of Bliss is not a place even of healthy animalism, or indeed of activity of any kind. Acrasia herself *does* nothing: she is merely "discovered," posed

on a sofa beside a sleeping young man, in suitably semitransparent rai-
ment. It is hardly necessary to add that her breast is "bare to ready
spoyle of hungry eies," [50] for eyes, greedy eyes ("which n'ote therewith
be fild") are the tyrants of that whole region. The Bower of Bliss is not
a picture of lawless, that is, unwedded, love as opposed to lawful love.
It is a picture, one of the most powerful ever painted, of the whole sexual nature in disease. There is not a kiss or an embrace in the island:
only male prurience and female provocation. Against it we should set
not only the Garden of Adonis, but the rapturous reunion of Scudamour
with Amoret,[51] or the singularly fresh and frank account of Arthur's
meeting with Gloriana.[52] It is not to be supposed of course that Spenser
wrote as a scientific "sexologist" or consciously designed his Bower of
Bliss as a picture of sexual perversion. Acrasia indeed does not represent
sexual vice in particular, but vicious pleasure in general.[53] Spenser's
conscious intention, no doubt, was merely to produce a picture which
should do justice both to the pleasantness and to the vice. He has done
this in the only way possible—namely, by filling his Bower of Bliss with
sweetness showered upon sweetness and yet contriving that there should
be something subtly wrong throughout. But perhaps "contriving" is a
bad word. When he wishes to paint disease, the exquisite health of his
own imagination shows him what images to exclude. . . .

For the purposes of our particular study the third and fourth books
of *The Faerie Queene* are by far the most important, for in them Spenser, as I promised, becomes our collaborator and tells the final stages of
the history of courtly love. I do not mean, of course, that he would have
understood the phrase "history of courtly love," nor that he knew he
was ending a story. But it is in his mind, none the less, that the last phase
of the long process becomes conscious.

The subjects of these two books are respectively Chastity and
Friendship, but we are justified in treating them as a single book on the
subject of love. Chastity, in the person of Britomart, turns out to mean
not virginity but virtuous love: and friends are found to be merely "another sort of lovers" [54] in the Temple of Venus. The Proem to the legend
of Friendship deals entirely with "lovers deare debate," [55] and its story
is equally concerned with friendship, reconciliation and marriage. In the
ninth canto Spenser explicitly classifies Eros, Storgë, and Philia as "three
kinds of love." [56] Finally, his conception of love is enlarged so as to include even the harmonies of the inanimate world, and we have the

wedding of Thames and Medway. For this all-embracing interpretation of love Spenser, of course, has precedent in ancient philosophy, and specially in the *Symposium*. His subject-matter in these two books is therefore extremely complex: and as, in these same books, the non-allegorical fringe becomes wider and more brilliant than ever, there is some excuse for the bewilderment of those critics (too quick despairers!) who suppose that Spenser has abandoned his original design. But those who have learned to look for the allegorical centres will not go astray.

A few pages ago we were considering the difference between the Bower of Bliss and the Garden of Adonis. While we did so I carefully excluded a much more interesting question—that of the difference between the Bower of Bliss and the Houses of Malecasta and Busirane. It is now time to rectify this omission. The Bower, it will be remembered, turned out to be a place not of lawless loves or even lawless lusts, but of disease and paralysis in appetite itself. It will be remembered that the Bower is the home not of vicious sexuality in particular, but of vicious Pleasure in general.[57] The poet has selected one kind of pleasure chiefly because it is the only kind that can be treated at length in serious poetry. The Bower is connected with sex at all only through the medium of Pleasure. And this is borne out by the fact—very remarkable to any one well read in previous allegory—that Cupid is never mentioned in the Bower, a clear indication that we are not yet dealing with love. The Bower is not the foe of Chastity but of Continence—of that elementary psychic integration which is presupposed even in unlawful loves. To find the real foe of Chastity, the real portrait of false love, we must turn to Malecasta and Busirane. The moment we do so, we find that Malecasta and Busirane are nothing else than the main subject of this study—Courtly Love; and that Courtly Love is in Spenser's view the chief opponent of Chastity. But Chastity for him means Britomart, married love. The story he tells is therefore part of my story: the final struggle between the romance of marriage and the romance of adultery.

Malecasta lives in Castle Joyeous amid the "courteous and comely glee" of gracious ladies and gentle knights.[58] Somebody must be paying for it all, but one cannot find out who. The Venus in her tapestries entices Adonis "as well that art she knew":[59] we are back in the world of the Vekke and the commandments of Love. In the rooms of the castle there is "dauncing and reveling both day and night," and "Cupid still emongst them kindles lustfull fyres."[60] The six knights with whom Britomart contends at its gate (Gardante, Parlante, and the rest) might have stepped straight out of the *Roman de la Rose,* and in the very next stanza the simile of the rose itself occurs.[61] The place is dangerous to spirits who would have gone through the Bower of Bliss without noticing its existence. Britomart gets a flesh wound there,[62] and Holiness himself is glad to be helped in his fight against Malecasta's champions by Britomart; by which the honest poet intends, no doubt, to let us know that even a religious man need not disdain the support which a happy marriage will give him against fashionable gallantry. For Britomart is married love.

Malecasta clearly represents the dangerous attractions of courtly love—the attractions that drew a Surrey or a Sydney. Hers is the face that it shows to us at first. But the House of Busirane is the bitter ending of it. In these vast, silent rooms, dazzling with snake-like gold, and endlessly pictured with "Cupid's warres and cruell battailes," [63] scrawled over with "a thousand monstrous formes" [64] of false love, where Britomart awaits her hidden enemy for a day and a night, shut in, entombed, cut off from the dawn which comes outside "calling men to their daily exercize," [65] Spenser has painted for us an unforgettable picture not of lust but of love—love as understood by the traditional French novel or by Guillaume de Lorris—in all its heartbreaking glitter, its sterility, its suffocating monotony. And when at last the ominous door opens and the Mask of Cupid comes out, what is this but a picture of the deep human suffering which underlies such loves?

> Unquiet care and fond Unthriftyhead;
> Lewd Losse of Time, and Sorrow seeming dead,
> Inconstant Chaunge, and false Disloyalty;
> Consuming Riotise, and guilty Dread
> Of heavenly vengeaunce: faint Infirmity;
> Vile Poverty; and, lastly, Death with infamy.[66]

The Mask, in fact embodies all the sorrows of Isoud among the lepers, and Launcelot mad in the woods, of Guinevere at the stake or Guinevere made nun and penitent, of Troilus waiting on the wall, of Petrarch writing *vergogna è'l frutto* and Sydney rejecting the love that reaches but to dust; or of Donne writing his fierce poems *from* the house of Busirane soon after Spenser had written *of* it. When Britomart rescues Amoret from this place of death she is ending some five centuries of human experience, predominantly painful. The only thing Spenser does not know is that Britomart is the daughter of Busirane—that his ideal of married love grew out of courtly love.

Who, then, is Amoret? She is the twin sister of Belphoebe and both were begotten by the Sun,

> pure and unspotted from all loathly crime
> That is ingenerate in fleshly slime[67]

The meaning of which is best understood by comparison with Spenser's sonnet,

> More then most faire, full of the living fire,
> Kindled above unto the maker neare.[68]

And we know that the Sun is an image of the Good for Plato,[69] and therefore of God for Spenser. The first important event in the life of these twins was their adoption by Venus and Diana: Diana the goddess of virginity, and Venus from whose house "all the world derives the glorious features of beautie." [70] Now the circumstances which led up to this adoption are related in one of the most medieval passages in the whole *Faerie Queene*—a *débat* between Venus and Diana;[71] but this *débat* has two remarkable features. In the first place, the Venus who takes part in it is a Venus severed from Cupid, and Cupid, as we have already seen, is associated with courtly love. I say "associated" because we are dealing with what was merely a feeling in Spenser's mind, not a piece of intellectual and historical knowledge, as it is to us. There is therefore no consistent and conscious identification of Cupid with courtly love, but Cupid tends to appear in one kind of context and to be absent from another kind. And when he does appear in contexts approved by our domestic poet, he usually appears with some kind of reservation. He is allowed into the Garden of Adonis on condition of his "laying his sad dartes asyde":[72] in the Temple of Venus it is only his younger brothers who flutter round the neck of the goddess.[73] We are therefore fully justified in stressing the fact that Venus finds Amoret only because she has lost Cupid, and finally adopts Amoret *instead of* Cupid.[74] The other important novelty is that this *débat* ends with a reconciliation; Spenser is claiming to have settled the old quarrel between Venus and Diana, and that after a singularly frank statement of the claims of each. And when the two goddesses have agreed, their young wards

> twixt them two did share
> The heritage of all celestiall grace;
> That all the rest it seemd they robbed bare,[75]

and one of them, Amoret, became

> th'ensample of true love alone
> And Lodestarre of all chaste affection.[76]

She was taken by Venus to be reared in the Garden of Adonis, guarded by Genius the lord of generation, among happy lovers and flowers (the two are here indistinguishable) whose fecundity never ceases to obey the Divine Command. This was her nursery: her school or university was the Temple of Venus. This is a region neither purely natural, like the Garden, nor artificial in the bad sense, like the Bower of Bliss: a region where,

> all that nature did omit,
> Art, playing second natures part, supplyed it.[77]

Here Amoret no longer grows like a plant, but is committed to the care of Womanhood; the innocent sensuousness of the garden is replaced by "sober Modestie," "comely Curtesie,"

> Soft Silence and submisse Obedience,

which are gifts of God and protect His saints "against their foes offence."[78] Indeed the whole island is strongly protected, partly by Nature,[79] and partly by such immemorial champions of maidenhead in the Rose tradition, as Doubt, Delay, and Daunger.[80] But when the lover comes he defeats all these and plucks Amoret from her place among the modest virtues. The struggle in his own mind before he does so, his sense of "Beauty too rich for use, for earth too dear," is a beautiful gift made by the humilities of medieval love poetry to Spenser at the very moment of his victory over the medieval tradition:

> my hart gan throb
> And wade in doubt what best were to be donne;
> For sacrilege me seem'd the Church to rob,
> And folly seem'd to leave the thing undonne.[81]

Amoret, however, cannot withdraw her hand, and the conclusion of the adventure may be given in the words of the poet who has studied most deeply this part of *The Faerie Queene:*

she what was Honour knew,
And with obsequious Majestie approv'd
My pleaded reason.

The natural conclusion is marriage, but Busirane for centuries has stood
in the way. That is why it is from the marriage feast that Busirane carries Amoret away,[82] to pine for an indefinite period in his tomblike
house. When once Britomart has rescued her thence, the two lovers become one flesh—for that is the meaning of the daring simile of the
Hermaphrodite in the original conclusion of Book III.[83] But even after
this, Amoret is in danger if she strays from Britomart's side; she will
then fall into a world of wild beasts where she has no comfort or guide,[84]
and may even become the victim of monsters who live on the "spoile of
women." [85]

If it is difficult to write down in prose the *significacio* of all this, the
difficulty arises from the fact that the poetic version has almost too much
meaning for prose to overtake. Thus, in general, it is plain that Amoret
is simply love—begotten by heaven, raised to its natural perfection in
the Garden and to its civil and spiritual perfections in the Temple,
wrongly separated from marriage by the ideals of courtly gallantry, and
at last restored to it by Chastity—as Spenser conceives chastity. But the
danger of such analysis is that some stupid person will ask us "Who,
then, is Scudamour? And if Chastity means (for Spenser) married love,
and that is Britomart, then what is the difference between Britomart and
Amoret?" Now, if we must, we can of course answer such questions. We
can say that while Scudamour and Amoret united by Britomart are a
picture of one thing—Marriage—yet Scudamour, taken by himself, is
hardly a personification at all; he is the lover, the husband, any husband,
or even *homo* in search of love. Or we can say that while Britomart
represents Chastity attained—the triumphant union of romantic passion
with Christian monogamy—Amoret, in isolation, represents the romantic
passion which Chastity must so unite. We can even go on to say that
whereas Amoret is the passion, Florimel is the object of the passion, The
Beautiful or Loveable, and that her sufferings illustrate the miseries to
which this object is exposed outside marriage: that the false Florimel is
the false Loveable grasped by Courtly Love: and we might point out
that the girdle which will fit only the true Florimel (and Amoret)[86] was
made for Venus, but for Venus, once more, carefully dissociated from

courtly love.[87] But I have no intention of following this plan. The very speed and ease with which the "false secondary power" produces these interpretations, warns us that if once we give it its head we shall never be done. The more concrete and vital the poetry is, the more hopelessly complicated it will become in analysis: but the imagination receives it as a simple—in both senses of the word. Oddly as it may sound, I conceive that it is the chief duty of the interpreter to begin analyses and to leave them unfinished. They are not meant as substitutes for the imaginative apprehension of the poem. Their only use is to awaken, first of all, the reader's conscious knowledge of life and books in so far as it is relevant, and then to stir those less conscious elements in him which alone can fully respond to the poem. And perhaps I have already done too much. Perhaps all we need to know is that the twins Amoret and Belphoebe represent Spenser's view that there are two kinds of chastity, both heaven-born.

The less allegorical parts group themselves easily enough round this core. The swashbucklers—the Paridells and Blandamours—are an almost literal picture of court life. In Book IV they are the enemies of true friendship; they are the young men, described by Aristotle, who change their friends several times in the same day.[88] In Book III, Paridell wooing Hellenore, is a picture of courtly love in action: he is the *learned* lover and knows all the Ovidian tricks.[89] That is why the one constant element in him is his hatred of Scudamour.[90] Marinell is a sort of pendant to Belphoebe: she represents virginity as an ideal, while he avoids love on prudential grounds, which Spenser disapproves. His marriage with Florimel probably expresses no allegorical relation; it comes in, like the wedding of the rivers, or Arthur's reconciliation of Poeana and Amyas, to illustrate the general theme of the book, which is Reconciliation rather than what we should call Friendship. Concord is for Spenser the resolution of discord: her two sons are Hate and Love, and Hate is the elder.[91] That is why we meet Ate, and her works, long before we meet Concord, and also why the titular heroes of the book are friends who were once foes; and the same theme of reconciliation connects Arthur's activities with the main subject.

In addition to such merely typical adventures, we have, as usual, passages that are quite free from allegory. Such are the beautiful "episode" of Timias and Belphoebe, and the prophecies of Merlin. We also have, so to speak, "islands" of pure allegory such as that of Malbecco or the House of Care, which are not closely connected with the central allegorical action. The two books, taken together, are a kind of central *massif* in *The Faerie Queene,* in which the poet's originality is at its highest and his command (for his own purposes) of the Italian art of interweaving is most perfect. It is very unfortunate that they also contain some of his worst writing; but this must not be taken as proof that he is tiring of his design. It comes mainly from the very simple cause, that in these books Spenser is facing the necessity, incumbent on a professed disciple of Ariosto, of giving us some big, set battlepieces, and Spenser, like all the Elizabethans, does this kind of thing very badly. It is idle to seek deep spiritual causes for literary phenomena which mere incompetence can explain. If a man who cannot draw horses is illustrating a book, the pictures that involve horses will be the bad pictures, let his spiritual condition be what it may. . . .

The sixth book is distinguished from its predecessors by distinct traces of the influence of Malory (a welcome novelty) and by the high proportion of unallegorical, or faintly allegorical, scenes. This last feature easily gives rise to the impression that Spenser is losing grip on the original conception of his poem; and it suggests a grave structural fault in *The Faerie Queene* in so far as the poem begins with its loftiest and most solemn book and thence, after a gradual descent, sinks away into its loosest and most idyllic. But this criticism overlooks the fact that the poem is unfinished. The proportion of allegoric core to typical, or purely fictional, fringe has varied all along from book to book; and the loose texture of the sixth is a suitable relief after the very high proportion of pure allegory in the fifth. The only fragment of any succeeding book which we have proves that the poem was to rise from the valley of humiliation into allegory as vast and august as that of the first book.

In the poem as a whole our understanding is limited by the absence of the allegorical centre, the union of Arthur and Gloriana. In the Mutabilitie cantos the opposite difficulty occurs—we have there the core of a book without the fringe. The fact that this should be so is interesting because it suggests (what is likely enough *a priori*) that Spenser was in the habit of writing his "cores" first and then draping the rest round them. But we lose much by not seeing the theme of change and permanence played out on the lower levels of chivalrous adventure. It is obvious, of course, that the adventures would have illustrated the theme of constancy and inconstancy, and that the mighty opposites would have appeared in the form of Mutabilitie and the Gods only at the central allegorical gable of the book—which is the bit we have. It is obvious too, that the Titaness, despite her beauty, is an evil force. Her very name "bold Alteration," [92] and the fact that she rises against the gods, put her at once among the enemies for any reader who understands Spenser's conceptions of health, concord, and subordination. The state of affairs which she would fain upset in heaven and has already upset in earth, is precisely that state which Spenser (or Aristotle) would have described as just and harmonious,

> all which Nature had establisht first
> In good estate, and in meet order ranged
> She did pervert.[93]

She is, in fact, Corruption, and since corruption, "subjecting the creature to vanity," came in with the Fall, Spenser practically identifies his Titaness with sin, or makes her the force behind the sin of Adam. She it is who

> Wrong of right, and bad of good did make
> And death for life exchanged foolishly:
> Since which all living wights have learn'd to die,
> And all the world is woxen daily worse.
> O pittious worke of Mutability,
> By which we all are subject to that curse,
> And death, instead of life, have sucked from our Nurse![94]

The full impact of that last line can be felt only when we have read the whole *Faerie Queene*. The enemies of Mutability are, first, the gods, and then *Nature*. Taken together they represent the Divine order in the universe—the concord, the health, the justice, the harmony, the Life, which, under many names, is the real heroine of the whole poem. If we take them apart, however, then the gods represent precisely what we should call "nature," the laws of the phenomenal universe. That is why the Titaness so far prevails with them—they are that world over which, even in the highest regions, she asserts some claim. But *Nature*, taken apart, is the ground of the phenomenal world. The reverence with which Spenser approaches this symbol contrasts favourably with the hardier attempts of Tasso and Milton to bring God, undisguised, upon the stage —and indeed it would be a pleasant task, if this chapter were not already too long, to show how much more religious a poem *The Faerie*

Queene is than the *Paradise Lost*. Mutability's appeal, it should be noticed, is not in the first instance to Nature at all, but

> to the highest him, that is behight
> Father of Gods and men of equall might,
> To weete the God of Nature.[95]

Yet when this appeal is answered it is the goddess *Natura* who appears, as in Claudian, Bernardus, Alanus, and Jean de Meun,

> This great Grandmother of all creatures bred,
> Great Nature, ever young, yet full of eld;
> Still mooving, yet unmoved from her sted,
> Unseene of any, yet of all beheld.[96]

The woody pavilion (unlike those fashioned by the "idle skill" of craftsmen)[97] which rises up to receive her, the "flowers that voluntary grow" beneath her feet, and the homage of the river-god, are all in the same tradition. Yet at the same time Spenser can compare her garments to those of Our Lord on the mount of Transfiguration, and even put into the mouth of Mutability words that separate *Nature* by a great gulf from the mere gods:

> Sith heaven and earth are both alike to thee,
> And gods no more then men thou doest esteeme;
> For even the gods to thee, as men to gods, do seeme.[98]

The modern reader is tempted to inquire whether Spenser, then, equates God with Nature: to which the answer is, "Of course not. He was a Christian, not a pantheist." His procedure in this passage would have been well understood by all his contemporaries: the practice of using mythological forms to hint theological truths was well established and lasted as late as the composition of *Comus*. It is, for most poets and in most poems, by far the best method of writing poetry which is religious without being devotional—that is, without being an act of worship to the reader. In the medieval allegories and the renaissance mask, God, if we may say so without irreverence, appears frequently, but always *incognito*. Every one understood what was happening, but the occasion remained an imaginative, not a devotional, one. The poet thus retains liberties which would be denied him if he removed the veil. For even Spenser, daring though he is in such matters, could hardly have descended so suddenly and delightfully as he does from the high court of the universe to the grotesque antimask of Faunus ("A foolish Faune indeed"),[99] if he had placed the Almighty undisguised instead of "Nature" on the bench of that high court; though in the long run this intermeddling of the high and low—the poet's eye glancing not only from earth to heaven but from the shapeless, funny gambollings of instinct to the heights of contemplation—is as grave, perhaps even as religious, as the decorum that would, in a different convention, have forbidden it.

I find the significance of the whole *débat* hard to determine with precision because of the deep obscurity of the lines in which Nature gives her sentence; but the general outlines of the meaning I think I have grasped. It is a magnificent instance of Spenser's last-moment withdrawal from dualism. The universe is a battlefield in which Change and Permanence contend. And these are evil and good—the gods, the divine order, stand for Permanence; Change is rebellion and corruption. But behind this endless contention arises the deeper truth—that Change is but the mode in which Permanence expresses itself, that Reality (like Adonis) "is eterne in mutabilitie," [100] and that the more Mutability succeeds the more she fails, even here and now—not to speak of her more ultimate ruin when we reach the

> rest of all things, firmely stayd
> Upon the pillars of Eternity.[101]

To praise this fragment seems almost an impertinence. In it all the powers of the poet are more happily united than ever before; the sublime and the ridiculous, the rarified beauties of august mythology and the homely glimpses of daily life in the procession of the months, combine to give us an unsurpassed impression of the harmonious complexity of the world. And in these cantos Spenser seems to have soared above all the usual infirmities of his style. His verse has never been more musical, his language never so strong and so sweet. Such poetry, coming at the very end of the six books, serves to remind us that the existing *Faerie Queene* is unfinished, and that the poet broke off, perhaps, with many of his greatest triumphs still ahead. Our loss is incalculable; at least as great as that we sustained by the early death of Keats.

If this chapter is not radically erroneous, then the history of Spenserian criticism, with one or perhaps two honourable exceptions, is a history of gross underestimation. I have not tried to conceal his faults; on some of them I have spoken more severely than most of his professed admirers. His prosaic, and even prosy, tendencies I almost claim to have set for the first time in their true light. I have exposed, without extenuation, those unpleasing passages where he becomes a bad poet because he is, in certain respects, a bad man. But they must be set beside the barbarity of Homer, the hatreds of Dante, the pride of Milton—and perhaps we may add, Shakespeare's apparently contented acquiescence in the ethical tomfoolery of honour and revenge. I do not mention these things with the absurd intention of exalting Spenser by depreciating others. I wish merely to indicate the level on which Spenser stands, the poets with whom he is to be compared.

My claim for Spenser may take the form of the old eulogy—*totam vitae imaginem expressit;* but perhaps my meaning will be clearer if we omit the word *totam,* if we say simply *vitae imaginem.* Certainly this will help to clear up a common misunderstanding. People find a "likeness" or "truth" to life in Shakespeare because the persons, passions and events which we meet in his plays are like those which we meet in our own lives: he excels, in fact, in what the old critics called "nature," or the probable. When they find nothing of the sort in Spenser, they are apt to conclude that he has nothing to do with "life"—that he writes that poetry of escape or recreation which (for some reason or other) is so intensely hated at present. But they do not notice that *The Faerie Queene* is "like life" in a different sense, in a much more literal sense. When I say that it is like life, I do not mean that the places and people in it are like those which life produces. I mean precisely what I say—that it is like life itself, not like the products of life. It is an image of the *natura naturans,* not of the *natura naturata.* The things we read about in it are not like life, but the experience of reading it is like living. The clashing antitheses which meet and resolve themselves into higher unities, the lights streaming out from the great allegorical *foci* to turn into a hundred different colours as they reach the lower levels of complex adventure, the adventures gathering themselves together and revealing their true nature as we draw near the *foci,* the constant reappearance of certain basic ideas, which transform themselves without end and yet ever remain the same (eterne in mutability), the unwearied variety and seamless continuity of the whole—all this is Spenser's true likeness to life. It is this which gives us, while we read him, a sensation akin to that which Hegelians are said to get from Hegel—a feeling that we have before us not so much an image as a sublime instance of the universal process—

that this is not so much a poet writing about the fundamental forms of life as those forms themselves spontaneously displaying their activities to us through the imagination of a poet. The invocation of the Muse hardly seems to be a convention in Spenser. We feel that his poetry has really tapped sources not easily accessible to discursive thought. He makes imaginable inner realities so vast and simple that they ordinarily escape us as the largely printed names of continents escape us on the map—too big for our notice, too visible for sight. Milton has well selected wisdom as his peculiar excellence—wisdom of that kind which rarely penetrates into literature because it exists most often in inarticulate people. It is this that has kept children and poets true to him for three centuries, while the intellectuals (on whom the office of criticism naturally devolves) have been baffled even to irritation by a spell which they could not explain. To our own troubled and inquiring age this wisdom will perhaps show its most welcome aspect in the complete integration, the harmony, of Spenser's mind. His work is one, like a growing thing, a tree; like the world-ash-tree itself, with branches reaching to heaven and roots to hell. It reaches up to the songs of angels or the vision of the New Jerusalem and admits among its shining ones the veiled image of God Himself: it reaches down to the horror of fertile chaos beneath the Garden of Adonis and to the grotesque satyrs who protect Una or debauch Hellenore with equal truth to their nature. And between these two extremes comes all the multiplicity of human life, transmuted but not falsified by the conventions of chivalrous romance. The "great golden chain of Concord" has united the whole of his world. What he feels on one level, he feels on all. When the good and fair appear to him, the whole man responds; the satyrs gambol, the lances splinter, the shining ones rise up. There is a place for everything and everything is in its place. Nothing is repressed; nothing is insubordinate. To read him is to grow in mental health.

With Spenser my story comes to an end. His chivalrous and allegorical poem was already a little out of date when it first appeared, as great poems not infrequently are. Its literary influence is much more important for the student of Milton and the Romantics than for the student of the Elizabethans. There is a history of great literature which has a slower rhythm than that of literature in general, and which goes on in a higher region. The biggest things do not work quickly. It is only after centuries that Spenser's position becomes apparent; and then he appears as the great mediator between the Middle Ages and the modern poets, the man who saved us from the catastrophe of too thorough a renaissance. To Hurd and the Wartons and Scott he appeared chiefly as a medieval poet, to Keats and Shelley as the poet of the marvellous. What the romantics learned from him was something different from allegory; but perhaps he could not have taught it unless he had been an allegorist. In the history of sentiment he is the greatest among the founders of that romantic conception of marriage which is the basis of all our love literature from Shakespeare to Meredith. The synthesis which he helped to effect was so successful that this aspect of his work escaped notice in the last century: all that Britomart stands for was platitude to our fathers. It is platitude no longer. The whole conception is now being attacked. Feminism in politics, reviving asceticism in religion, animalism in imaginative literature, and, above all, the discoveries of the psychoanalysts, have undermined that monogamic idealism about sex which served us for three centuries. Whether society will gain or lose by the revolution, I need not try to predict; but Spenser ought to gain. What once was platitude should now have for some the brave appeal of a cause nearly lost, and for others the interest of a highly specialized historical phenomenon—the peculiar flower of a peculiar civilization, important whether for good or ill and well worth our understanding.

NOTES

1. See Greenlaw, Osgood, Padelford, *Works of Spenser,* vol. i, Baltimore, 1932, p. 389.
2. Op. cit., ibid.
3. Op. cit., p. 395.
4. V. Owst, *Literature and Pulpit in Medieval England,* specially cap. 2.
5. *F.Q.* I. viii. 36, and V. xi. 19, 20.
6. Ibid. V. xi. 9.
7. Ibid. I. xi. 12.
8. Ibid. I. v. 30.
9. Ibid. III. ii. 28.
10. Ibid. xii. I.
11. Ibid. V. iv. 45.
12. Ibid. III. iv. 59.
13. Ibid. I. ii. 22, vii. 43, xii. 26.
14. Ibid. v. 21.
15. Ibid. III, Proem 2.
16. Ibid. I. v. 25.
17. Ibid. i. 5.
18. Ibid. IV. x. 34.
19. Ibid. I. v. 42.
20. Ibid. iv. 20, 23, 26, 29, 32, 35.

21. Ibid. v. 40.
22. Ibid. II. i. 3.
23. Ibid. I. ix. 54.
24. Ibid. III. x. 59.
25. Ibid. II. xii. 48.
26. Ibid. vi. I.
27. Ibid. I. xi. 49.
28. Ibid. I. x. 30.
29. Ibid. III. v. 33.
30. Ibid. vi. 34.
31. Ibid. vi. 41.
32. Ibid. I. iii. 4.
33. Ibid. IV. iii. 43.
34. Ibid. VI. v, vi.
35. Ibid. II. v. 29.
36. Ibid. xii. 50.
37. Ibid. II. xii. 58.
38. Ibid. xii. 61.
39. Ibid. III. vi. 29.
40. Ibid. III. vi. 34.
41. Ibid. vi. 44.
42. Ibid. II. xii. 44, 45.
43. Ibid. III. vi. 45.
44. *v. supra,* p. 151 [of Professor Lewis' book]. The fact that all the references to Art in the Bower are copied from Tasso does not invalidate my argument: the opposite passages in the Garden are not.
45. *F.Q.* II. xii. 63 et seq.; VI. x. II et seq.
46. Ibid. III. vi. 46.
47. Ibid. i. 36.
48. Ibid. II. v. 34.
49. Ibid. III. vi. 41.
50. Ibid. II. xii. 78.
51. Ibid. III. xii (First Version), 43-7.
52. Ibid. I. ix. 9-15.
53. Ibid. II. xii. I.
54. Ibid. IV. x. 26.
55. Ibid. IV, Proem. I.
56. Ibid. IV. ix. I.
57. Ibid. II. xii. I.
58. Ibid. III. i. 31.
59. Ibid. III. i. 35.
60. Ibid. III. i. 39.
61. Ibid. III. i. 45, 46.
62. Ibid. III. i. 65.
63. Ibid. III. xi. 29.
64. Ibid. III. xi. 51.
65. Ibid. III. xii. 28.
66. Ibid. III. xii. 25.
67. Ibid. III. vi. 3.
68. *Amoretti,* viii.
69. *Republic,* 507 D et seq.
70. Ibid. III. vi. 12.
71. Ibid. III. vi. 11-25.
72. Ibid. III. vi. 49.
73. Ibid. IV. x. 42.

74. Ibid. III. vi. 28.
75. Ibid. III. vi. 4.
76. **Ibid. III. vi. 52.**
77. Ibid. IV. x. 21.
78. Ibid. IV. x. 51.
79. Ibid. IV. x. 6.
80. Ibid. IV. x. 12, 13, 17.
81. Ibid. IV. x. 53.
82. Ibid. IV. i. 3.
83. Ibid. III. xii (1st version), 46.
84. Ibid. IV. vii. 2.
85. Ibid. IV. vii. 12.
86. Ibid. IV. v. 19.
87. Ibid. IV. v. 3-6.
88. *Ethics,* 1156 B.
89. *F.Q.* III. ix. 28, 29, 30: x. 6, 7, 8.
90. Ibid. IV. i. 39.
91. Ibid. IV. x. 32.
92. Ibid. *Mut.* vii, Argument. On the influence of Giordano Bruno, see B. E. C. Davis, *Edmund Spenser,* pp. 232 et seq.
93. *F.Q.* Mut. vi. 5.
94. Ibid. *Mut.* vi. 6.
95. Ibid. *Mut.* vi. 35.
96. Ibid. *Mut.* vii. 13.
97. Ibid. *Mut.* vii. 8.
98. Ibid. *Mut.* vii. 15.
99. Ibid. vi. 46.
100. Ibid. III vi. 47.
101. Ibid. *Mut.* viii. 2.

FOURTEEN

W. B. C. WATKINS

*The Kingdom of Our Language (1949)**

Spenser, so counter to present taste, might appear in the stocks more often if he seemed to our critics important enough.[1] Only Mr. William Van O'Connor has recently troubled to pillory him:

In the first four lines Spenser presents the theme:

> Oft when my spirit doth spred her bolder winges
> In mind to mount up to the purest sky,
> It down is weighd with thoght of earthly things,
> And clogd with burden of mortality:

In the next four lines the reader expects to find some exploration of the theme, but finds, instead, simply further statement:

> Where, when that soverayne beauty it doth spy,
> Resembling heavens glory in her light,
> Drawne with sweet pleasures bayt, it back doth fly,
> And unto heaven forgets her former flight.

In the well constructed lyric one would expect in the last lines to discover the intellectual resolution. Here, however, there is no dramatic emotional situation to be resolved. There is merely further explanation couched in terms of graceful tribute:

> There my fraile fancy, fed with full delight,
> Doth bath in blisse, and mantleth most at ease;
> Ne thinks of other heaven, but how it might

---

*This essay appeared in *The Hudson Review*, II (Autumn, 1949), 343-376, and as chapter eight (pp. 259-285) of *Shakespeare and Spenser*, Princeton University Press, 1950. Parts I, II, and III have been reprinted from *The Hudson Review*.

Her harts desire with most contentment please.
Hart need not wish none other happinesse,
But here on earth to have such hevens blisse.

The difference between the poems of Herrick and Stevens and Spenser
is the distinction between the poetry of exploration and the poetry of
exposition. Herrick and Stevens present material for the reader to *work*
through; Spenser presents an imagined experience unequivocally stated.
There is in the first two poems an intellectual and emotional problem to be
settled in terms of the materials presented. Spenser, as a Christian, represents and illustrates a Christian attitude; he does not *re-experience* it. He
does not *earn* his attitude.[2]

This does not arouse spirited defense of the *Amoretti,* of all Spenser's mature poems the least exciting, especially if one agrees that Herrick's *Mad Maid's Song* and Stevens' *Peter Quince at the Clavier* are
finer poems than this particular sonnet. The sonnet, however, is in its
way well constructed and contains more of the qualities which Mr.
O'Connor demands than he seems to realize. It is not dramatic, yet there
is more sinew in the convolutions of its neo-Platonic thought than casually appears; there is even more surprise and tension, since underlying
the whole sonnet is the pull between heaven and earth. The first four
lines express the soul's aspirations heavenward defeated by mortality; the
next four are statement, but "exploratory statement" essential to partic-
ularize "mortality," showing the soul, snared by desire, accepting a substitute heaven. The octave leaves us with a sense of true heaven forgotten
in earthly illusion. The opening lines of the sestet, expatiating on this
earthly bliss, are the only part of the poem which can be dismissed as
merely "further explanation," since the concluding couplet suddenly re-
verses the neo-Platonism and the *substitute* nature of earthly love, pro-
claiming the paradox of heaven on earth. In thus forcing a system of
philosophy to bow to his mistress Spenser shows no intense spiritual conflict; he stays, as he intends to stay, within the bounds of graceful,
playful tribute. Is there no room in poetry for this?

But the implications in Mr. O'Connor's complaint, reaching beyond
a casually chosen sonnet, disturb me more than his disparagement of
Spenser—particularly certain basic assumptions: the "well constructed
lyric," a formula reminiscent of the "well made play"; the necessity for
an "intellectual resolution" to a "dramatic emotional situation." The

lyric, seemingly, not only *must be* dramatic; it should be "an intellectual and emotional problem" to be solved, "an attitude to be earned."

Mr. O'Connor's is indisputably a voice of our time, and his preferences speak at least in part for many of us. In rejecting poetry like this sonnet because it lacks intensity, compression, drama, our generation is doing very much what Shakespeare and his fellows did. But if most of the Elizabethans forsook the *Amoretti* vein (Spenser with them), they by no means forsook all that Spenser accomplished and stood for in poetry, nor did they define drama so narrowly. The danger of present-day criticism, which has done so much to vindicate "inclusive" poetry, is of slipping unaware into an exclusive view, a new absolutism. Dr. Johnson sitting in judgment on the Metaphysicals is having the tables turned, while we risk freezing our own poetic taste into a set of neo-Metaphysical rules. Overly partial to the dramatic, we are likely to ignore not only narrative, which the poets have surrendered to the novelists, but the interdependence of narrative and drama.

A greater poetic passage than this sonnet of Spenser's is also "unequivocally stated":

> Nature that fram'd us of foure Elements,
> Warring within our breasts for regiment,
> Doth teach us all to have aspyring minds:
> Oure soules, whose faculties can comprehend
> The wondrous Architecture of the world;
> And measure every wandring plannets course,
> Still climing after knowledge infinite,
> And alwaies moving as the restles Spheares,
> Wills us to weare our selves and never rest,
> Untill we reach the ripest fruit of all,
> That perfect blisse and sole felicitie,
> The sweet fruition of an earthly crowne.

Marlowe, not yet himself mature, is writing in a still immature form—English drama, and with a shackled grandeur that no one wishes edited by a Bentley. Marlowe's weakness is not exposition and statement, which he never abandons, though he develops in the direction of drama; his weakness is imperfect articulation, since the potentially fine structure of the passage is faulty. As in Spenser's sonnet, the aspiring soul stoops to earthly fruition; but heaven and earth are not in balance. While in this instance we prefer Marlowe's failure to Spenser's success, Spenser at least achieves his end. It is the end which leaves us cold.

We have lost pleasure in the purely formal; and it is precisely the formal statement of three themes one after the other, then combined at the end, which gives the opening sonnet of the *Amoretti* (a simpler, more uncompromising example than Mr. O'Connor's choice) the effect of a thematic musical exercise:

> *Happy ye leaves* when as those lilly hands,
>   which hold my life in their dead doing might,
>   shall handle you and hold in loves soft bands,
>   lyke captives trembling at the victors sight.
> And *happy lines,* on which with starry light,
>   those lamping eyes will deigne sometimes to look
>   and reade the sorrowes of my dying spright,
>   written with teares in harts close bleeding book,
> And *happy rymes* bath'd in the sacred brooke,
>   of Helicon whence she derived is,
>   when ye behold that Angels blessed looke,
>   my soules long lacked foode, my heavens blis,
> *Leaves, lines,* and *rymes,* seek her to *please* alone,
>   *whom if ye please, I care for other none.*

This is low in emotional key, not intense, not exciting. Yet this is all that Spenser set out to accomplish—simple but expert statement, contrived in a pattern of intricate verbal sounds so skillful that only careful analysis would reveal it. The balance of meaning and sound is maintained, however; internal and external rhymes, alliteration, assonance do not blur the statement, or, as with Swinburne, hypnotize us so that meaning seems not to matter.

This kind of formality, with its description and exposition, lends itself to drama better than one might suppose. In Richard Second's last soliloquy is a conceit latently metaphysical, but sighs and tears and groans are used as formal elements of structure:

> For now hath time made me his numbering clock:
> My thoughts are minutes; and with *sighs* they jar
> Their watches on unto mine eyes, the outward watch,
> Whereto my finger, like a dial's point,
> Is pointing still, in cleansing them from *tears.*
> Now sir, the sound that tells what hour it is

> Are clamorous *groans,* which strike upon my heart,
> Which is the bell: so *sighs* and *tears* and *groans*
> Show *minutes, times,* and *hours:* but my time
> Runs posting on in Bolingbroke's proud joy,
> While I stand fooling here, his Jack o' the clock.

Though like Marlowe Shakespeare shortly moves away from Spenser toward more dramatic condensation of thought and feeling, he never abandons the formal, which we find metamorphosed in the technique of *King Lear.*

Richard's transitional soliloquies are predominantly lyrical statement, though especially in this instance the intellectual element (itself formal) is prominent. The kinship to Spenser and the difference from him are highlighted if we compare a stanza from Arthur's soliloquy to Night after fruitless pursuit of Florimell and sleep:

> But well I wote, that to an heavy hart
> Thou art the root and nurse of bitter cares,
> *Breeder of new, renewer of old smarts:*
> In stead of rest thou lendest rayling teares,
> In stead of sleepe thou sendest troublous feares,
> And dreadfull visions, in the which alive
> The drearie image of sad death appeares:
> So from the wearie spirit thou doest drive
> Desired rest, and men of happiness deprive.

Both soliloquies are reflective, but Richard's is introspective and analytical to a degree not true of Arthur's, which is of course more stylized. Richard's conceits forecast metaphysical wit; Arthur's play on words is not the kind of verbal extravagance typical at this period of Shakespeare, but closer to the felicity of phrase admired by Jonson, later by Dryden, Pope, and Johnson. Not by paradox, but by placement and natural emphasis in the line, *new* and *old* are contrasted and assimilated to *smarts; old* and *new* are reconciled in *renew.*

This stanza reveals two of Spenser's primary technical faults, which he must share the responsibility of propagating among his followers through the centuries: the loosening of structure by excessive particles and auxiliaries, and the weak epithet. "Drearie image" and "wearie spirit" rely too much on the adjective, though Spenser is more justified than many of his followers because he is clearly composing for the ear: besides the double alliteration (*dr*eadfull-*dr*earie), *drearie* and *wearie* contribute internal rhyme to an elaborate sound pattern. On the credit side is a mastery of words which this adjectival weakness may obscure, and a control of syntax which Marlowe and even Shakespeare were some time in rivaling. Spenser's sentence unfolds with ease in the confines of his complex stanza.

Rather than defend Spenser from specific charges, some of which he deserves, it will be more profitable to consider his poetic craftsmanship in relation to Shakespeare's. Like Shakespeare he has range and variety; he is master of more than one style. Heretofore no one—not even Shakespeare—has had a more catholic appeal to the *profession*. Besides shoals of minor poets, among his debtors are Marlowe, Shakespeare, Milton, Dryden, Pope, Thomson, Burns, Wordsworth, Keats, Byron, Shelley, Tennyson, Yeats. In bearing the responsibilities of this eminence (several of these poets show up his weaknesses), he should be judged with perspective.

Spenser has not stood the test of time so well as Shakespeare; much of his work, like Jonson's, requires historical orientation for full understanding; some is unrecoverable. None the less, he and Shakespeare represent two great traditions, narrative and dramatic, two primary ways of using language, direct and oblique; furthermore, while thus supplementary, they are in many ways complementary. No other two taken together so fully represent the achievement of English poetry. The technical triumph of the Elizabethan age and the richness of its poetic language cannot be illustrated by Shakespeare alone, or by Shakespeare in combination with any other poet than Spenser.

II

The *Shepheardes Calender* is an aqueduct flung back across the morass of Tudor poetry to Chaucer, the "well of English undefyled." In that morass are several streams of fine poetry—Dunbar, Skelton, Wyatt, Surrey, Sackville. Some lost themselves. Skelton wandered merrily into the rushes. A few found their way back into the main current—Surrey and Sackville through Spenser; Wyatt through Sidney's sonnets, Shakespeare, and Donne. Though in his *Induction* Sackville demonstrated an astonishing mastery, which he could not repeat, and Wyatt left a handful of first rate poems, on the whole the Tudor efforts at reclamation were premature. Wyatt had the originality and power, but lacked the skill; Surrey had the skill, but lacked originality and power. Spenser had all three, plus faith and audacity and will.

Five editions in Spenser's lifetime indicate that the poets read the *Shepheardes Calender* even if they did not always know the author's identity, and profited even when they did not altogether approve. To recognize Spenser's influence only among the so-called Spenserians— Drayton, the Fletchers, Drummond—is myopic; it has never been limited to kindred spirits nor to mere imitation. Spenser's intense concern with the craft and medium of poetry makes him a focal figure; to ignore or neglect him is to distort the whole tradition.

This problem of words—not just vocabulary, but syntax, words in meaningful patterns—occupied Spenser even when he was in the Merchant Taylors' School, where the admirable and lively Mulcaster spread joy in his native tongue. Earlier humanists, if they did not like More write primarily in Latin, deplored the poverty of English. Poetry (or those who felt responsible for it) was scrambling after classic prosody from a real sense of the inadequacy of poulter's measure, and from a false scorn of barbaric rhyme and beat. Spenser was sufficiently impressed to quibble with Harvey and Dyer over the quantitative values of homely English syllables, over troublesome vowels already dissolving into diphthongs or virtually disappearing into a common sound. In *September* he makes Diggon complain:

> Then playnely to speak of shepheards most what
> Badde is the best *(this English is flat)*.

But this conventional protest is off-key in a poem which is a proclamation of emancipation. "Why, a God's name may we not have the kingdom of our language?" Spenser explodes to Harvey in 1581.

He met Harvey's objection by pointing to Marot and Bellay, who had determinedly caught up with the Italians, and to Chaucer, who had made the English of his day sufficient for great poetry. None could complain of the expressiveness of Chaucer, however rough his meter in a faulty text wrongly read. Though Mr. C. S. Lewis, somewhat overwhelmed by Ariosto, still maintains that "his discipleship to Chaucer exists only in profession, not in practice," Spenser's tributes to Chaucer are more than nationalistic bravura. The poet who had already mastered a slightly artificial but thoroughly English style (in contrast to Milton) in the *Shepheardes Calender,* where continental influences are classical and French, not Italian, and in *Mother Hubberds Tale,* before he progressed very far on the first draft of the *Faerie Queene,* learns many new devices of narration and transition from Ariosto, but does not unlearn his language.

Even in his archaisms, paralleling the procedure of Bellay, Spenser follows Chaucer's example in selecting from contemporary dialects outside London more than he pillages Chaucer's Middle English. These archaisms Sidney in a neoclassical moment censures long before Jonson; even E. K. (with Spenser conniving) is conciliatory. Like most innovators Spenser goes too far. But he is consciously seeking words, homely as well as elevated, of fresher and more precise meaning. Many of his resurrections are stillborn; others survive till later poets strangle them. He abandons his extreme archaism, just as he repeats only three of the thirteen metrical forms, ten of which were first introduced to the Elizabethans in the *Calender.*

Spenser learns more from Chaucer than judicious selection of current dialects—the importance of skillfully handled syntax, the metrical value of the short syllable, effective for melodic purposes and for swift-moving, effortless narrative. With an equal predilection for description and meditation, like Chaucer he is capable also of dramatic narration when it suits his purpose. As he matures Spenser becomes more restrained in his borrowings, more skillful in adaptation, in taking over language principles rather than special practices. And with a swiftness more remarkable, though less famous, than Marlowe's lightning development of blank verse, Spenser molds a style that is rich, varied, fluid, adaptable to racy, homely satire and to conversational directness, as well as to the elegant formality of the *Amoretti* or the lofty idealism of the *Faerie Queene.* Since drama evolves from narrative, it is not surprising to find in Spenser's early poetry, if we trouble to look, a mastery of colloquial verse and dialogue unsurpassed in the drama for another fifteen years.

These bold borrowings, adaptations, innovations in language and metrical form point the way for the rest of the Elizabethans. His successes justify his failures. Shakespeare has as many faults of abuse and excess. Othello asks that Desdemona be sent to him,

> With such accommodation and *besort*
> As levels with her breeding.

When Prospero wants Miranda to see Ferdinand approaching, he says:

The fringed curtains of thine eyes advance
And say what thou seest yond.

Isolated, these speeches are slightly ridiculous. In their context they create a deliberate remoteness—Othello, noble, exotic; Prospero, long exiled from his kind, stately master of his own rare world. Similarly, Spenser's language is adapted to the creation of the special world of the *Faerie Queene,* though even there and everywhere in his minor poems he introduces colloquialism as daringly as Shakespeare, or Mr. Eliot, or Mr. Auden. Abstractions and personifications are frequent in Shakespeare as in Spenser, and neither hesitates to make up words or twist old words to new meanings.

Spenser's language is more consistent than Shakespeare's, but each poet alters diction and syntax according to the effect he desires. In the considerable exposition of thought and action in his plays Shakespeare resorts to direct statement; few maintain, except by implication, that on these occasions poetry flies out of the window. In his complex allegory Spenser not only writes most of the time in elaborate metaphor; he also uses language dramatically at crucial points in his story, and repetitive imagery is as essential to his symbolism as to Shakespeare's mature plays. There is a large area in the use of language where they overlap. But in general we may say that Spenser exemplifies the direct, logical statement of the narrative tradition going back to Chaucer and enriched by Ariosto and Tasso; Shakespeare the oblique statement, the double or triple meaning, the elliptical phrase of drama. Spenser secures a cumulative effect by slow elaboration; Shakespeare intensity by the greatest possible compression.

The direct statement, the denotative use of language, has been in ill repute among poets and critics, except for a few like Mr. Eliot, since the end of the nineteenth century; the explicit has been abandoned to prose. In using *implicit* and *explicit,* as Miss Josephine Miles remarks, we should remember that what becomes through familiarity explicit was less so perhaps when first written. The terms are slippery and will remain so until the semanticists lead us out of the wilderness. In distinguishing so far as one can in brief space these two uses of language, I shall limit myself primarily, not systematically, to diction, syntax, figure, and imagery. The first two bring us at once to "the qualities which good verse shares with good prose." Syntax provides an index not only to the logical processes of the mind but to the structure of the sensibility.[3]

Chaucer's hand in Spenser's syntax and narrative style is evident in such fables as the Oak and the Briar in *Februarie,* the Kid and the Fox in *May;* but is most apparent in *Mother Hubberds Tale,* written about 1580 though unpublished for ten years. Spenser promises a plain, unvarnished tale:

> No Muses aide me needes hereto to call;
> Base is the style, and matter meane withall.

It is a fabliau, supposedly told by a "plain, good woman." Spenser does not pretend to capture in the telling the psychology of the narrator, as Wordsworth, with only partial success, was to do later in poems like *The Thorn.* Mother Hubberd is used merely for a certain flavor, and skillfully Chaucerianized Elizabethan for the purportedly "base" style:

> *It was the month, in which the righteous Maide,*
> *That for disdaine of sinfull worlds upbraide,*
> *Fled back to heaven, whence she was first conceived,*
> Into her silver bowre the Sunne received;
> And the hot Syrian Dog on him awayting,
> After the chased Lyons cruell bayting,
> Corrupted had th'ayre with his noysome breath,
> *And powr'd on th'earth plague, pestilence, and death.*
> *Amongst the rest a wicked maladie*
> *Raign'd amongst men, that manie did to die,*
> Depriv'd of sense and ordinarie reason;
> That it to Leaches seemed strange and geason.
> My fortune was mongst manie others moe,
> To be partakers of their common woe;
> And my weake bodie set on fire with griefe,
> Was rob'd of rest, and naturall reliefe.
> *In this ill plight, there came to visite mee*
> *Some friends, who sorie my sad case to see,*
> *Began to comfort me in chearfull wise,*
> *And meanes of gladsome solace to devise.*
> *But seeing kindly sleep refuse to doe*
> *His office, and my feeble eyes·forgoe,*
> *They sought my troubled sense how to deceave*
> *With talke, that might unquiet fancies reave*
> *And sitting all in seates about me round,*

> *With pleasant tales (fit for that idle stound)*
> *They cast in course to waste the wearie howres. . . .*

In this simple magic of straightforward, unpretentious storytelling in verse Spenser recaptures a power lost since Chaucer, a style as old as poetry, as new as any present. The unobtrusive intimacy and personal tone, so different from the Romantics, of the opening device is at once that of the folk tale of common origin and of the highly sophisticated frame of the Platonic dialogues, to which Tudor and early Elizabethan prose pieces like the *Utopia,* the *Schoolmaster,* the *Defense of Poesy* also owe their peculiar charm. For if Chaucer is in the immediate background, one feels in *Mother Hubberds Tale* the interfusion of centuries of tradition in folklore and philosophic meditation.

Spenser gets on with his story:

> Whilome (said she) before the world was civill,
> The Foxe and th' Ape disliking of their evill
> And hard estate, determinéd to seeke
> Their fortunes farre abroad, lyeke with his lyeke:
> For both were craftie and unhappie witted;
> Two fellowes might no where be better fitted.
> The Foxe, that first this cause of griefe did finde,
> Gan first thus plaine his case with words unkinde,
> Neighbour Ape, and my Gossip eke beside,
> (Both two sure bands in friendship to be tide,)
> To whom may I more trustelý complaine
> The evill plight, that doth me sore constraine,
> And hope thereof to finde due remedie?
> Heare then my paine and inward agonie.
> Thus manie yeares I now have spent and worne,
> In meane regard, and basest fortunes scorne,
> Doing my Country service as I might,
> No lesse I dare saie than the prowdest wight;
> And still I hoped to be up advancéd,
> For my good parts; but still it hath mischauncéd.
> *Now therefore that no lenger hope I see*
> *But froward fortune still to follow mee,*
> *And losels lifted high, where I did looke,*
> *I meane to turne the next leafe of the booke.*

The verse flows into the crannies of character and the vagaries of dialogue with undiminished ease. We hardly notice that our simple story has now assumed two simultaneous levels—beast and human—and is beginning to develop overtones of social and political satire. The ridicule of the self-righteous, envious grumbler, determined no longer to acquiesce, is so timeless that topical reference can be either ignored or supplied from any contemporary scene.

These couplets are free-flowing. There is no sign of strain in the adjustment of sentence to metrical pattern; while the sentences are frequently complex, they are clear and straightforward. That they are not more closely knit is attributable to the deliberately colloquial style rather than to any failure in structural sense. Speech rhythms are adjusted to the meter with skill and variety, producing considerable variation in the beats of the line (trochees for iambs) without destroying the fundamental rhythmic pattern. The frequent enjambment is chiefly on unaccented syllables, but occasionally on accented:

> Amongst the rest a wicked maladie
> Raign'd amongst men, that manie did to die.

But Spenser does not depend too much on enjambment for fluidity. The syntax of the Fox's speech shows that it is not built up line by line, but conceived as a whole; we are carried through the passage by the structure of thought more than by mechanical devices. Even the alliterative pattern here—no mere decorative "searching the letter"—seems a characteristic rhetorical trick of speech in the glib Fox; "froward fortune" and "losels lifted high" are the stock proverbial phrases of the demagogue, and the homely figure of the last line, as abrupt as his decision, is individual flavor. Colloquial rhythm pervades the narrative as well as the dialogue and is apparent from the beginning.

Many of the qualities which we associate with dramatic verse are equally the property of narrative, and Spenser had fully mastered those qualities in the couplet long before the dramatists learned to loosen the bonds of blank verse. This gift of poetic speech so admirably adapted to drama Spenser uses sparingly in the *Faerie Queene,* but in a few instances he evolves some ten years before *King Lear* a terse poetic dialogue not unlike Goneril's.[4] And his colloquial rhythms from 1579 on are taken up at once by the sonneteers beginning with Sidney, partly through them passing on to the dramatists.

Spenser's master in this familiar style, so far as he needed one, is clear from this portrait in a consciously Chaucerian manner:

> Which when the Priest beheld, he view'd it nere,
> As if therin some text he studying were,
> But little else (God wote) could thereof skill:
> For read he could not evidence, nor will,
> Ne tell a written word, ne write a letter,
> Ne make one title worse, ne make one better:
> Of such deep learning little had he neede,
> Ne yet of Latine, ne of Greeke, that breede
> Doubts mongst Divines, and difference of texts,
> From which arise diversitie of sects,
> And hatefull heresies, of God abhor'd:
> But this good Sir did follow the plaine word,
> Ne medled with their controversies vaine,
> All his care was, his service well to saine,
> And to read Homelies upon holidayes:
> When that was done, he might attend his playes.

The shifts of pace and variety of pauses here are admirable, playing speech rhythm against metrical beat or making them skillfully coincide:

> All his care was/his service well to saine.

This satirical analysis of the priest's ignorance is a rationalization in semi-soliloquy, with its bewilderment, its slight hesitations followed by rush of words. The satire is all the better for being equivocal, poised between self-righteousness and discomfort; the priest is undermined by his inability to "follow the plaine word" except so far as he has learned his text and homilies by rote. Indignation is softened by sly humor. At other times Spenser's scorn is full of sheer animal spirits, anticipating Samuel Butler:

> The Pasport ended, both they forward went,
> The Ape clad Souldierlike, fit for th'intent,
> In a blew jacket / with a crosse of redd
> And manie slits, as if that he had shedd
> Much blood through many wounds therein receaved,
> Which had the use of his right arme bereaved;
> Upon his head an old Scotch cap he wore,
> With a plume feather all to peeces tore:
> His breeches were made after the new cut,
> *Al Portugese,* loose like an emptie gut.

But most of all, Spenser as a satirist is the Elizabethan Dryden, for Dryden is closer in temper to Spenser than to his great follower, Pope. The kinship is in basic humanity and generosity, largeness of view, easy vigor, and verve. Occasionally Spenser strikes the very quality which is to be pre-empted by Dryden as "raillery"; good nature tempers satire which is not so much wit as a kind of exuberant fun:

> Be you the Souldier, for you likest are
> For manly semblance, and small skill in warre.

Yet Mr. Eliot calls Dryden "a successor of Jonson, and therefore the descendant of Marlowe." And Mr. Oscar Campbell in his study of Elizabethan satire ignores Spenser altogether. Outside the drama, no Elizabethan satirist, not even Donne, is greater than Spenser, who also happens to be one of the few masters of the familiar style in English poetry.

Spenser maintains the same fluency when he lays aside the couplet for ottava rima in *Muiopotmos: the Fate of the Butterflie,* which also deserves rescue from the dreary *Complaints.* The changes in diction and style are determined not by the stanza, but by the demands of mock-heroic, as delicate and skillful as the *Rape of the Lock,* another poem in debt to Spenser, who himself never forgot *Sir Thopas.* Such phrases as "deadly dolorous debate" are partly self-satire in this burlesque of epic and the heroic style:

> I sing of deadly dolorous debate,
> Stirr'd up through wrathfull Nemesis despight,
> Betwixt two mightie ones of great estate,
> Drawne into armes, and proofe of mortall fight,
> Through prowd ambition, and hart swelling hate,
> Whilest neither could the others greater might
> And sdeignfull scorne endure; that from small jarre
> Their wraths at length broke into open warre.
>
> The roote whereof and tragicall effect,
> Vouchsafe, O thou the mournfulst Muse of nyne,
> That wontst the tragick stage for to direct,
> In funerall complaints and waylfull tyne,
> Reveale to me, and all the meanes detect,
> Through which sad Clarion did at last declyne
> To lowest wretchedness; and is there then
> Such rancour in the harts of mightie men?

These two opening stanzas are a triumph of "straight-face" comedy. They are poetically fine enough to be taken as serious poetry, and, as in all great mock-heroic, this serious poetic quality is essential to the complex effect. The next stanza, by giving away the heroes, announces the parody already caught by the subtle ear.

At first glance, the opening of *Muiopotmos* seems to be composed line by line like *Tamburlaine,* until the sudden overflow into the seventh and eighth lines. But Elizabethan punctuation is misleading. While such devices as the strong initial beat of the fourth line modify the rhythm and prevent monotony, it is the syntax which prevents looseness and the deadliness of end-stopped verse. This structural unity is clearer in the second stanza, where the more convoluted sentence shows careful arrangement of primary and subordinate clauses and postponement of verbs. Placement of *vouchsafe* and *reveale* and reliance on grammatical logic (instead of repeating subject of the second verb) suggest that condensation is to Spenser a means to secure structure rather than intensity. Furthermore, the position of the opening phrase (*whereof* ties in directly with *warre*) and the inversion make the sense continuous, so that the two stanzas are really one. Such technical virtuosity was certainly not lost on Milton, who, together with Spenser, teaches Pope the difficult art of weaving self-contained heroic couplets into "paragraphs."

This organic unity differs from the almost mathematically formal structure of the first *Amoretti* sonnet. Both types of structure are found in the *Faerie Queene,* where the verse ranges from elaboration to simplicity. Any of Spenser's direct addresses to the reader, so frequent at the opening of a canto, illustrates a mastery of simple statement as marked as *Mother Hubberds Tale,* though completely different in tempo and quality:

> The noble hart, that harbours vertuous thought,
> And is with child of glorious great intent,
> Can never rest, untill it forth have brought,
> Th'eternall brood of glorie excellent:
> Such restlesse passion did all night torment
> The flaming corage of that Faery knight,
> Devizing, how that doughtie turnament
> With greatest honour he atchieven might;
> Still did he wake, and still did watch for dawning light.

This is equally admirable as prose or poetry. With the exception of the inversion in the eighth line, there is nothing unnatural or forced in syntax perfectly fitted into the confines of an exacting stanza; there is no conflict between metrical demands and meaning, but the poise of reconciliation.

We are no longer geared to the leisurely unfolding of the *Faerie Queene.* We read it too rapidly, partly under the psychological oppression of its length; consequently to most it has a monotony which more carefully spaced reading dissipates. Spenser is to be read aloud for delight as well as profit; only when approached thus does the richness and variety of his art unfold. And if we turn from the first six books to the *Mutabilitie Cantos,* we find a change in his style so great as to make it difficult to see how these two cantos, supposedly the core of a Seventh Book, could have been successfully brought into focus with the rest.

In the *Mutabilitie Cantos* is little suggestion of Ariosto or Tasso. Romance-epic shifts from romance to epic. Diction and style have greater simplicity and an authority as fine in its way as Milton's—close to what Keats was attempting when, in painstaking revision of *Hyperion,* he turned from Milton to Dante. Always aware of what he is doing, Spenser calls it "sternenesse" of style: syntax becomes simpler, nearer to the metrical pattern, and the more sparing inversions and indirections have too much justification to seem *tours de force.* Meter and sentence beat almost in unison:

> Ah! whither dost thou now thou greater Muse
> Me from these woods and pleasing forrests bring?
> And my fraile spirit (that doth oft refuse
> This too high flight, unfit for her weake wing)
> Lift up aloft, to tell of heavens King
> (Thy soveraine Sire) his fortunate successe,
> And victory, in bigger notes to sing,
> Which he obtain'd against that Titanesse,
> That him of heavens Empire sought to dispossesse.

> Yet sith I needs must follow thy behest,
> Do thou my weaker wit with skill inspire,
> Fit for this turne; and in my feeble brest
> Kindle fresh sparks of that immortall fire,
> Which learned minds inflameth with desire
> Of heavenly things: for, who but thou alone,
> That art yborne of heaven and heavenly Sire,

> Can tell things doen in heaven so long ygone;
> So farre past memory of man that may be knowne.

Spenser still flavors his style with the antique—*sith, yborne, ygone*—which are at the same time slight metrical helps; but he no longer needs easy aids, and there is no suspicion of quaintness in this slight, deliberate resort to archaism.

If in his last period he strikes out on the one hand in the direction of a sterner heroic style, on the other he carries his mastery of metrical complexity to heights unsurpassed in English. In *Prothalamion* the elaborate canzone is sustained by the structure of the sentence:

> Calm was the day, and through the trembling ayre,
> Sweete breathing Zephyrus did softly play
> A gentle spirit, that lightly did delay
> Hot Titans beames, which then did glyster fayre:
> When I whom sullen care,
> Through discontent of my long fruitlesse stay
> In Princesse Court, and expectation vayne
> Of idle hopes, which still doe fly away,
> Like empty shaddows, did aflict my brayne,
> Walkt forth to ease my payne
> Along the shoare of silver streaming Themmes,
> Whose rutty Bancke, the which his River hemmes,
> Was paynted all with variable flowers,
> And all the meades adornd with daintie gemmes,
> Fit to decke maydens bowres,
> And crowne their Paramours,
> Against the Brydale day, which is not long:
> Sweete Themmes runne softly, till I end my Song.

The skeletal statement may be transposed thus: *Calm was the be-throthal day when I walked forth to ease my pain along the Thames.* The elaboration is contrived by development of four elements in the sentence: the calmness of the day, the personal pain, the easing of pain by the river's beauty, the coming ceremony. But these elements are not formally treated as in the *Amoretti*. Suspense is built up by what was to become Milton's favorite device—postponement of the main idea—though, grammatically speaking, Spenser begins with an inversion of the main clause. Calm, the mood of the whole poem, is first established in nature, then contrasted to a discordant personal mood with its equally discordant artificial background (the Court), then offered as a solace; but this seeming resolution is modified by the sudden introduction of the fourth element (harmonious with the day) in a coda. We have already seen in *Mother Hubberds Tale* that Spenser early learned the structural potentialities of relatives used often with deliberate looseness, and of careful placement of subordinate clauses. Now he no longer bothers to maintain exact balance between importance of substance and grammatical logic. This kind of intentional structural ambiguity is typical of the later Shakespeare.

In *Prothalamion* diction is for the most part simple, almost plain. *Mead* and *paramours* are the only obvious poeticisms, though we may include such words as *glyster, rutty, adorned, variable,* which were subsequently worked into a poetic diction and squandered. Description of nature is beautifully poised between artifice and reality; yet the pictorial is not only subordinated to emotional complexity, to the deliberate clash of moods; it is also of no more importance than the modulation of sound. Art is consummate here and appears less contrived than Tennyson's lyric beginning:

> Calm is the morn without a sound,
>   Calm as to suit a calmer grief,
>   And only through the faded leaf
> The chestnut pattering to the ground.

Spenser and Tennyson are frequently berated for describing rather than dramatizing emotion. Such direct statement as theirs seems to us often less truly *direct* than the half-articulate cry, the ellipsis, the psychologically revealing surprise. We prefer one kind of artifice to another.

III

One manifestation of explicit as distinct from implicit use of language is preference for simile over metaphor. We cannot say that Spenser is a poet of simile, Shakespeare of metaphor; for neither confines himself to one exclusively. Their range is too wide, their use of language too rich and varied to distinguish more than general tendencies. A few examples will indicate the divergence.

My first choice is not fair, the poetic advantage being too conspicuously Shakespeare's; its value is similarity in the comparison. Spenser writes in *Januarie:*

> You naked trees, whose shady leaves are lost,
> Wherein the byrds were wont to build their bowre:
> And now are clothd with mosse and hoary frost,
> Instede of blossmes, wherewith your buds did flowre:
> I see your teares, that from your boughes doe raine,
> Whose drops in drery isicles remaine.
>
> All so my lustfull leafe is drye and sere,
> My timely buds with wayling all are wasted:
> The blossome, which my braunch of youth did beare,
> With breathed sighes is blowne away, and blasted
> And from mine eyes the drizling teares descend,
> As on your boughes the isicles depend.

Shakespeare may be partially indebted to this passage in his familiar *Sonnet LXXIII:*

> That time of year thou mayst in me behold
> When yellow leaves, or none, or few do hang
> Upon those boughs which shake against the cold,
> Bare ruin'd choirs where late the sweet birds sang.

He condenses into four lines as much as Spenser says in twelve—even more. His fourth line, ostensibly in simple apposition, actually carries much of the poetic meaning. He is using a form which demands compression, whereas Spenser's form allows him to set his own limit; but primarily Shakespeare achieves compression by metaphor and by exploiting fully the multiple meanings of certain key words. *Bare* is made to work on several levels of meaning simultaneously:

1. My middle age is *bare*.
2. The boughs are *bare* of leaves.
3. The trees are *bare* of birds.
4. The choirs are *bare* of singers.

Thus the barrenness of middle age is made intensely visual and audible. Only the fourth meaning is directly stated; the rest are implicit, made valid by stressing one point of similarity in middle age, boughs in winter, deserted choirs—the last two literal (birds and singers with actual voices), the first metaphorical. In these lines Shakespeare exhausts the associations and correspondences in the figure; later he strips these away to its essence when Macbeth complains:

> my way of life
> Is fall'n into the sear, the yellow leaf.

In each case, though metaphor is used, emotion is frankly stated; the statement becomes oblique through the deliberate multiplicity of implications. Incidentally, the adjective is paramount in Macbeth's condensation; *sear* especially, with its latent pun, carries most weight.

Spenser's comparison between a tree in winter and approaching age is explicit, elaborated in detail, like Richard's soliloquy on time. First we have the visualization of the naked trees, then the comparison—a method which strikes us as naive, even archaic, as lacking economy, since it involves repetition of all the elements compared, first stated in connection with trees, then recapitulated in terms of human aging. The second stanza contains the substance of the figure and is capable of standing alone; if we omit the simile bridge—"all so"—the first four lines of this stanza, already half metaphor, can as metaphor carry the central meaning in terms not dissimilar to Shakespeare's:

> . . . my lustfull leafe is drye and sere,
> My timely buds with wayling all are wasted:
> The blossome, which my braunch of youth did beare,
> With breathed sighes is blowne away, and blasted.

This is youthful verse, written at a time when English poetry was in a bad way—gauche, verbose, almost inarticulate. The redundancy is in part a fault of inexperience; but when we make due allowance for this and check against his mature work, we are struck by two things: (1) to some extent Spenser seems to be pulled half-consciously into metaphor in the second stanza by the very nature of the language; (2) the recapitulation is certainly intentional. Perhaps it helps to point to the device in music. Spenser's repetition is not only with variation, it is with alteration of meaning. He is not trying to do what Shakespeare does; he is not interested in economy but in elaboration. His poem is an eclogue to winter rather than a sonnet using natural imagery to portray a mental and emotional state. The sense of loss portrayed in these two stanzas expresses a different relation between personal and objective. Shakespeare suborns nature to personal ends; Spenser simply puts man and nature in the same key. The metaphorical condensation which I made above actually destroys this balance. On any count Shakespeare's lines

are superior to this studio work of Spenser's, but the fundamental difference is between two kinds of poetry.

The simile is not just a metaphor trailing its umbilical cord. Nor
does it merely "add" and never develop. Often the epic simile attracts
attention to itself rather than to the object which it is supposed to illum-
inate, but not always. The very elaboration in Spenser, whose effects are
built up by accumulation, at times acquires a certain symbolism from
the general context and a metaphorical dimension quite different from
metaphorical framework. Though the end result is not unlike, the
method differs from Shakespeare's.

Shakespeare by no means neglects the simile even in his mature
plays, especially when he seeks a formal effect:

> *Iago.* Patience, I say; your mind perhaps may change.
> *Othello.* Never, Iago. Like to the Pontic sea,
> Whose icy currents and compulsive course
> Ne'er feels retiring ebb, but keeps due on
> To the Propontic and the Hellespont,
> Even so my bloody thoughts, with violent pace,
> Shall ne'er look back, ne'er ebb to humble love,
> Till that a capable and wide revenge
> Swallow them up.

Othello's character is epic, his associations not with familiar English
streams, but with exotic tides which literally defy nature's law. Shakespeare is not engaged in a psychological study of a Moor, yet he does
contrive a specific way of thinking and feeling for Othello which goes
beyond a sprinkling of exotic words; except in those psychologically
realistic moments of the play when a broken phrase—little more than
an ejaculation—becomes the shorthand of his torment, in all Othello's
speeches there is a suggestion of the grandiloquent artifice used earlier
for Richard Second and for some moments of Hotspur.

Spenser describes the ebb and flow of battle between Cambello and
Triamond:

> Like as the tide that comes from th'Ocean mayne,
> Flowes up the Shenan with contrarie forse,
> And overruling him in his owne rayne,
> Drives backe the current of his kindly course,
> And makes it seeme to have some other sourse:

> But when the floud is *spent,* then backe againe
> His *borrowed* waters forst to *redisbourse,*
> He sends the sea his owne with *double gaine,*
> And *tribute* eke withall, as to his Sovereigne.

> Thus did the battell varie to and fro,
> With diverse fortune doubtfull to be deemed.

At first glance the last four lines of the simile seem elaboration beyond the point of comparison, for its own sake or to fill out the stanza. The tide is not subordinated to the fight so definitely as the Pontic tide to Othello's anger. Spenser's simile, indeed, almost halts the struggle, yet it presents the whole nature of that struggle better than his account of the action. And while it does not show the careful, logical expansion of detail of the simile in *Januarie,* it represents the same kind of sensibility, the same balance between man and nature. Later, in the second stanza broken off above, Spenser introduces a secondary simile:

> And all the while the disentrayled blood
> Adowne their sides *like litle rivers stremed,*
> *That with the wasting of his vitall flood,*
> Sir Triamond at last full faint and feeble stood.

This is in perfect imaginative agreement with the "tribute" drawn back into the sea by the retreating tide. If we look again at the first stanza we can see what happens: "floud is *spent"* suggests to Spenser, in the midst of his simile's flight, a secondary meaning which he develops spontaneously without pausing. The waters of the sea are not really "spent," but "borrowed" to be "redisboursed" with "double gaine" in "tribute" owed the sea as "sovereign." The basic simile is still at work, only it has passed into the metaphorical dimension though still technically simile. Finally, some lines later the same simile with the same metaphorical meaning recurs as the particular wasting of one man's life through little rivers of blood is related to the elemental mystery of the sea's demands upon the land, and to the life-giving, death-bringing force of earth and water. The epic simile is not necessarily an ornamental excrescence in the *Faerie Queene.*

If Spenser seldom achieves the tension of Shakespeare's dramatic compression, he sets up a kind of vibration of interrelated meanings among various simple, direct statements. The centers of radiation in the broadest sense are usually the allegorical cores of the books; in a manner impossible to explain fully and to analyze, seemingly disconnected and widely separated passages acquire from the context of the poem an additional vitality. Occasionally even incidental passages isolated from the poem retain this cumulative energy.

Besides the almond-tree type, where simile flashes through metaphor,[5] or the expanded simile, like the Shannon tides which develop inside themselves related metaphor, there is a further qualification to Spenser's preference for similes. His metaphors are less obtrusive. Often he casts a whole stanza in a metaphor so simple that it may pass unobserved, like this one—another river—with its rich overtones of irony:

> God of the world and worldlings I me call,
> Great Mammon, greatest god below the skye,
> *That of my plenty poure out unto all,*
> And unto none my graces do envye:
> Riches, renowne, and principality,
> Honour, estate, and all this worldes good,
> For which men swincke and sweat incessantly,
> *From me do flow into an ample flood,*
> And *in the hollow earth* have their eternal brood.

In the context of its underworld canto, this simple metaphor has a compression and complexity of its own. The river of materialism pours out its "graces" with ironical impartiality, breeding forms of life ("eternal brood") like the fertile Nile; only, along with Cocytus and Acheron and Styx, it is a river of hell.

NOTES

1. An exception is the perceptive appreciation of Spenser in Mr. Donald Stauffer's *Nature of Poetry.*
2. "Tension and Structure of Poetry," *Sewanee Review*, Autumn 1943.
3. In a short poem like a sonnet structure is frequently only the syntax of a sentence adjusted to the form; the quality of the sentence is the quality of the poem.
4. For example, *F. Q.* 5. 6:

> *Even in the dore him meeting, she begun:*
> 'And where is thy Lord, and how far hence?
> Declare at once; and hath he lost or won?'

> . . . .
> *Till she againe thus sayd:* 'Talus be bold,
> And tell what ever it be, good or bad,
> That from thy tongue thy hearts intent doth hold.'

To whom he thus, at length. 'The tidings sad,
That I would hide, will needs, I see, be rad.
My Lord, your love, by hard mishap doth lie
In wretched bondage, wofully bestad.'

'Ay me,' *quoth she,* 'what wicked destinie?
And is he vanquisht by his tyrant enemy?'

'Not by that Tyrant, his intended foe;
But by a Tyrannesse,' *he then replied,*
'That him captived hath in haplesse woe.'

'Cease thou bad newes-man, badly doest thou hide
Thy maisters shame, in harlots bondage tide.
The rest my selfe too readily can spell.'
With that in rage she turn'd from him aside. . . .

Upon the top of all his loftie crest,
A bunch of haires discolourd diversly,
With sprincled pearle, and gold full richly drest,
Did shake, and seem'd to daunce for jollity,
Like to an Almond tree ymounted hye
On top of greene Selinis all alone,
With blossomes brave bedecked daintily;
Whose tender locks do tremble every one
At *every little breath,* that under heaven is blowne.